A CULTURAL
HISTORY OF ANIMALS

VOLUME 1

A CULTURAL HISTORY OF ANIMALS

GENERAL EDITORS: LINDA KALOF AND BRIGITTE RESL

Volume 1
A CULTURAL HISTORY OF ANIMALS IN ANTIQUITY
Edited by LINDA KALOF

Volume 2
A CULTURAL HISTORY OF ANIMALS IN THE MEDIEVAL AGE
Edited by BRIGITTE RESL

Volume 3
A CULTURAL HISTORY OF ANIMALS IN THE RENAISSANCE
Edited by BRUCE BOEHRER

Volume 4
A CULTURAL HISTORY OF ANIMALS IN THE AGE OF ENLIGHTENMENT
Edited by MATTHEW SENIOR

Volume 5
A CULTURAL HISTORY OF ANIMALS IN THE AGE OF EMPIRE
Edited by KATHLEEN KETE

Volume 6
A CULTURAL HISTORY OF ANIMALS IN THE MODERN AGE
Edited by RANDY MALAMUD

A CULTURAL HISTORY OF ANIMALS

IN ANTIQUITY

Edited by Linda Kalof

BERG

Oxford • New York

English edition
First published in 2007 by
Berg

Editorial offices:
First Floor, Angel Court, 81 St Clements Street, Oxford OX4 1AW, UK
175 Fifth Avenue, New York, NY 10010, USA

Paperback edition published in 2011
© Linda Kalof 2007, 2011

Berg is the imprint of Oxford International Publishers Ltd.

Library of Congress Cataloging-in-Publication Data

A cultural history of animals / edited by Linda Kalof and Brigitte Resl.
    p. cm.
  Includes bibliographical references and index.
  ISBN-13: 978-1-84520-496-9 (cloth)
  ISBN-10: 1-84520-496-4 (cloth)
  1. Animals and civilization. 2. Human-animal relationships—History. I. Kalof,
Linda. II. Pohl-Resl, Brigitte.

  QL85C85   2007
  590—dc22   2007031782

British Library Cataloguing-in-Publication Data

A catalogue record for this book is available from the British Library.

ISBN 978 1 84520 361 0 (volume 1, cloth)
     978 1 84788 817 4 (volume 1, paper)
     978 1 84520 496 9 (set, cloth)
     978 1 84788 823 5 (set, paper)

Typeset by Apex Publishing, LLC, Madison, WI

Printed in the United Kingdom by the MPG Books Group

www.bergpublishers.com

CONTENTS

ILLUSTRATIONS

SERIES PREFACE

A Cultural History of Animals is a six-volume series reviewing the changing roles of animals in society and culture throughout history. Each volume follows the same basic structure, and begins with an outline account of the main characteristics of the roles of animals in the period under consideration. Following from that, specialists closely examine major aspects of the subject under seven key headings: symbolism, hunting, domestication, entertainment, science, philosophy, and art. The reader, therefore, has the choice between synchronic and diachronic approaches: A single volume can be read to obtain a thorough knowledge of the subject in a given period from a variety of perspectives, or one of the seven main aspects can be followed through time by reading the relevant chapters of all six volumes, thus providing a thematic understanding of changes and developments over the long term.

The six volumes divide the topic as follows:

Volume 1: A Cultural History of Animals in Antiquity (2500 BCE–1000 CE)

Volume 2: A Cultural History of Animals in the Medieval Age (1000–1400)

Volume 3: A Cultural History of Animals in the Renaissance (1400–1600)

Volume 4: A Cultural History of Animals in the Age of Enlightenment (1600–1800)

Volume 5: A Cultural History of Animals in the Age of Empire (1800–1920)

Volume 6: A Cultural History of Animals in the Modern Age (1920–2000)

General Editors, Linda Kalof and Brigitte Resl

Ancient Animals

LINDA KALOF

When the earliest versions of the story of Gilgamesh were being written on clay tablets around 2100 BCE, the role of animals in ancient human societies was critical, compelling, and pervasive. But the centrality of animals to human cultures was nothing new, even at that very early time in history.[1] As long ago as 30,000 BCE, Paleolithic humans were expressing their awe and admiration for animals by painting their images on the walls of caves and carefully placing their bones in ceremonial positions throughout the underground chambers. In one cave, a bear skull was intentionally placed on a flat rock in the center of the chamber, another bear skull was marked with black lines, bear teeth were inserted in the small hollows of rocks, and a few bear forelimbs were driven into the floor at the entrance of the cave.[2] While it is possible that the positioning of these animal body parts was the work of the natural environment, perhaps from the water or mud that flooded the cave from time to time, it is also possible that humans did the deed in their veneration of the huge, powerful Paleolithic bear. My vote is for the second hypothesis. Indeed, some argue that the bones of bears were sacred and honored even earlier in our history. There is evidence of a 60,000-year-old Paleolithic bear cult in which the bones and skulls of now-extinct cave bears were ritually stored, positioned, and arranged, most likely in connection with human burials, suggesting that our early ancestors may not have distinguished clearly between the death of humans and the death of animals.[3] And it is possible that wolves were venerated even earlier in human history. Archaeological evidence from the south of France indicates that 125,000 years ago, Paleolithic humans built shelters inside a cave with the skull of a wolf placed intentionally at the entrance.[4]

Many thousands of years later animals—particularly cattle—were still central to the human perception of creation, birth, life, and death.[5] Archaeological evidence documents that cattle were worshipped in 6000 BCE at Çatal Hüyük, an ancient city in the area of present-day Turkey. In that culture, cattle were important components of rituals and ceremonies. Taurine images were dominant in the art of the third millennium BCE throughout most of the world, including Mesopotamia, Egypt, Anatolia, the Gulf and the Caucasus, western central Asia, and the Indus Valley.[6] Humans had a close identification with bovines in antiquity, and the strong, brave and libidinous wild bull was a model for male power and fertility, particularly for chiefs and early kings,[7] as told in the story of the friendship between the king Gilgamesh and the beast-(bull)-man Enkidu.

Bulls were not only important as models of masculinity, but also provided the first source of animal power in the production of food that gave rise to a surplus system and a leisure class, with cattle ownership a sign of wealth.[8] In his analysis of the role of cattle in the ancient world, Calvin Schwabe documents that the word *chattel* is related to cattle, and *capital* originally referred to head of cattle. In Sanskrit the word for "to fight" meant "to raid for cattle" and "leader" meant "lord of cattle."[9] Even the origins of modern English financial terms such as stock, stock market, and watered stock reflect the importance of cattle. Writing evolved out of the need to record cattle wealth, and the first symbol for the things to be counted as wealth was the horned bovine head (*capital*), the first letter in alphabetic writing systems, which is drawn in cuneiform as an upside-down triangle, on its side with curved horns as in the Greek α, or on its back as in English *A*.[10] In Egypt during the Old Kingdom (2649–2134 BCE), the length of a king's reign was measured by the number of official cattle counts held during his rule.[11]

With the creation of cities, the accumulation of wealth, and increased trading and fighting, humans deployed images of wild, ferocious animals to symbolize struggle, violence, and warring kingdoms. In the earliest examples, animals were carved into stone cylinder seals around 3500 BCE in Mesopotamia. These small cylinders were then rolled onto clay, and the resultant seal was used to secure and record valuables inside containers (or, if pierced from end to end, the cylinders could be worn on a string as decorative jewelry). As the only visual records we have of life in ancient Mesopotamia, cylinder seals provide an important record of a 3,000-year-old human–animal relationship, illustrating the increasing perception of animals, particularly bulls, as linked to struggle, strife, and victory in war.[12]

According to Francis Klingender, the animal images on the cylinder seals fall into three major categories: (1) a symmetrical frieze in which animals are depicted moving single file in one direction, or sometimes for balance two files are shown, each moving in opposite directions, one placed above the other; (2) pairs of animals and/or humans are shown in confrontation, such as the depiction of a nude hero and a bull man fighting with rampant bulls; and (3) a continuous frieze of fighting animals, often lions and other predators attacking cattle, with humans defending flocks of domesticated animals. A photograph of a stone cylinder seal from Mesopotamia that dates to about 2400 BCE is shown in Figure 1.5 in chapter 1. The cylinder itself is shown on the left, and the impression the seal made when rolled in clay appears on the right, with the image a depiction of the use of animal scenes to reflect the continuous struggle between the tame and the wild and the civilized and uncivilized in the ancient world.[13]

Eventually, the symmetrical style of animal representation was abandoned for a more naturalistic approach that provided details of the physical and behavioral characteristics of a diversity of animal species, such as lions, bears, hyenas, and jackals. Most likely based on firsthand observations, Mesopotamian artists began to sculpt lifelike, naturalistic animal representations, using their skills to convey the essence of individual species. For example, images of the much loved bull were used to decorate musical instruments; the core was made of wood, while the head and horns were made of gold sheet, the eyeballs of inset shell, and the pupils and eyelids of lapis lazuli, a deep sky blue–colored mineral.[14] Below the wooden core of the bull's head, the instruments were often decorated with a series of panels depicting fight scenes with humans and animals, bulls with human heads and animals engaged in human-like behaviors.

The day-to-day lives of animals were also well documented in ancient art. Donkeys walk across threshing floors, cattle graze under trees, and goats feed from mangers. Goats were a popular art motif in the ancient world. One famous representation of animal behavior from the third millennium BCE is a sculpture of a rearing male goat with his front legs resting on the branches of a budding plant, sometimes called Rearing Goat in a Flowering Plant or, more often, Ram Caught in a Thicket (this last based on the biblical story of Abraham's discovery of a ram caught by the horns in a bush, which he disentangled and then sacrificed instead of his son). But in fact the animal depicted in the sculpture is not a ram but a goat, although he was originally "caught"—his forelegs had been tied to the plant with a silver chain. Scholars believe that the sculpture represents the ancients' concern with the fertility of plants and animals.[15] The goat's rearing stance has multiple interpretations. First, the goat is very successful at reproduction, second only to the bull, and the rearing stance he assumes in the statue is the same as the position he assumes for sex. Second, the rearing stance has been interpreted as climbing the tree, a reflection of the goat's ability to climb trees to feed on hard-to-reach leaves.[16]

Some aspects of the lives of domesticated animals in early antiquity are well documented in ancient limestone carvings. There are numerous Egyptian images of nurturing and bonding among cattle, such as mother cows gazing at or licking their calves, and also of humans caring for cattle. A standard representation of the time shows cattle fording bodies of water, with both young and old bovines appearing anxious about the safety of the young calves that had to be carried or pulled along by humans. Tomb art from 2400 BCE shows long-horned cattle deployed in Egyptian agriculture to pull wooden scratch plows, with the plow attached to their horns with a rope. At this time, domesticated donkeys and horses were commonly used for riding, carrying loads, and pulling carts, sleds, and chariots.[17] Bulls provided substantial animal power once domesticated and controlled through ringing their noses, cutting off the sharp tips (or all) of the horns, and castration,[18] and by 1400 BCE, oxen were being used for a variety of draught tasks.

In addition to oxen, horses were also critical to the developing city-states. As a source of speed and stamina for the rulers of cattle-rich areas, the horse provided the means to engage in long-distance trade and conquer foreign lands. The horse became a symbol of status and wealth, just as cattle conferred wealth on the people of the earliest civilizations; the upper classes were referred to by names indicating horse ownership, such as the *hippeis* in Athens and the *equites* in Rome.[19]

Visual records from ancient Egypt, Mesopotamia, and Greece show that hunters, warriors, and kings rode around in chariots harnessed to small, stocky horses.[20] While commonly used to haul chariots and carts, horses were not used to pull very heavy loads until the Middle Ages. Ancient horses were harnessed in such a way that their heads were pulled back, forcing a strong arch in the neck and precluding their pulling heavy loads (severe penalties were meted out to those who harnessed their horses to loads in excess of 500 kilograms). Although a controversial thesis, it has been argued that the Greeks and Romans did not know how to harness horses properly, but rather used an oxen-yoking mechanism, such that when the horse began to pull, it was forced to raise his head to avoid strangulation.[21] Because most ancient images of ridden horses show the animals with open mouths and strained facial expressions, it has been argued that the ancients used painful mouth bits that allowed riders to control their horses (a good example is the frieze from the Parthenon of Alexander astride his beloved Bucephalas, shown in Figure 3.5 in chapter 3). Another good example is a horse-and-jockey sculpture that dates to about 140 BCE. This bronze statue of a galloping horse ridden by a young jockey (on display at the Athens Archeological Museum) emphasizes the movement in the horse's flexed muscles and the front hooves raised off the ground, and on the horse's face we see what some might label agony in the marked contractions of the cheek muscles, laid-back ears, wide eyes, flaring nostrils, and open mouth.

There is archaeological evidence that in the seventh century BCE, horses were ridden with the help of cheek-pieces and mouth bits.[22] And in *Gilgamesh*, a hot-blooded stallion is described as doomed to gallop endlessly with a bit in his mouth, indicating that horse bits were used as long ago as 1700 BCE.

Selective breeding of animals, particularly cattle, sheep, and dogs, was well under way in both Babylonia and Egypt by 1900 BCE.[23] Most early Egyptian representations of animals reflect affection for a wide variety of species, and the popularity of domestic scenes suggests that Egyptians were fond of living with animals. Dogs of many shapes and sizes are found in ancient Egyptian art, including large hunting dogs that look much like the contemporary mastiff and slim dogs that look like greyhounds, suggesting that these two canine breeds have remained relatively unchanged for thousands of years.[24] Egyptian artists drew pictures of dogs wearing wide collars that proudly announced the animal's name (such as "Town Dog"), made toys in the shape of animals, such as an ivory dog whose lower jaw could be moved by a lever, and painted household scenes depicting monkeys and cats playing with other household pets, for example, teasing geese.[25]

Cats were among the most highly regarded animals in ancient Egypt (see Figure 3.4 in chapter 3). One version of the story of the Persian King Cambyses' conquest of Egypt in 525 BCE was that his victory was assured when he had his soldiers hold cats aloft as they advanced on the enemy—the Egyptians ceased all defensive tactics since they were loathe to harm the advancing cats.[26] Herodotus wrote that it was forbidden to kill a cat, and members of a household were required to shave their eyebrows when one of their cats died of natural causes. However, some cats were purposefully killed. Evidence from mummified cats at London's Natural History Museum reveals that many were young and had been killed by having their necks broken, perhaps so that they could be sold as votive offerings.[27] The ancient Egyptians mummified numerous species of animals, including bulls, cats, and very many birds. Excavations at Saqqara, Egypt, have uncovered miles of tunnels that had thousands of little holes carved into them, each containing a mummified bird.[28]

Tomb adornments in the form of animal images were also popular with the Greeks. Stunning sculptures in marble and stone depict animals sleeping next to children, dogs gazing lovingly up at their human companions, and birds and hares cradled in the hands of children. Birds were particularly important to the ancients as childhood companions, or perhaps as toys. Numerous statues depict children holding a bird in one hand and adults offering birds to children.

The ancients often used domesticated animals as weapons and decoys in their wars, like the cats used by Cambyses and his army and the elephants used as war equipment by the Greeks. Elephants were elaborately decorated with ornaments such as headpieces and clanging bells and occasionally given fermented wine to drink, encouraging them to behave wildly.[29] The use of elephants on the front lines was probably intended primarily to terrify the enemy with a display of strength; their practical use as a war animal was likely limited. Elephants are not effective in fighting human wars; if bombarded by arrows, an elephant will simply turn around and retreat, often inflicting more damage on his own army than on the enemy.[30] Further, a female elephant will refuse to fight if separated from her young, and she would immediately abandon all military duties and rush to the rescue if her offspring squealed when wounded or trampled.[31]

Bovines were also deployed as war equipment in antiquity. In 217 BCE, strategizing a way to bypass Roman resistance to his march through a guarded area, Hannibal had his troops tie bundles of sticks to the horns of two thousand bovines captured during the Carthaginians' trek through Italy.[32] Come nightfall they set fire to the bundles and herded the cattle toward the enemy. As the animals moved forward, the surrounding trees and bushes caught fire from the burning bundles, and when the lit bundles burned down to the animals' heads, they went into a wild panic. Hannibal and his men easily sneaked by the Romans who were kept busy dealing with the frenzy of the fire and the frenetic animals.

As in every era of human history, hunting occupied much of the leisure time of the elite in antiquity. In Egypt during the New Kingdom, it was common for the lives of important, wealthy individuals to be recorded on the walls of tombs, and many of those visual representations are devoted to hunting. The palace of King Ashurbanipal at Nineveh is covered with limestone carvings of hunting scenes (see Figure 3.3 in chapter 3), many in enclosed parks (an ancient canned hunt). Indeed, as early as 2446 BCE, hunting in Egypt often occurred in confined areas, and royal hunters slaughtered wild animals driven to the site and corralled by attendants.[33] The pictures at Nineveh document that lions were released from wooden enclosures and driven toward their slaughterers by attendants banging cymbals, while the king "hunted" from the safety of his horse-drawn chariot (which was often driven by another attendant, allowing the king to focus on bringing down the "enemy") or while hiding in a pit. Frightened, cornered, and desperate, the animals were easily overcome, and ancient artists depicted their last moments as they vomited blood and dragged their wounded bodies across the "battlefield." Meanwhile, crowds of people watched the hunt from the sidelines. The hunt was not only a spectator sport for the public, but also a public display of the king's power.[34]

Ancient hunting practices have often been closely linked to battle. For example, an association between hunting and war is evident in the visual representations of hunting in the southern Greek societies of Mycenae[35] and Sparta.[36] And after examining 121 examples of nonmythological boar and deer hunts depicted on Greek vases painted between 600–425 BCE, one scholar concluded that, hunting in ancient Greece was reserved for the wealthy, served elite interests, and provided young elite youths with a right of passage to adulthood as well as practice for participation in both warfare and civic affairs.[37] One of the most vivid and lively descriptions of a proper hunting excursion was provided by the Greek historian, Xenophon (434–355 BCE):

The sportsman himself should sally forth in a loose, light hunting dress, and footgear to match; he should carry a stout stick in his hand, the net-keeper following. They should proceed to the hunting-field in silence, to prevent the hare, if by chance there should be one close by, from making off at the sound of voices. When they have reached the covert, he will tie the hounds to trees, each separately, so that they can be easily slipped from the leash, and proceed to fix the nets, funnel and hayes, as above described. When that is done, and while the net-keeper mounts guard, the master himself will take the hounds and sally forth to rouse the game. Then with prayer and promise to Apollo and to Artemis, our Lady of the Chase, to share with them the produce of spoil, he lets slip a single hound, the cunningest at scenting of the pack. [If it be winter, the hour will be sunrise, or if summer, before day-dawn, and in the other seasons at some hour midway.] As soon as the hound has unravelled the true line he will let slip another; and then, if these carry on the line, at rapid intervals he will slip the others one by one; and himself follow, without too great hurry, addressing each of the dogs by name every now and then, but not too frequently, for fear of over-exciting them before the proper moment … Meanwhile the hounds are busily at work; onwards they press with eager spirit, disentangling the line, double or treble, as the case may be. To and fro they weave a curious web, now across, now parallel with the line, whose threads are interlaced, here overlapped, and here revolving in a circle; now straight, now crooked; here close, there rare; at one time clear enough, at another dimly owned. Past one another the hounds jostle—tails waving fast, ears dropt, and eyes flashing.[38]

Large walled-off areas called "paradise parks" often enclosed animals for royal hunts and processionals and also accommodated gift animals from foreign leaders. Early empires including Assyria, Babylonia, and Egypt had animal parks, and the idea of a royal "paradise" (which served as a model for the garden of Eden) continued in the West until the end of the Roman Empire and in China until the 1800s.[39] Paradise parks were usually situated close to landowners' estates so that owners could hunt whenever they wished and so that the animals could be easily observed by the landowner and his guests. In one ancient account, the estate staff trained animals to appear at a certain

location for food, entertaining the guests as they watched the animals gather
to feed, (often represented in myth as lured together by Orpheus [see Figure 4.7 in chapter 4]):

> ... a trumpet was sounded at regular hours and you saw boars and wild
> goats come for their food ... at Hortensius's place at Laurentum, I saw
> the thing done more in the manner of the Thracian bard ... as we were
> banqueting Hortensius ordered Orpheus to be summoned. He came com-
> plete with robe and lute, and was bidden to sing. Thereupon he blew a
> trumpet, and such a multitude of stags and boars and other four-footed
> beasts came flooding round us that the sight seemed as beautiful to me as
> the hunts staged ... in the Circus Maximus—at least, the ones without
> African beasts.[40]

The public slaughter of animals and disenfranchised humans was a popular
form of entertainment for almost five centuries (ending in 281 CE). It was so
widespread that few Roman cities did not provide such entertainment.[41] In
support of the Roman social hierarchy, emperors sponsored lavish and exotic spectacles to please the public and ensure their own popularity with the
Roman people. Even though associated with a form of emperor worship, the
shows provided the opportunity for public participation in Rome, and Cicero
noted that the wishes of the Roman people were expressed in three places:
public assemblies, elections, and plays or gladiatorial shows.[42] Keith Hopkins
writes that as citizen participation in politics declined under emperor rule, the
arena shows and games provided opportunities for regular meetings between
emperors and the masses. Rome was unique among the large empires of antiquity in allowing the dramatic confrontation of the rulers and the ruled, and
the amphitheater was the people's parliament.[43] With several months of every
year devoted to celebrations, Rome had many festivals lasting several days at a
time, and about a third of the time that the emperor and public spent together
was when they were spectators at the shows.[44] The shows became a political arena, a place where, face-to-face with their emperor, the Roman crowd
could honor him, or demand that he grant them pleasures, or make political
demands of him. When the people applauded the shows, they celebrated the
emperor; when they booed, they berated him.[45]

Scholars have offered numerous theories to account for the public killing of
exotic animals in Rome. It has been argued that animals were publicly slaughtered in Rome to establish a sense of control over the strange and the spec-
tacular,[46] to display exotic animals as the novel booty of foreign exploits,[47] to
legitimately kill less powerful beings,[48] to prove wealth by destroying exotic
and expensive animals,[49] to fulfill a desire to watch animals by combining the

pleasure of killing and torture with the pleasure of watching the swift and spirited activity of wild beasts,[50] and to reduce the population of animals that destroyed valuable crops in order to promote the spread of agriculture.[51]

Killing large numbers of wild animals in public spectacles was a Roman tradition long before the arena slaughters, particularly in rural areas where predators of livestock and agricultural pests were killed in public festivities. Animals were used in rituals as both sacrificial victims and active participants in Roman festivals and holidays, such as the *Ludi Taurei*, the *Cerialia*, and the *Floralia*.[52] During the *Ludi Taurei*, bulls were released and hunted, some of whom may have been set on fire; during the *Cerialia*, an event that honored the goddess of Italian agriculture, foxes were set loose with flaming torches tied to their backs; and in the *Floralia*, hares and roebucks were hunted in commemoration of greater control over gardens and cultivated lands.[53]

The animal shows in urban Rome had their beginnings in the rural hunts of the countryside. Urban hunting spectacles were staged in part to earn the votes of town dwellers who had neither the opportunity nor the financial means to hunt, and men desiring political office brought the experience of hunting to the urban areas so that all could participate in the sport, "at least as spectators."[54] Simulated hunting experiences were staged in the Roman arena using hunters and weapons, the construction of natural, wooded scenery, and the resistance of dangerous and wild animals to the chase.[55]

Numerous narrative accounts from the ancient world document key aspects of the Roman slaughters. Surviving documents record the number of animals killed (3,500 during the reign of Augustus; 9,000 during the reign of Titus; 11,000 were butchered by Trajan to celebrate a war victory). Other records detail the elaborate construction of arena scenery to simulate the animals' natural habitat, details of ingenious technological apparatuses capable of elevating animals or humans into the air, and descriptions of the reluctance of some animals to fight in the arena.[56]

It is curious that there are no records to account for how the Romans disposed of the thousands upon thousands of dead animals and humans after their slaughter. We know that the carcasses were removed from the arena through the Doors of the Dead, which were situated under the seating area of the elite,[57] and that the disposal of many thousands of corpses over hundreds of years must have been extremely important to the Romans in efforts to avoid pollution. It has been speculated that while fire would not have been an efficient means of carcass disposal, probably some bodies were thrown into the Tiber River, some unclaimed corpses of social marginals and other outcasts were dumped in a field and exposed to dogs and birds, and some of the animals were eaten by the Roman people. Donald Kyle argues that "if the games led to distribution of meat, the emperor/patron as a master hunter was providing game as well as games for his people."[58]

While we do not know how the dead animals were disposed of after their slaughter, there is documentation on how living animals were captured and sent to Rome destined for the arena. There are numerous descriptions of the hunt and seizure of wild animals and their transport to Rome, such as this strikingly realistic description provided by Claudian:

> Whatsoever inspires fear with its teeth, wonder with its mane, awe with its horns and bristling coat—all the beauty, all the terror of the forest is taken. Guile protects them not; neither strength nor weight avails them; their speed saves not the fleet of foot. Some roar enmeshed in snares; some are thrust into wooden cages and carried off. There are not carpenters enough to fashion the wood; leafy prisons are constructed of unhewn beech and ash. Boats laden with some of the animals traverse seas and rivers; bloodless from terror the rower's hand is stayed, for the sailor fears the merchandise he carries. Others are transported over land in wagons that block the roads with the long procession, bearing the spoils of the mountains. The wild beast is borne a captive by those troubled cattle on whom in times past he sated his hunger, and each time that the oxen turned and looked at their burden they pull away in terror from the pole.[59]

A more recent scholar describes how wild animals were captured and conveyed to Rome for the shows.[60] Animals were rounded up by hired professional hunters and soldiers using pits and nets. In the pit method, a pillar was driven into the middle of an excavated hole, and a small animal, such as a puppy or a lamb, was tied to the top of the pole. As the predator ran up to snatch the prey, it would not see the pit and, in jumping to reach the decoy, would fall into the hole. A cage baited with meat would then be lowered into the pit, and when the beast entered the cage for the meat, it would be caught and hauled to the surface. In the net method of capture, animals were driven into runs or alleys, and then captured at the dead end with nets. After capture, large carnivorous animals were likely kept in dark, narrow boxes, which would keep them quiet and make them less likely to harm themselves during their journey to Rome; "inoffensive" animals might have been allowed to roam about the ship or, if traveling by land, trained to follow caravans.[61]

Animals were often reluctant participants in the arena shows. Having been dragged into Rome, caged, and kept out of sight in the dark cellars of the amphitheater, numerous strategies were needed to get recalcitrant animals from their cellar quarters out into the arena. The record of the last animal show in 281 CE documents that one hundred maned lions were slaughtered at the doors of their cages because they refused to leave.[62] According to Jennison,[63] the animals were kept in cages under the arena and either hoisted up onto the stage or transferred to a series of underground cages and at show time released into a passage and forced to move to the surface. Upon release, the animals often huddled against the back of their cages or took refuge under a wooden barrier. Burning straw or hot irons were used to make them leave their cages—the fronts of the cages were made to open wide and at the top rear, there was a small square opening to insert the blazing bundle of straw. Jennison quotes a line from Claudian that captures some of the reluctance of the animals to enter the arena: "The wild beasts, looking up mistrustfully at the thousands of spectators, become tame under stress of fear."[64] The animals' reluctance to fight in the arena was sometimes an added attraction for the spectators. Because of its reluctance to engage in combat, the rhinoceros was one of the most popular animals to place in combat with another species. When prodded by an arena attendant to fight, the rhinoceros would become angry, and once angered, he was invincible, tearing bulls apart and throwing bears into the air.[65] One of the most often repeated stories of animal resistance to fighting in the arena is based on a spectacle in 55 BCE of a combat between elephants and humans. The elephants abruptly ceased fighting their human tormentors, turned to the audience, trumpeted piteously, and appeared to beg for mercy, bringing the spectators to tears and to their feet, cursing the emperor (Pompey) for his cruelty. A retrospective account of the event was recorded by Dio Cassius:

> ... eighteen elephants fought against men in heavy armour. Some of these beasts were killed at the time and others a little later. For some of them, contrary to Pompey's wish, were pitied by the people when, after being wounded and ceasing to fight, they walked about with their trunks raised toward heaven, lamenting so bitterly as to give rise to the report that they did so not by mere chance, but were crying out against the oaths in which they had trusted when they crossed over from Africa, and were calling upon Heaven to avenge them. For it is said that they would not set foot upon the ships before they received a pledge under oath from their drivers that they should suffer no harm.[66]

The seating arrangement of the arena served as a distancing mechanism from the carnage, perhaps one reason the spectators rarely protested the public slaughters. Keith Hopkins argues that crowd social psychology may have provided some release from individual responsibility for the arena activities and/or an opportunity for spectators to identify with victory rather than defeat. Brutality was an integral part of Roman culture: owners had absolute control over slaves, fathers had absolute power over life and death in a strict patriarchal society, and state-controlled legitimate violence was established late in the empire, with capital punishment becoming a state monopoly only in the second century CE.[67] Further, it is argued that because the Romans had been active in battles and wars for centuries, the popularity of the gladiatorial contests was a residual of war, discipline, and death; public executions served as reminders that those who betrayed their country would be quickly and severely punished, with public punishment reestablishing the moral and political order and reconfirming the power of the state.[68]

Visual representations of arena scenes were standard images in the mosaics that decorated the floors and walls of the villas of the wealthy and on domestic objects such as lamps, ceramics, gems, funerary reliefs, and statues.[69] One scene painted on a Roman lamp illustrates the wide appeal of looking at combative situations between humans and animals: a lion lunges up a ramp toward a prisoner who is bound to a stake on top of a platform, just out of reach of the animal, thus increasing the uncertainty of the outcome and the enjoyment of the audience.[70] Scenes of blood, panic, and death depicted in mosaics decorated the houses of the wealthy and emphasized the distance of the audience from the death of animals (and disenfranchised humans).[71] Some of the most vivid animal scenes are depicted in floor mosaics in an ancient villa in Armerina, Sicily, where we can see the hunt and capture of wild animals in North Africa, their journey by ship to Rome (see Figure 4.8 in chapter 4), and their death in the arena. In a mosaic from Tunesia, two prisoners are shown with their arms strapped to their sides while they are being pushed toward their assailants by arena attendants in protective clothing; one of the prisoners is being mauled in the face by a leopard, while the other stares in wide-eyed terror at his animal attacker (see Figure 4.10 in chapter 4).[72] A first century CE mosaic from Zliten in Libya illustrates the visual nature of the Roman shows, which often had numerous "mini-performances" taking place simultaneously, for example, a hunting scene, a fight between a tethered bull and a bear, humans attacked by a lion and leopards, and an orchestra playing in the background.[73]

Baiting animals and humans in entertainment spectacles was also part of the early Etruscan culture. Several Etruscan wall paintings from a 510 BCE tomb in Tarquinia illustrate a "beast-master" character, called Phersu, in scenes that depict bloody competition, some between humans and animals.[74] In one painting, the masked and bearded Phersu, dressed in a multicolored shirt and a conical hat, incites a vicious dog to attack a wrestler who wields a club but is handicapped with a sack over his head. Phersu holds a length of rope intended to entangle the human as the dog attacks and tears into the flesh of the profusely bleeding wrestler. It is believed that this scene depicts a funereal event at which staged games and athletic contests were customary. It is argued that the Romans perceived their gladiatorial shows as distant descendents of these Etruscan funereal combats.[75]

Bullfighting was another popular animal entertainment for the ancients. Bullfight scenes were popular decorations in Egyptian tombs as long ago as 2600 BCE. The bullfight motif was linked to both farmyard life in ancient Egypt and to funerary texts celebrating the deceased's status as victor over a challenge by another potential leader.[76] Pliny the Elder claimed that the Thessalians of ancient Greece started killing bulls for sport by racing a horse alongside the bull, grabbing his horns and twisting his neck, and that Julius Caesar staged similar contests in Rome.[77] In 1450 BCE, bulls were used in sporting spectacles in Knossos when the Minoans participated in bull-leaping contests (see Figure 4.1 in chapter 4). Bull-leaping or bull-jumping appears to have been a form of Minoan sport entertainment that demonstrated agility, bravery, and strength. Most interpreters of the extant illustrations of bull-leaping argue that both men and women participated in the event, and no evidence indicates that either bulls or humans were harmed during the activities. However, bull-leaping was a forerunner of centuries of human-animal combat, anticipating both the arena games and the contemporary bullfight.

The ancients were also keen on the display of animals in more passive conditions, such as in menageries and animal parks. Veltre writes that the term "menagerie" is derived from the French *ménage*, "to manage," and *rie*, "a place," thus literally a place to manage animals, which, he argues, implies a place of containment, domination, and control.[78] Early menageries appeared with the rise of urbanization, which provided the large number of skilled laborers and artisans required to manage the animals. In addition, encounters with wild animals were not considered a novelty until the development of cities; the rise of urbanization might have brought about a desire for wild nature, and the menagerie became a kind of "art form" of contact with the wild.[79] Exotic animals were kept in Egypt as long ago as 2446 BCE. A limestone tomb carving of three Syrian bears shows them with slight smiles on their faces, collars around their necks, and short leashes tethering them to the ground; the bears were likely taken captive by Egyptian trading expeditions to the Phoenician coast or obtained through trade with Asians.[80] Numerous illustrations of tame Syrian bears held on leashes by foreigners are found on the walls of Theban tombs, and while it is believed that they were brought to Egypt as curiosities, there is no evidence that they were performing animals—the first performing bear in Egypt was exhibited during Roman times.[81] Elephants were popular as exotic animal performers, and some Romans were impressed with their intelligence, particularly Pliny the Elder:

> The elephant is the largest land animal and is closest to man as regards intelligence, because it understands the language of its native land, is obedient to commands, remembers the duties that it has been taught, and has a desire for affection and honour. Indeed the elephant has qualities rarely apparent even in man, namely honesty, good sense, justice, and also respect for the stars, sun and moon ... Some elephants, at the gladiatorial show staged by Germanicus Caesar, even performed clumsy gyrations like dancers.[82]

Plutarch also wrote at some length about the intelligence and affectionate nature of elephants in the ancient world:

> For the largest of the elephants had fallen athwart the gateway and lay there roaring, in the way of those who would have turned back; and another elephant, one of those which had gone on into the city, Nicon by name, seeking to recover his rider, who had fallen from his back in consequence of wounds, and dashing in the face of those who were trying to get out, crowded friends and foes alike together in a promiscuous throng, until, having found the body of his master, he took it up with his proboscis, laid it across his two tusks, and turned back as if crazed, overthrowing and killing those who came in his way.[83]

Many species of exotic animals were collected and kept in menageries in ancient Egypt. Queen Hatshepsut's (1495–1475 BCE) animal collection included baboons, leopards, cheetahs, monkeys, and giraffes, some of whom were clearly included in the royal household—one wall painting shows a pair of beautiful cheetahs wearing collars and led about on leashes.[84] Tuthmosis III also had an impressive collection of exotic animals; his limestone temple at Karnak is adorned with the images of 38 birds, 13 mammals, a tiny insect, and approximately 275 specimens of plant life—in Houlihan's words, a "natural history museum in stone."[85] The Museum of Alexandria, founded by Egyptian kings Ptolemy I (367–280 BCE) and Ptolemy II (309–247 BCE), was a research institute that maintained a large exhibition of a variety of exotic species, including elephants, antelope, camels, parrots, leopards, cheetahs, a chimpanzee, twenty-four "great lions," lynxes, Indian and African buffaloes, a rhinoceros, a polar bear, and a 45-foot-long python.[86]

Aristotle's descriptions of animal biology and zoology were based on his observations of animals sent to a zoo in Greece by Alexander the Great, Aristotle's student. Alexander sent animal specimens to Greece from his military expeditions, and it is possible that Aristotle also participated in animal dissections.[87] The Greeks exhibited a variety of small exotic animals, and the public was charged admission to visit the collections, the earliest recorded gate fee in history to see exhibited animals.[88] The Greeks had a general scientific interest in animals: they performed experiments on captive quail-like birds and school children took field trips to observe small animal collections.[89]

Even though the Romans greatly enjoyed watching animals go to their death in the arena, they also liked to observe animals in aviaries, fishponds, and small parks. People enjoyed viewing animals destined for the arena in holding areas called *vivaria*, and some animals were put on display at slaughter-free Roman celebrations and games.[90] The famous physician of the ancient world,

Galen, wrote that after their slaughter in the arena, elephants (and probably other species as well) were dissected by physicians to satisfy anatomical curiosity.[91] Galen is also known as the father of sports medicine, having gained experience in trauma and sports medicine while giving medical attention to the gladiators from 157–161 CE.[92]

It was common for the Romans to document their awe of the spectacles of nature, particularly combative struggles between animals. Pliny the Elder recorded numerous animal-on-animal fights in his work, such as a combat between an elephant and a snake, which he found a most entertaining natural spectacle, exclaiming "What other cause can one assign for such mighty strifes as these, except that Nature is desirous, as it were, to make an exhibition for herself, in pitting such opponents against each other?"[93] And writing on the nature of sea creatures, Pliny described the hostility between two species of whales:

> The balaena [a species of whale] penetrates to our seas even. It is said that they are not to be seen in the ocean of Gades before the winter solstice, and that at periodical seasons they retire and conceal themselves in some calm capacious bay, in which they take a delight in bringing forth. This fact, however, is known to the orca, an animal which is peculiarly hostile to the balaena, and the form of which cannot be in any way adequately described, but as an enormous mass of flesh armed with teeth. This animal attacks the balaenian [in] its places of retirement, and with its teeth tears its young, or else attacks the females which have just brought forth, and, indeed, while they are still pregnant: and as they rush upon them, it pierces them just as though they had been attacked by the beak of a Liburnian galley. The female balaena, devoid of all flexibility, without energy to defend themselves, and over-burdened by their own weight, weakened, too, by gestation, or else the pains of recent parturition, are well aware that their only resource is to take to flight in the open sea and to range over the whole face of the ocean; while the orcae, on the other hand, do all in their power to meet them in their flight, throw themselves in their way, and kill them either cooped up in a narrow passage, or else drive them on a shoal, or dash them to pieces against the rocks. When these battles are witnessed, it appears just as though the sea were infuriate against itself; not a breath of wind is there to be felt in the bay, and yet the waves by their pantings and their repeated blows are heaved aloft in a way which no whirlwind could effect.[94]

The Romans often took advantage of spontaneous opportunities to watch animals in elaborate nature spectacles. Again, Pliny the Elder, prolific writer that he was, recorded his firsthand observation of how the emperor Claudius put on a spontaneous spectacle involving a trapped whale:

> A killer whale was seen in Ostia harbour … It had come when … [Claudius] was building the harbour, tempted by the wreck of a cargo of hides imported from Gaul. Eating its fill of these for many days, the whale had made a furrow in the shallow sea-bed and the waves had banked up the sand to such a height that it was absolutely unable to turn round; its back stuck out of the water like a capsized boat. Claudius gave orders for a number of nets to be stretched across the entrances of the harbour and, setting out in person with the praetorian cohorts, provided the Roman people with a show. The soldiers hurled spears from ships against the creature as it leapt up, and I saw one of the ships sink after being filled with water from the spouting of the whale.[95]

With the collapse of the Roman Empire in 476 CE and the emergence of a period of relative economic decline, extravagant animal spectacles were no longer affordable.[96] However, the deployment of animals to entertain and amuse humans continued. Roving animal trainers and performers traveled the countryside with exotic animals, itinerant animal acts performed at medieval fairs, and local governments provided opportunities to view animals kept in moats, cages, and pits.[97] In the tenth century, manuscript drawings show that bears and apes were trained to perform human behaviors, and horses performed by dancing on ropes and beating drums.[98] Further, as the animal collections held by the Romans were dismantled, the practice of maintaining menageries was taken over by European royalty and other wealthy individuals. Royal menageries were filled with animals brought back to northern Europe from the Crusades, and collections of live trophy animals continued their ancient tradition of illustrating the importance of rulers and empires.

The authority of the ancients regarding animal behavior and anatomy went unquestioned until the 1200s when artists began to make firsthand observations in creating their work. In the absence of observation, the vivid descriptions of the physiology and behavior of the animals in the ancient world, such as those provided by Pliny the Elder, were essential. Alas, Pliny's careful documentation of ancient animals ended with his untimely death at age fifty-five. In his desire to observe firsthand the eruption of Vesuvius in 79 CE, he traveled by boat to Stabiae and on landing was overcome by sulphurous fumes.[99] Pliny the Elder's work had a major influence throughout the early Middle Ages. Indeed, his firsthand observations, such as that of the whale in Ostia harbor, were to be the last written or visual records based on looking at real animals for more than one thousand years, a central issue that will be taken up in volume 2 in the *Cultural History of Animals* series.

CHAPTER ONE

Animals

*From Souls and the Sacred in Prehistoric Times
to Symbols and Slaves in Antiquity*

JIM MASON

I begin this essay far away in time and topic from the focus of this volume. I do so because it is essential to understand the importance of animals to the human mind and consequently its expressions in arts, myths, rituals, symbolism, religions, literature, and other components of culture. As we shall learn, our lifeways—particularly our economic relationships with animals—determine our ways of seeing animals. Our ways of seeing animals have, in turn, much to do with our worldview, which includes views of nature, the supernatural/ divine, and—it must be emphasized—ourselves in it all. For the longest part of our existence as hominid animals, we had one kind of relationship with animals and then, rather recently in evolutionary time, we shifted to domestication and quite another kind of relationship. With the rise of the civilizations of antiquity, this "new" relationship was already several thousand years old and becoming settled; nevertheless, those civilizations were still struggling with the heavy baggage of the much older relationship. Much of the culture of the formative stages of these civilizations reflects this struggle. Thus, if we are to understand more fully the role of animals (and the emerging agrarian worldview) in antiquity, we must first stray from the theme at hand.

MOVERS OF THE MIND

Animals are more important than we think. Animals are—to use a computer-era metaphor—hardwired into the basic circuits of our minds. Throughout the five to ten million years of our hominid evolution, we have lived among animals—noisy, lively, eating, drinking, sleeping, shivering, fighting, playing, copulating, urinating, defecating, bleeding, dying *others* that fascinated us and provoked thought. Somewhat like us, yet somewhat different, animals forced comparisons, categories, and conclusions. Animals moved our minds even as our minds were evolving. And they are still alive, well, and kicking at the deepest levels of our minds today.

Unfortunately, too few fully understand this. The late biologist Paul Shepard explained it best in *Thinking Animals: Animals and the Development of Human Intelligence:* "There is a profound, inescapable need for animals that is in all people everywhere," he wrote; as shapers of the human mind and thought, there is "no substitute" for them.[1] This need for animals, Shepard says,

> is no vague, romantic, or intangible yearning, no simple sop to our loneliness or nostalgia for Paradise. It is as hard and unavoidable as the compounds of our inner chemistry. It is universal but poorly recognized. It is the peculiar way that animals are used in the growth and development of the human person, in those most priceless qualities, which we lump together as "mind." It is the role of animal images and form in the shaping of personality, identity, and social consciousness. Animals are among the first inhabitants of the mind's eye. They are basic to the development of speech and thought. Because of their part in the growth of consciousness, they are inseparable from a series of events in each human life, indispensable to our becoming human in the fullest sense.[2]

Our prevailing worldview may block our understanding of this. We are too used to thinking of animals as important only in the economic sense—for food, materials, work, and, lately, as tools for finding cures for diseases. And human superiority, we think, gives us these entitlements over "lower" animals. Ironically, we can hardly think about their importance to the very capacities—mind, speech, and intelligence—on which we base our claims of superiority.

IMPRINTING A FULL DECK

What evolved in humans, Paul Shepard says, "was not intelligence, but a development process."[3] Genetics sets down the equipment—the brain, nervous system, and other organs—but it does not complete the process. Take vision, for example. Put a patch over the eye of a newborn animal, and it cannot, in the absence of light, develop those final nerve connections and so remains blind even after the patch is removed. Similarly, the human brain needs animal types to help it make the connections that put the mind—and the external world—in order. Animal types are, Shepard says, "a necessary ingredient, like light shining on the eye of the newborn."[4]

Second, in producing the human brain, natural selection did not turn out an organ "that could assimilate an infinitely complex world like a stomach digesting meat."[5] Instead, natural selection produced a linking device, one that takes "advice" on types, categories, and the order of things from the types, categories, and order of things in the living world. "The clever brain employed the existing composition of plants and animals of the ecosystem itself as a master model. To have done it differently would have involved vastly more information storage of DNA and cumbersome connections and tissues."[6] We do not come into the world with a full deck, in other words; we have to print—or imprint—it ourselves. Thus, the development of the mind and intelligence had to become part of the development of each individual—to be repeated with each new human life. Fortunately, each new life does not have to start completely from scratch, as it is born into a family, a tribe, and a culture. From these, the cumulative wisdom about types, groups, names, and the order in the world gets passed on.

Third, this whole setup makes the human animal highly adaptable to variations in environment and culture. If we had been born with brains already loaded with fixed ideas geared to a specific ecosystem, they would have served us only in that ecosystem. When the ecosystem changed with geologic and climatic events, we would have had no mental equipment to help us migrate or otherwise cope with the changes. As it is, we have an organ, the brain, which has the capacity for speech, thought, and the other activities we call *mind* so long as it is duly imprinted and informed by its environment in the developing years. In this way, our minds enabled our ancestors to spread out all over the world and live in greatly varying environments. As environments varied, the "advice" and imprinting varied, and consequently human beings produced a great many kinds of cumulative wisdom about the world. These are the thousands of cultures of the world. To the eye, they appear to differ greatly in their beliefs, rituals, arts, and tools, but these very differences flow from the same source—the spongelike brain/mind that takes its shape and finds its order by sopping up the images, categories, and order in the world immediately around it.

Throughout evolution, human mind-sopping came largely from observing animals moving and doing their things. Trees, rocks, mountains, and other objects offered the mind rather simple, straightforward things to categorize and name. But the behavior of animals offered a way of making sense of concepts and intangible things, and these are important to human culture—that is, the transmission of learning and human experience from one generation to the next. Shepard explains:

> The kind of learning that culture carries ... is born on the symbolic vehicle of speech which, among other things, denotes intangible qualities, invisible events (as in the past or at a distance), spatial relations, personality traits, spiritual forces, and the whole adjectival realm of description. To the early humans and to the young human mind, these things are not perceptible; they are imageless. They cannot be seen in the self or even in other people. They are discoverable only as they inhere in other creatures. Friskiness, hunger, and patience can be seen respectively in pups, the searching coyote, or the waiting hawk atop a tree.[7]

Animals' behavior patterns could also provoke deeper thoughts about ourselves and the world—thoughts like *who are they?* and *who are we?* and the other whys and wherefores of existence. Animals were indeed food for thought; they offered a constant moving feast of wonders and puzzles for the mind. They offered sounds, body shapes, movement, and behavior that were strikingly similar to those of humans. The bear and the ape stood on their hind legs and lifted morsels to their mouths with "hands." Bison, elk, wolves, beavers, and many other animals called to each other, and they foraged, moved, and lived in groups like people. Much more compelling to the human mind, though, would have been the obvious similarities of sexual acts and bodily functions. We are so very squeamish and silly about these today because our culture operates to distance ourselves from, and deny our biological kinship with, other animals. Our early ancestors, however, were intimate with the living world, not alienated from and hostile to it. When they followed a bison herd and watched a bull, penis red and dripping with semen, mount and move his loins against a cow, they would surely vividly recall their own sexual experiences. On their daily foraging rounds, they were likely to see animals eating, drinking, defecating, and urinating—acts that are daily human experiences as well.

THE POWER OF ANIMAL IMAGES

The presence of animals in our minds and culture becomes apparent in their prominence in art. The earliest known artworks are scenes of animals painted on the walls of caves in Europe and Asia (see Figure 1.1). The suggestion that those paintings reflect the food wishes of hunters is simplistic. Lord Kenneth Clark disputes this: "Personally I believe that the animals in the cave paintings are records of admiration. 'This is what we want to be like,' they say, in unmistakable accents; 'these are the most admirable of our kinsmen ...'"[8] The great bulk of our ancestors' diet came from plants, yet animals were the main things on their minds. We ought to think about why they were so much more fascinated with deer than acorns.

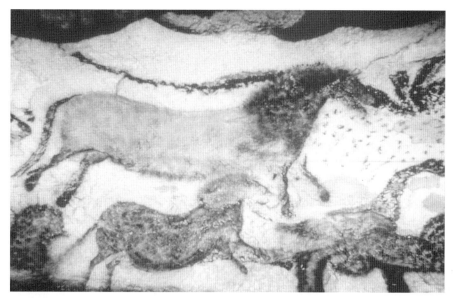

FIGURE 1.1: *Herd of Horses*. Serigraph transcription of prehistoric cave painting. Location: Lascaux Cave, Perigord, Dordogne, France. Photo Credit: Art Resource, NY; ART 44240.

In all of art since the cave paintings, it is probable that animals are represented more often than any other class of things in nature.[9] Animals, as artists are well aware, can be used to convey many kinds of messages—even those that words cannot. In religious art, animals are often the major symbols for teachings and moral themes. The dove symbolizes peace, the lamb innocence and Christian compassion. In the bestiaries, the moral storybooks of the Middle Ages, "animal pictures became a kind of pictorial shorthand, a reminder of the Christian truths embodied in every creation of the natural world."[10]

In addition to their symbolic value, animals add feelings to art. As any serious lover of art knows, animals often set the mood of a painting. In bucolic landscapes, it is the cows chewing their cud and dozing in the shade that convey the utter tranquility and dreaminess of country life. In paintings of battle scenes, it is the twisted bodies of horses with fear in their eyes that shout out the cruelty and violence of war. In his masterpiece *Guernica*, Pablo Picasso used such a figure to convey the horror of the Fascists' surprise bombing raid on a small village during the Spanish Civil War. Many of our great works of art would not be nearly so powerful, or so tender, if the animals were removed.

ANIMALS EMBEDDED

In *Thinking Animals*, Shepard tells about "concealed creatures" and "embedded figures"—more evidence that animals are, to use computer-speak, wired into our minds. Animals are moved by other things in nature to flee, breed, feed, fight, and so forth. With our more complex minds, animals often mean not only a meal or danger, but clues, signs, symbols—a whole language embedded in our minds. He tells of an experiment in which a man was given a brief glimpse of a silhouette of a tree stump. Its roots, branches, and contours formed the image of a duck. Asked what he saw, the man did not indicate that he saw the duck. Then he was asked to describe a scene or tell a story. The story he told was full of references to feathers, nests, flight, ponds, and other things related to ducks. This kind of perceptual activity goes on all the time, Shepard says. "As adults, we see creatures to which we do not attend, and … we weave them continuously into the flow of thought, from which they shed telltale signs into our conscious life."[11] People suffering from some forms of schizophrenia are especially prone to spotting these embedded animals. In their withdrawal from the real world, perhaps the primitive, deeply embedded animal figures are more prominent in their minds. Shepard also notes how widely animal figures are used in intelligence tests, personality studies, psychological therapy, and perceptual research. "The whole realm of visual figure use in psychology, especially in the study of children, is shot through with animals."[12] Consider the Rorschach test, in which the subject describes a scene or tells a story after being shown various inkblots. "The blots are usually seen as animals," he notes, "but the journals, books, and papers on Rorschach theory devote little attention to the most fundamental question that it raises."[13] That these meaningless shapes are commonly seen as animal shapes is simply accepted.

THE POWER OF ANIMAL STORIES

Language and folklore also depend heavily on animals to convey messages from human mind to mind. Joseph D. Clark's book *Beastly Folklore* reveals nearly five thousand examples of animal-based expressions. We say, for example, that a person is "mousy" or "sheepish." People "play possum," "grouse" about things, or "badger" someone. Anyone can list hundreds of examples and see how animals are the source of vivid expressions in human language. According to Clark, no other set of things in the universe is found so often in speech.[14] This constant animal presence in language, like that in art, tells us much about the importance of animals to the human mind.

Because they play into the "wiring," animal stories and images resonate, which gives them extra kick and clout. Aesop, a Greek slave in the sixth century BCE, was one of the first to use their potency to get moral and political messages across to a wide, popular audience. Francis Klingender explains that Aesop's fables worked because of their "power to harness more primitive layers of the imagination."[15] So effective were they that Gautama, the Enlightened

One, or Buddha, borrowed several of them for his own spiritual teachings. Of his "Birth Stories," or *Jatakas,* more than a hundred are animal fables of the same stock as Aesop's.[16] We find the same use of animals' power on the imagination in children's books and stories. As Margaret Blount explains in *Animal Land,* "an animal fantasy is a kind of imaginative launching ground that gives a built-in power of insight to narrative—one is half-way there before one has noticed."[17]

PLAYING ANIMAL

Once they are old enough to walk and run, children the world over get much of their fun and exercise by "playing animal"—that is, by imitating animal postures, sounds, and behavior. In my own first- and second-grade years, my playmates and I spent most of our recesses cavorting about the playground as the animal of the day. Some of us would play like wolves and chase after each other. A classmate named Carolyn specialized in the horse, and she usually went into character as soon as the bell rang. Sometimes she would gallop, buck, and rear for nearly the whole play period. When the bell rang again, Carolyn would return to her desk, trotting and whinnying.

Much of the fun is the simple thrill of exercise and the joy of using our newly discovered hands, feet, muscles, and limbs. Play makes us try out our bodies and test them against gravity, space, and the other people and things around us. Playfulness in our "dub years" is one of the things we have in common with other mammals. The instinct for it is stamped into the mammalian genetic code because it has such tremendous survival value in aiding the development of muscles, senses, coordination, and agility.

In humans, however, the playacting is an important part of another kind of growth. Because we are such conscious animals, we have awareness of not only our body but also the vague, indefinable thing called "self." Thus, in humans, self-actualization—or figuring out the *self*—is a critical developmental process. This awareness of the self in humans produces a corresponding awareness of the *Other,* the people and things around one's Self. So we have the psychic chore of coming to terms with not only the Self, but the Other as well. Our collective failure to do so can lead to social problems—that is, problems among various people, or Selves. As we playact the various animals by exaggerating their traits (as in leapfrog, horseplay, monkeyshines, fox-and-geese, "chicken," etc.), we find out that they are really not us and we are really not them. We take on their traits and, at the same time, we put them off. In imitating the Other, we establish its reality as a separate being, for if we have to imitate it, we cannot *be* it. All that the child is aware of here, of course, is laughter and great fun, but deeper down, the child is working out the psychic boundaries between the Self and Others.

TOTEMISM AND HUMAN SOCIETY

Totemism derives from the Algonquian (Chippewa) word for brother-sister kin, *ototeman*, which, in its original context, referred to the lineal descent of a clan's members from its founding spirits—animal, plant, or other natural or supernatural beings. At the core of this view of the world is a set of myths or stories about how the world came into being—creation myths, we call them. In totemic culture, these stories usually explain not only how the world began, but also how the tribe came into being. They provide a base for a whole body of tribal legends and lore that give the tribe a sense of place and purpose in the world. This body of stories and ideas about the world is an extension of the child's process of self-actualization. It provides the social group, the tribe or clan, with an identity, a history, and a model for its lifeways. Just as the child uses animals to find its personal Self, the tribe uses animals (sometimes other natural beings, but primarily animals) to find its social Self.

Into adulthood, in totemic cultures at least, human beings continue to follow the teaching of animals—the most fascinating, informative beings in the world. As their creation myths suggest, totemic cultures see animals as First Beings, ancestors, and teachers. This view was best expressed by the Pawnee chieftain Letakots-Lesa when he told anthropologist Natalie Curtis in 1904:

> In the beginning of all things, wisdom and knowledge were with the animals; for Tirawa, the One Above, did not speak directly to man. He sent certain animals to tell men that he showed himself through the beasts, and that from them, and from the stars and the sun and the moon, man should learn.[18]

The most important myth of a society is its creation story, for it sets out the elements of the people's worldview. Universal in creation stories is the prominence of animals, especially the most fascinating species of the region. These stories are surprisingly similar the world over. In *Red Man's Religion*, anthropologist Ruth Underhill says that there are very few basic plots. Common in eastern Asia and North America is the story of the Earth Diver, in which the world at first is only water. The first beings are diving birds or mammals—usually one of the species found in the tribe's domain lands. One of these divers brings up a piece of soil from which the earth is made. Then a First Being appears who commands the divers. In another plot, the solid earth was always here; it just required some shaping by the First Beings when they appeared. In another, there is no world at all in the beginning; a First Being comes out of the nothingness and makes the earth and seas by force of will or by using pieces of its own body.

Whatever the origins of the land and seas, the First Beings in them are usually animals. Typically, they are animals with human abilities: They have animal forms, but they speak and behave like humans. The subject of a great many stories and tales, they are often the creatures who transformed and shaped the earth to its present condition, and in many cultures, they are the ancestors of human beings. Generally, this First Being is the most wily and intelligent animal in the tribal area. Among North American peoples, it is the mink, raven, or blue jay in the Northwest; in the Plains, it is coyote or grandmother spider; in the Northeast, it is the white arctic hare. In Guyana, for example, people "traced their primordial beginnings to animals (tigers [West Indian for jaguars], snakes, the water *camoodi* [a giant water snake]) or from animal-human procreation. The Carib nation … was born from the fragments of a snake."[19] In African traditions, "animals with a powerful relationship to nature—the lion, tiger, elephant, and leopard—are most commonly found as totemic beasts, but, of course, an animal with cunning and mental alertness such as the spider might also take on this symbolic role."[20] Among the !Kung San people of South Africa, who hunt their Master Animal, the eland, "the first eland appears in a curiously ambiguous relationship to their creator-god and trickster-hero, Kaggen ('Mantis')."[21]

After these First Beings, humans come into the world. In most creation stories they are practically helpless, like infants. The older, wiser animal-people teach them how to make fire, tools, and clothing and how to find food and cook. They also teach the first humans how to perform the dances, chants, and ceremonies. Then, typically, the animal-people go back to the forests and streams and become animals as we know them. Their descendants are the animals of the tribe's homeland. The human beings, the tribe's human ancestors, are now on their own, but they must continue to live and perform the ceremonies as they were taught. If they do not, the world will fall out of order. The attention to lifeways and the ceremonies, then, is not so much worship in the modern religious sense as an obligation. It is what the tribe must do to carry out its end of the ancestral deal with the First Beings.

PRIMAL GUILT

What I have said about the awe and fascination toward animals—the sense of kinship with them, the reliance on them as teachers and world shapers—begs an obvious question: If primal (early totemic) people had such feelings and ideas about animals, how could they hunt, kill, and eat them? We know that they had none of the sort of feelings toward animals that today we call humane or compassionate. But we do see evidence in the form of certain beliefs and rituals that they had some feelings of discomfort, or guilt, about hunting and killing. This may seem off base unless we remember that they viewed prey animals as equals and, in some cases, as kin. An Inuit hunter's statement reveals this feeling:

> The greatest peril in life lies in the fact that human food consists entirely
> of souls. All the creatures that we have to kill and eat, all those that we
> have to strike down and destroy to make clothes for ourselves, have souls
> like we have, souls that do not perish with the body, and which must
> therefore be propitiated lest they should avenge themselves on us for taking away their bodies.[22]

The mythologist Joseph Campbell, among others, notes a sense of actual guilt among foragers who hunted and killed animals for food. It was set up, in part, by their view of animals as ancestors, kin, and fellow beings. From this, "a psychology of tension is thereby established on many levels, which it is the function of hunting rituals and their mythologies to resolve."[23] These rites, he says, are evidence of guilt. Feelings of guilt or apprehension were resolved, in part, by belief systems that allowed the killing to be either painless or permitted by the supernaturals. Societies that rely primarily on hunting for subsistence usually have a myth of a supernatural being known as the Master of the Animals. This figure is like a chief of the animal to be hunted—say, the caribou. According to typical tribal legends, a tribal ancestor had long ago made an agreement with the Master Animal that allowed the tribe to hunt and eat the caribou so long as the ceremonies were performed to show proper respect for the caribou herd. In *Of Wolves and Men,* Barry Lopez describes this belief among the Naskapi people of the Labrador Peninsula in eastern Canada:

> The agreement is mythic in origin, made with an Owner of the Animals.
> In the Naskapi world this is the Animal Master of the caribou because
> the caribou is the mainstay of the Naskapi diet. The Animal Master is a
> single animal in a great mythic herd. He is both timeless and indestructible, an archetype of the species. It is he who "gives" the hunter the animal to be killed and who has the power to keep the animals away from
> the hunter if he is unworthy. In the foundation myths of every hunting
> culture there is a story of how all this came about.[24]

In other types of hunter belief systems, the hunters must perform ceremonies of purification before and after the hunt. These are, according to Campbell, usually rituals of atonement indicative of some feelings of guilt. Campbell notes that the guilt and its ceremonial component are greater when the prey animal is closer to human size and shape. He gives the example of the Ainu of Japan, who have elaborate atonement rituals for the killing of bears, which they believe to be their ancestors and kinfolk. Essentially, the ceremony expresses their belief that the bear is a great spirit who wants to be freed from his earthly body so that he can return to his home in the spirit world. The Ainu word for this sacrificial killing means, literally, "to send away." Campbell reports that in spite of all the ritual, the Ainu still show ambivalence about the killing. Often the women who have suckled the bear cubs alternately laugh and cry during the ceremonies.

In many other cultures with bear cult sacrifices, similar guilt-reducing ceremonies are practiced. "When the bear has been slain," Campbell notes, "it is usual to disclaim responsibility for his death. In northern Siberia today, the Ostyaks, Votyaks, Koryaks, Kamchadals, Gilyaks, Yakuts, Yukahir, and Tungus will say: 'Grandfather, it wasn't I, it was the Russians, who made use of me, who killed you. I am sorry! Very sorry! Don't be angry with *me*.'"[25]

British scholar James Serpell has described evidence of actual guilt by tribal hunters in Africa, South America, India, and Indochina: "Although it varies in detail from place to place, the undercurrent of guilt and the need for some form of atonement for animal slaughter is common among hunting people."[26]

HUNTING IN PERSPECTIVE

We came to be human, the popular story goes, "because for millions upon millions of evolving years we killed for a living."[27] So wrote Robert Ardrey, the best known of the popularizers, in his 1976 best seller, *The Hunting Hypothesis*. From the beginnings of *Homo erectus* in Africa, he wrote, "we had to be pre-adapted to a diet consisting exclusively of meat and equipped with the skills of the chase that could guarantee survival."[28] A recent book by Donna Hart and Robert W. Sussman stands the Ardrey thesis on its head, suggesting that early humans were more the hunt*ed* than the hunt*ers,* that our ancestors developed brains, tools, and social cooperation to avoid being killed by animals. That and more balanced views have not been as popular as those of Ardrey and his ilk. The contributors to *The Evolution of Human Hunting* say that early humans were more scavengers/collectors than hunters and that true hunting—socially coordinated stalking and killing with special tools—did not begin until about twenty thousand years ago. Why such a late start? Joseph Campbell speculates that ice age conditions expanded prairies and savannas, which in turn greatly expanded the migrating herds of hoofed animals across the continents of the northern hemisphere. Many totemic societies became specialized hunters and as such could travel as far as the herd ranged—even into unfamiliar ecosystems. The "Great Hunt," he says, spanned from Europe across Asia into North America; a second wave extended into northern Africa.

ANIMAL POWERS

This strictly materialist view may not tell the whole story. It does not consider what might have been going on in the minds and culture of our species some twenty thousand years ago. They may not have been simply opportunists, as the above model suggests. Since all views on prehistoric hunting are based on ambiguous evidence and much speculation, I feel entitled to offer my own: Perhaps some tribes tilted toward hunting because of totemic cultural views prevailing at the time. I have in mind two rather large areas of prevailing ideas: ideas about animals and ideas about sex and gender. Animals intrigued our ancestors with their size, speed, strength, and behavior; they were First Beings, world shapers, teachers, and ancestors of the tribe. Animals gave early humans a handy way to "see" the vague, formless, chaotic rest of nature. According to author Yi Fu Tuan, "When people want to express their sense of the force of nature, both in the external world and in themselves, they have found and still do find it natural to use animal images."[29] Animals embodied or represented all the mysterious powers of the world that humans did not have, which is why Campbell described totemic culture as "the way of the animal powers."

FEMALE POWERS

The other great and powerful mystery in primal or early totemic culture was the notion of the female powers. Women's roles as childbearers, midwives, food gatherers, food preparers, food sharers, healers, shamans, and all-around nurturers contributed to considerable female status. In an age when the kin group was everything, females carried on the life of the kin group via children, food, herbal medicines, and much of the knowledge of the magical powers in the world that could help or hurt their kinfolk. The mother role was central, of course, but it was bolstered by women's embeddedness in the weave of primal lifeways. To be female was to be in continuity with the major mysteries of childbirth, the silent but potent plant world, the fecundity of other animals, and the growth and regeneration of the living world (which we now sterilize and make into an abstraction with words like *nature* and *environment*). Of all these roles, the procreative was the most compelling. It gave females a strong sense of personal identity and security as well as power and status within the kin group. Thus, the female gender identity is automatically defined by the mother role. Because women have built-in ways of showing their womanhood, men strive for ways to display their manhood. Anthropologist Henry S. Sharp, in his study of northern Canada's Chipewyan people, put it this way: "To be female is to be power, to be male is to acquire power."[30]

Bear in mind that primal people had no way of understanding reproductive and birth cycles. With nine months separating the act of coitus from the birth event, it is unlikely that they could have connected the two. From hunting, they had intimate and specialized knowledge of the habits of animals for the purpose of locating and following them to make a kill. It is unlikely, however, that they could have maintained contact with one animal or a few specific animals over a

FIGURE 1.2: *Venus of Willendorf* (side view). Limestone figure. Aurignacian (late Paleolithic). 25th millenium BCE. Location: Naturhistorisches Museum, Vienna, Austria. Photo Credit: Erich Lessing/Art Resource, NY; ART 29898.

long enough period of time to see how copulation is linked to birth. The discovery of fatherhood would have to wait until people began to domesticate animals and to live continuously with the same few individual animals over a long period of time. But until then, women "owned" the birth mystery and were revered as the givers of life. The primal explanation of this most powerful mystery was that women had close connections to the awesome powers of nature. Indeed, primal people believed that women were *part of* these forces of nature that could either sustain or destroy, could either bring forth human life or take it away.

These female powers inspired the other type of first art: the "Venus" figurines or "naked goddesses" of the late Stone Age (see Figure 1.2). They, too, reflect what was most fascinating to the primal mind, what things were seen as the most powerful mysteries and forces in the world. Whereas the cave paintings depicted the animal powers, these first sculptures depicted the mysteries of the female—pregnancy, childbirth, fecundity, continuing life for the kin group. One such figurine found in a burial site suggests a female role in receiving the dead and the delivering of their souls to rebirth. We do not know exactly how primal people used these figurines. They may have used them as fetishes to aid childbirth, as idols/protectresses of the family hearth, or as sacred objects in ceremonies having to do with the life and fecundity of the kin group. Nevertheless, archaeologists have found them all across Europe and Asia in sites that date from thousands of years before agriculture begins. They are evidence of a mythology in which the outstanding human powers and their form were female. This mythology flourished until well into the agricultural period when the Naked Goddess came to be called Lady of the Wild Things, Protectress of the Hearth, Consort of the Moonbull, and many other names.

WHY HUNTING?

But back to the question of why men took up organized hunting. I submit that men hunted to enhance their own status in the kin group. Males needed some means of achieving a balance of power against the female powers. Every animal killed and eaten offered a bit of the animal powers. "Like the sun, the moon, and the stars, animals [were] aspects of the natural order, every species endowed with a power of its own, which [was] manifest in its individuals."[31] The hunt, in my view, was not so much about acquiring food as it was about acquiring power—the animal's power. Taking the carcass back and eating it with one's family and kinfolk enabled the whole group to share in the taking of the animal's power. The attitude was similar to that of cannibals, who eat the flesh of their respected enemies and heroes to acquire their power, not their protein. In addition to the prestige gained by taking an animal's power, hunting gave men some role, and hence some status, as food providers. Women's foraging consistently brought in the bulk of the diet, but it brought no excitement. The hunt required much preparation, and it produced much excitement, which, of course, grew out of people's emotional conflicts, which in turn grew out of their sense of the animal powers. Richard Leakey noted this hunt excitement in the !Kung San people of southern Africa:

> … there was almost certainly more excitement about the men's contribution than the women's, even though the plant foods essentially kept everyone alive. There is a mystique about hunting: men pit their wits and skill against another animal, producing the silent tension of stalking, the burst of energy and adrenaline of the chase, and the elation of success at the kill. The challenge of a hunt is overt and visually impressive, the more so the bigger and fiercer the prey. Meanwhile the undoubted cerebral skills in mapping the distribution of plant foods, and knowing which will be ripe when, are much more calm, covert, and apparently unimpressive.[32]

I have not dwelled on the totemic culture of primal societies in prehistoric times too much. It is important to understand their views of the living world if we are to fully understand how domestication sparks the transformation into an agrarian society and culture that is well under way even before the historical period. For primal society, the living world was neither an abstract concept like *nature* or *environment,* nor a warehouse full of resources as we see it today. The world out there was alive and full of beings, souls, and powers. Other living beings, especially animals, were regarded simply as other kinds of beings with lives, spirits, and powers of their own. Sometimes people saw them as friendly, sometimes not; in any case, they saw animals as having powerful spirits. The deities/gods/supernaturals—the powerful spirits or the sacred—were *in* and *of* the living world. They dwelled in it. On occasion, they could take the form of an animal, plant, or other thing. Under this worldview, then, things seen as close to nature shared the powers and were given considerable status and respect. I emphasize this point because we will refer to it again and again as we follow the transformation into agrarian society and its new worldview. As we have seen, women especially drew their identity, status, and generally powerful place in primal society from the perception that they were somehow close to the mysteries and powers in nature. Men acquired theirs by mastering ways to take nature's powers—in the form of large, impressive animals. In either case, being seen as close to nature was good and powerful in primal society.

A NEW RELATIONSHIP WITH ANIMALS

About thirteen thousand years ago, the earth's most recent great glacial ice cap was melting away because of a warming trend. No one knows for sure exactly how and why, but by about ten thousand years ago human groups at scattered locations from northern Africa eastward to India and Southeast Asia were gathering wild plant seeds and sowing and cultivating them. At about the same time, their hunting turned into tending herds of indigenous sheep and goats and, before long, cattle and other familiar barnyard animals. Hunter-gatherers—foragers—gradually became farmers. The transition occurred in fits and starts. The first farmers still moved with the seasons and kept up many of their foraging ways. But over time, foraging gave way to farming, sedentary lifestyles, village life, and dependence on domesticated plants and animals for food. I leave it to others to discuss the nuances of the various theories about why foragers turned to farming. Here, it is enough to say that they all boil down to human population density as the prime mover. In some ecosystems, human numbers crept upwards and people had to intensify food procurement—by gathering, hunting, planting, and herding.

In the hilly regions of what is today the Kurdish region of northeastern Iraq, some tribes who specialized in hunting wild sheep and goats began to assert greater control over the herds. They were probably responding to the population pressures in the region, and they intensified what they already knew best—hunting. They may have begun by selecting certain animals—males and the younger animals. Over time these selective, systematic killings became, in effect, a primitive form of herd management. As they were still totemic and respectful of the animal powers, perhaps mythic and ritual elements drove the selections. A band of foragers may have attached itself to a particular herd, which became "their" herd to follow, cull, and live from. Along with systematic culling, the band asserted some control over the movements of their herd to the best grazing and watering areas. Little by little, these first herders learned the rudiments of animal husbandry—techniques for controlling the mobility, diet, growth, and reproductive lives of their herd. In the course of centuries, perhaps millennia, they learned about the dynamics of sex, reproduction, and the roles of male and female. They learned selective breeding, that is, the selection of males and females to breed for offspring with desirable characteristics. In its earliest stages, the desired characteristics may have been coat color and pattern, horn shapes, or other features to help the "owner" band distinguish their animals from those of neighboring bands.[33]

FROM POWERS TO COMMODITIES

Domestication and animal husbandry brought economic advantages, but they also brought about an unsettling of the very old and deeply held totemic ways of seeing animals and the living world with awe. After centuries of animal husbandry, men gained conscious control over animals and their once-mysterious life processes. Castrated, yoked, harnessed, hobbled, penned, shackled, and their sex lives controlled for human gain, domestic animals were thoroughly subdued. They had none of the wild, mysterious power of their ancestors.

They were *disempowered* and *reduced,* and they came to be seen more with contempt than awe. In reducing domesticated animals, farmers reduced animals in general and with them the living world that animals had symbolized. Crop-conscious farmers saw wild animals as pests and natural elements as threats. But it was the reduction of animals through husbandry that was the main driver of the radically different worldview that came with the transition from foraging to farming, for it broke up the old totemic ideas of kinship and continuity with the living world. This, more than any other factor, accelerated human alienation from the living world.

FROM TOTEM ANIMALS TO SACRED HERD

The reduction of animals came gradually with the long transition from foraging to farming culture. Well into historical times, agrarian societies had their bull gods, ram gods, and many other animal-shaped deities that were a carry-over from the older totemic times. Francis Klingender has traced this continuity in the art of Egypt and North Africa and found that "as the various clans began to breed cattle and live on their milk, they transferred to their herds the notions of sanctity and kinship which formerly belonged to species of wild animals."[34] The sanctity of totem animals and the animal powers in general went into decline. In the earliest stages, the Master of the Animals became the sacred bull or ram. This imaginary animal was a deity who was the spirit of the herd and was worshipped or appeased to ensure the protection of the herd. In herder cultures, chiefs/kings often identified themselves with this sacred animal to enhance their power and prestige with the spirit animals' cult followers. Eventually, the kings used the association to enhance their own pretensions to deity, so that the king himself was the personification of the sacred bull or ram (see Figure 1.3). In their capital cities, these rulers maintained sacred flocks of sheep or herds of cattle that could not be killed or eaten except through ritual sacrifice.

THE HERDER LEGACIES

The Fertile Crescent of the Middle East was the epicenter of domestication of the large herd animals—sheep, goats, cattle, horses, and camels. Two points should be noted: First, this added a unique ingredient to the development of Western culture from the very start. As Alfred Crosby says, "The most important contrast between the Sumerians and their heirs, on the one hand, and the rest of humanity, on the other, involves the matter of livestock."[35] Second, this ingredient created huge repercussions—results that are significantly out of proportion to the simple beginnings of animal domestication. As German sociologist and zoologist Richard Lewinsohn put it half a century ago, "the specific variations produced by domestication may be small in a zoological sense but they are enormous from the sociological point of view, for they have effected deep-reaching transformations in the history of both human beings and animals."[36]

The term pastoralists, used by anthropologists for herding societies, seems a misnomer as it evokes images of gentle shepherds watching over tranquil flocks and fields. As Lewinsohn says, "Only in pastoral poetry were the shepherd folk peace-loving. In reality they were not far behind hunters in rapacity and

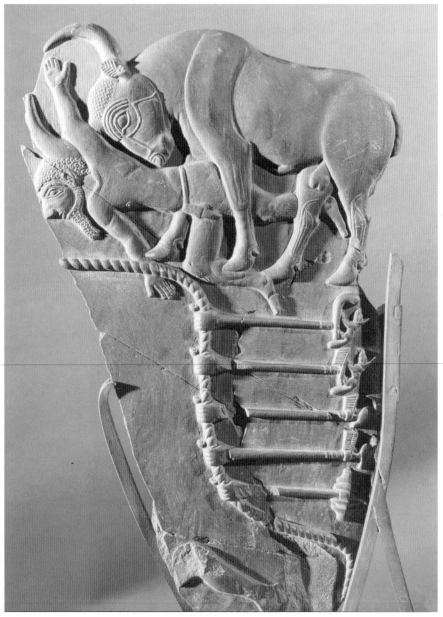

FIGURE 1.3: *The king as a bull*. Green slate. Location: Louvre, Paris, France. Photo Credit: Erich Lessing/Art Resource, NY; ART 26631.

belligerence."[37] Herding societies tend to be obsessed with their herds, for the animals constitute both their tribal identity and their livelihood. The herd is everything to them, and nothing gets between their herd and the best pasture and water. If anything does, the obsession turns to ruthlessness, defiance, and violence. Shepard comments:

> Around the world common elements run through their cultures: an obsession with the goat, cow, horse, sheep, or camel so extreme that every aspect of life mediates or embellishes its image; aggressive hostility to outsiders, the armed family, feuding and raiding in a male-centered hierarchical organization, the substitution of war for hunting, elaborate arts of sacrifice, monomaniacal pride and suspicion.[38]

British anthropologist B.A.L. Cranstone corroborates these views of herder culture after looking at herdspeople in Melanesia, North Africa, Syria, and Russian Turkestan. Since animals are the only form of wealth that is self-mobile, he says, their keepers need to be constantly on guard. "People who depend heavily on animals are, therefore, usually warlike because they have to be prepared to defend their herds."[39] More warlike are those who herd camels and horses, for these are powerful animals and valuable because they can run far and fast. Less warlike are people who herd sheep, goats, and other smaller, more controllable animals. Anthropologist and popular writer Marvin Harris has studied a variety of human cultures looking for common elements. In *Cannibals and Kings,* he noted that "most nomadic or seminomadic pre-state pastoral societies are expansionist and extremely militaristic."[40]

THE SHEPHERD-FLOCK MODEL

Joseph Campbell says of human societies, "The earliest model was of the animal world and the hunt, where the animals slain were the sacrifice..."[41] Just as animals provided a model for totemic society, so they did—though to a lesser degree—in agrarian society. Sir Keith Thomas wrote that "domestication ... became the archetypal pattern for other kinds of social subordination. The model was a paternal one, with the ruler a good shepherd—like the bishop with his pastoral staff. Loyal, docile animals obeying a considerate master were an example to all employees."[42] This model and these pastoral images are pervasive in Western culture. We look reverently upon notions of the Good Shepherd and the benevolent patriarch because our agrarian culture is so heavily weighted with the herders' legacies. The good, civilized man *shepherds* or *husbands* his family and property, his household, his community, his nation, and, by extension, the entire living world. The Good Shepherd model produced the modern secular idea of stewardship, which is supposed to

FIGURE 1.4: *Lunette with Christ as Good Shepherd*. Early Christian mosaic. Location: Mausoleum of Galla Placidia, Ravenna, Italy. Photo Credit: Scala/Art Resource, NY; ART 47899.

be the benign control and exploitation of the living world. It provided a model for the patriarchal nation-states of early civilization: The good king tended his fold of subjects. The king had absolute authority over his people just as the shepherd ruled over his flock and the patriarch ruled over his clan. The subjects owed complete loyalty and submission to the king just as the sheep obeyed the shepherd and the clan obeyed the patriarch. Over time, the model elevated many Middle Eastern kings to the level of gods. And the model grew, of course, into the West's monotheistic religions, whose great king of heaven and earth tends over the flock of the faithful (see Figure 1.4). Sociologist Gerhard Lenski finds the same concept of one all-powerful god in many herding societies: "In forty of the fifty herding groups for which [George Peter] Murdock provides data, there is belief in a Supreme Deity who created the world and remains actively concerned with its affairs, especially with a people's moral conduct."[43] Lenski says that the occurrence of belief in this kind of god "varies directly with the importance of herding activities to the particular group."[44] Lenski notes some other features of herding societies: "…marked social inequality … hereditary slavery … raiding and warfare … military advantage over their less mobile agrarian neighbors…"[45]

Some may object that dictatorship, warfare, and slavery naturally accompany the growth of the agrarian state. These horrors occur even in Mesoamerica, where dogs and turkeys were probably the only domesticated animals. But in the Middle East, royal power, wars, raiding, and slavery take on larger dimensions because of the cultural influence of the herding peoples there. Remember that these large animal domesticators came from a long tradition of specialized hunters, so they had retained their hunter-warrior skills. Obviously, these went a long way toward helping them build up their herds—their wealth and security. From the perspective of a hunter-warrior, how much more glorious (as well as easier and faster) it was to increase the herd by raiding than by slow, plodding husbandry. Warrior skills also helped keep the wealth, for a prosperous tribe had to be constantly on guard against raids by others. Herders were markedly more expansionist than ordinary farmers. Planter folks were confined to a few acres in a valley or along a river bank, and they expanded their fields relatively slowly—over years. Herders, on the other hand, arrogantly dominated an entire region through military force, thus ensuring access to the best range land and water sources. In the Middle Eastern center, at least, herders were the best positioned to fill the warrior class, out of which arose the ruling elites and kings. Consequently, the entire hierarchy and culture in the region was imbued with the herder's fierce, expansionist values. When these became integrated into the agrarian state's religion, military, and other governing institutions, they made for ruthless nations and frequent wars of conquest.[46]

ANIMAL SACRIFICE

As farming regions became more populous and urban settlements grew larger, hunting could not provide enough meat to satisfy the masses. Domestic animals were at hand, but guilt and the vestiges of old totemic beliefs, especially the sense of kinship with the sacred herd, did not permit their wholesale slaughter. As Lord Clark puts it, "While men still felt a kinship with animals, to eat them was a crime against the group, and expiation could be achieved only by a ritual feast in which all were involved."[47] So guilt-spreading and communion—or redistribution—were the first bases for animal sacrifice. The practice took on layers of religious importance over the centuries. The belief emerged that the gods could be pleased by the sacrifices and that they would protect the crops and the people from disasters. Eventually, as rulers associated themselves with the sacred herd and conspired with the priestly class to conduct the state religion, animal sacrifices became an assertion of royal and priestly authority. Throughout the ancient world, animal sacrifice followed the same basic formula: The animal was delivered to the temple, and after a ceremony designed to make the animal appear willing to be slaughtered, a priest carried out the ritual killing. The priest then burned a small amount of the fat or meat as an offering to the god or goddess. The rest of the animal's carcass was either returned to the owner, redistributed to cult followers, or sold to others. The ceremony was set up to make the gods responsible, according to Serpell. "According to an ancient Babylonian text, the head priest actually bent down to the ear of the slaughtered [animal] victim and whispered, 'this deed was done by all the gods; I did not do it.' "[48] Note that this blame-shifting device is identical to some of the older forms of ritual killing practiced by primal hunters.

These ritual sacrifices became more and more frequent as the kings and priests conspired to buy peace and public support through more and more lavish public feasts. In time, the king's sacred herd became increasingly less sacred, and the temple where the ritual slaughtering was done took on ever more the character of a commercial slaughterhouse. The scale and the frequency of the rituals, says Serpell, indicate that they were "little more than 'a transparent excuse for festive feasting.' "[49] Lord Clark tells of "the enormous scale on which it took place from early times. In the *Odyssey*, no feast, no landfall, no hospitable welcome, no gift-laden departure, is conceivable without the sacrifice of animals … and the Parthenon is said to have stunk like a slaughterhouse."[50]

In time, animal sacrifice lost its usefulness as a redistributive feast. Society was getting too large, and rulers simply could no longer provide meat for everybody as they did in earlier times. It ended, too, because of agrarian society's emerging ideas about property and ownership. Wealthy herders and farmers would have resented the priesthood's monopoly on slaughtering their animals. The practice was like a tax, and it hampered trade in animals and their products; it made no sense to have the trade restricted by old-fashioned religious ideas. Animals would have to have less spiritual value and more secular value; they would have to stop being gods if they were to serve as money. But the waning of animal sacrifice did not put animals in higher regard. On the contrary, agrarian society's growing need for them called for another wave of reduction.

MISOTHERY: ANIMAL HATING

I have coined the word *misothery* (miz OTH uh ree) to refer to a body of negative ideas about animals and nature. It comes from two Greek words for "hatred" or "contempt" and "animal." Literally, then, misothery is hatred and contempt for animals. And since animals are so representative of nature in general, it can mean hatred and contempt for nature—especially its animal-like aspects. Tennyson described nature as "red in tooth and claw," that is, bloodthirsty like a predatory animal. In another version of the same idea, we say it is a "dog-eat-dog" world. These are misotherous ideas, for they regard animals and nature as vicious, cruel, base, and contemptible. We sometimes use such expressions to describe human nature. Among the meanings for the word *animal* in most dictionaries are: *an inhuman person, brutish, bestial.* In the *Concise Oxford Dictionary* (9th ed.), *bestial* is defined as "brutish, cruel, savage, sexually depraved." Thus we call someone an "animal" when we want to insult and debase him or her. It is an epithet applied to the cruelest, most heinous criminals. Serial killers are usually referred to as "animals" in the popular press. We describe horrible human beings as "animals," "beasts," or "brutes" (an old word for *animal*) when we want to describe their egoism, insatiable greed, insatiable sexuality, cruelty, senseless slaughter of other beings, and the mass slaughter of human beings—all of the kinds of behavior that are, as John Rodman wrote in his "Dolphin Papers," "more frequently observed on the part of men than of beasts."[51]

I have deliberately constructed the word misothery for its similarity to the word misogyny, a reasonably common word for an attitude of hatred and contempt toward women. The similarity of the two words reflects the similarity of the two bodies of attitudes and ideas. In both cases, the ideas reduce the power, status, and dignity of others. Misogyny reduces female power/status/dignity and so aids and abets the supremacy of males in patriarchal culture. Misothery reduces the power/status/dignity of animals and nature and so aids and abets the supremacy of human beings in our dominionist culture. In the Middle East, where exploitation of domestic animals was key to the wealth of budding nations, agrarians invented misothery to push the reduction. The builders of the bustling city-states preached misothery in their arts and in their rising, new agrarian religions. In these, the essential message was to debase animals and nature and to elevate human beings over them. The effect, spiritually speaking, was to turn the world upside down: Before domestication, the powerful souls or supernaturals (or gods) were animal, and primal people looked up to them; after domestication, the gods were humanoid, and people looked down on animals. The agrarian's god might be a living Sumerian or Assyrian king, or it might be Zeus, Jupiter, Aphrodite, Venus, Artemis, Diana, or any of the other human-shaped gods of Greek and Roman polytheism, or it might be the superman Yahweh, God, or Allah of Middle Eastern monotheism. At any rate animal-using agrarians stripped animals of their souls and powers and put them in what they perceived to be their proper place: in the service of superior humankind.

BEAST FIGHTS IN SUMERIAN ART

We can see graphic evidence of animal reduction and developing misothery in Mesopotamia. Here the favorite motifs are scenes of animal processions, animals fighting, and men fighting animals. These scenes are found on temples, murals, and pottery and in sculpture. According to Klingender, they show up in great numbers on the famous cylinder seals, and they "provide a continuous record of the changing fashions in Mesopotamian art for almost three thousand years, from the middle of the fourth millennium to the collapse of the Persian Empire in the fourth century BCE."[52] In the earliest, protoliterate stage known as the Uruk period, the prevailing themes were "serenely pastoral, in marked contrast to the later subjects of Mesopotamian art."[53] Early on, the main theme was the sacred temple herd. The animals—cattle or sheep—are depicted in a peaceful procession, usually in natural settings. These are docile domestic animals moving in single file to the fields. These "animal file" scenes evoke the bucolic calm and order of a well-to-do agrarian city-state. Then, gradually, a second major category of scenes appears on the cylinder seals. In these "beast-hero" scenes, the animals are reared up, usually in confrontation, as on heraldic coats of arms. On some, a pair of heroes—possibly Gilgamesh and Enkidu—grapple with bulls or other beasts (see Figure 1.5). On others, "a hero may grapple simultaneously with a beast on either side, thus forming a triad representing a kind of fighting antithesis to the tree-of-life," says Klingender.[54] Later on a third major theme appears, one that "consists of a continuous frieze of fighting creatures, usually lions and other beasts of prey attacking cattle, with herdsmen defending their flocks."[55]

By the thousands, the cylinder seals illustrate Mesopotamia's changing views of animals and nature. In the process, says Klingender, "detachment was achieved" when the lifelike, naturalistic animals of the early period, when animals were still sacred under the remnants of totemic ideas, are shown distorted and stylized in the later periods, when animals had been reduced to symbols. "This probably reflects the taste of the barbarians who invaded Mesopotamia."[56] These would have been horse-mounted warrior peoples who burst out of the northern Middle East in the third and fourth millennia BCE. In waves of raiding to the south, they left their mark on Mesopotamia, its art, and, ap-

FIGURE 1.5: *Lapis lazuli cylinder seal,* from Mesopotamia. Early Dynastic Period, ca. 2600–2400 BCE. Scene of human-headed bulls protected from an attack of lion-headed birds by a hero and a bull-man. Location: British Museum, London, Great Britain. Photo Credit: Heritage Image Partnership/Art Resource, NY; ART 181533.

parently, its views of animals and nature. These developments in art reflected a deeper psychic/cultural shift: the reduction of animals from lively, ensouled, kindred beings to frozen symbols of human power over nature. In Mesopotamia, according to Lord Clark, "the sense of kinship with animals has been superseded by an overawed recognition of their strength, which can be used to symbolize the terrible power of the king."[57]

Klingender says that "animal art of later civilizations in Western Asia was wholly under the sway of this [Mesopotamian] achievement."[58] He notes that these rampant, fighting beast motifs show up on a gigantic scale in Hittite palaces and temples. Others are found at Assyrian sites and, later still, at Nebuchadnezzar's Babylon and in the palaces of Persian kings at Suza and Persepolis. "Their influence on the other great styles is no less remarkable: they contributed decisive elements to the arts of early Greece, the later Roman Empire, Sassanid Persia, Byzantium, the Muslim world and medieval Europe."[59] He means, of course, the motifs, themes, and scenes—the style of the art. But we know that art reflects a society's deepest ideas about the world, so the widespread popularity of these styles also tells us something about the spread of Middle Eastern agrarian culture. Obviously, its ideas about the order of humans, animals, and nature had appeal far and wide wherever domestication had begun. And the Mesopotamians, with some help from the hordes of horse-warriors from the north, furnished the graphics that best illustrated this new order. They were the first propagandists for misothery, and these notions were thoroughly ingrained in the cultures of the region by the time of Abraham and the beginnings of the monotheism that endures today.

PATRIARCHY

Male usurpation of female power came from the joining of three forces: First, males were jealous of the female powers discussed above. This institutionalized male envy carried over into the agricultural period, when sedentary living, population density, and the growth of towns and cities made hunting less practical and successful. Thus hunting and its rituals gradually ceased to offer men a means of compensating or counterbalancing the female powers. Male envy then turned on the female principles (and on women) and worked to reduce and co-opt them and bring them under male control. Second, the female powers gradually eroded as agriculture demystified nature. These powers, as noted, had been grounded in women's association with the mysteries of procreation specifically and nature's mysteries in general. As society took greater control over nature through irrigation, clearing, plowing, and other methods of intensified agriculture, it came to regard nature—and thereby women—with less and less awe. In battling weeds, pests, predators, drought, and capricious storms, farming society came to regard nature as more foe than friend. Farmers learned contempt for what they could control in nature, and they learned fear and hostility for what they could not control. Insofar as women had been associated with nature, their powers, status, and essence tended to change accordingly. Third, the discovery of fatherhood struck the most overt blow to female prominence. As noted, procreation—the most powerful mystery in nature—had been exclusively women's domain. After centuries of animal husbandry, ideas about male fertility began to emerge—especially in the Middle East, the epicenter of herd animal domestication. These would have been at war with the much older yet still prevailing ideas about the female powers and their manifestations in goddesses and fertility cults. Feminist author Kate Millet wrote in 1970:

> The circumstance which might drastically redirect such attitudes would be the discovery of paternity. There is some evidence that fertility cults in ancient society at some point took a turn toward patriarchy, displacing and downgrading female function in procreation and attributing the power of life to the phallus alone. Patriarchal religion could consolidate this position by the creation of a male God or gods, demoting, discrediting, or eliminating goddesses and constructing a theology whose basic postulates are male supremacist, and one of whose central functions is to uphold and validate the patriarchal structure.[60]

Patriarchy, like any other cause on the make, needed to have God and morality on its side. As we might expect, in the ideological warfare that ensued between the emerging male rule and the older female-powered egalitarian order, both religion and ethics were invoked to reduce women and to elevate men. Myth, as Kate Millett notes, "is a felicitous advance in the level of propaganda, since it so often bases its arguments on ethics or theories or origins."[61] In Western culture, there are two leading origin-of-evil myths—that is, myths that purport to explain why the world is so full of toil and trouble. One is Hebrew, the other Greek—the two principal feeders of Western thought and culture. Both are crassly misogynist. Both have their taproots in herder culture. The Greek story of Pandora's box credited woman with opening the box and releasing evil into the world. According to Millet, the myth served two purposes: It discredited and reduced Pandora, who was probably one of the older fertility goddesses of the Mediterranean, and it promoted the idea of feminine evil and destructive influence. In his account of the myth, the Greek poet Hesiod described Pandora as the original of "the damnable race of women—a plague which men must live with." She introduced evil through what the patriarchal Greek mind saw as a uniquely female product: sexuality. In his *Works and Days*, Hesiod described Pandora as a dangerous temptress with "the mind of a bitch and a thievish nature." She had "the cruelty of desire and longings that wear out the body." She was full of "lies and cunning words and a deceitful soul." Pandora was a snare sent by Zeus to be "the ruin of men." Millet notes the hypocrisy and mendacity of the Greeks' patriarchal propaganda: "When it wishe[d] to exalt sexuality, it celebrate[d] fertility through the phallus; when it wishe[d] to denigrate sexuality, it cite[d] Pandora."[62]

The Hebrew myth of the fall from grace is strikingly similar to that of Pandora. It is, however, much more central to the Judeo-Christian-Islamic tradition and to our present worldview. Even for the nonreligious, says Millet, "this mythic version of the female as the cause of human suffering, knowledge, and sin is still the foundation of sexual attitudes, for it represents the most crucial argument of the patriarchal tradition in the West."[63] The story of Eve and the fall in Hebrew tradition also suggests that Eve, like Pandora, may have been a fertility goddess in earlier times. At one point in Genesis, it says that Adam named her Eve "because she was the mother of all living things." So, like the Pandora myth, the Hebrew myth was double-barreled propaganda: It demoted a female deity while reducing women in general. Millet explains that the monotheistic, patriarchal Hebrews lived in a continual state of war with the fertility cults of their neighbors. In this situation, the story of Eve and the fall helped to solidify Hebrew identity against the wickedness and backwardness of their enemies. Another parallel to the Pandora myth is that woman's sexuality tempted man and brought about original sin, shame, and evil in the world. In the Eve myth, the sex act is disguised in language about eating forbidden fruit from the tree of knowledge of good and evil. Scholars have pointed out that the Hebrew word for "eat" can also mean coitus, and that throughout the Bible the word "knowing" is synonymous with the sex act—as in *carnal knowledge* or *he lay with her and knew her.* Again, as in the Pandora myth, a god-the-father figure punished his subjects for engaging in sinful sex. Adam and men were condemned to endless toil and adversity, while Eve and women were sentenced to inferiority and the pains and sorrows of childbirth. As Millet notes, "the connection of women, sex, and sin constitute[d] the fundamental pattern of Western patriarchal thought thereafter."[64]

SPREADING THE SEEDS OF A WORLDVIEW

Over the many centuries that it took to build agrarian society, male-dominant herding peoples with their values of aggression, expansion, and warfare naturally took over. When they conquered and annexed a region, they put the stamp of their culture on it, and herder ways and views came to dominate the Middle East both geographically and culturally. Over time, herder culture provided the dominant threads in the agrarian culture of the Middle East. Only in that center of civilization was such a powerfully male-supremacist worldview woven so early into the usual fabric of agricultural society. There, herder culture colored the entire process—from the early increase in the scale of society to the emergence of classes, ruling elites, and labor specialization, and, finally, the building of the agrarian state itself with its taxes, bureaucrats, patriotism, and wars of conquest. Early on, herder culture gave hue and pattern to the formation of Western civilization, and its motif was a world for males only, with every other kind of living being in service to them.

We can see much of this process unfold in the early history of Mesopotamia, which began about 3000 BCE. Historian Gerda Lerner believes that this was the beginning point of a 2,500-year process in which female power and status gradually fell while male power and status rose.[65] Before this process began, male-female relations were roughly egalitarian, although the greatest spirit-powers or deities were female; at the end of the process, men ruled over women as they ruled over the livestock, and there was one deity—an all-powerful male god, the Great Shepherd. In the process, she says, military strong men became chieftains over villages, established dominance over temple lands and herds that had previously been held communally, gradually pushed the priests into the background, and took on the role and symbolic trappings of the priests' closeness to the gods. Eventually, the strongest of these chieftains would become kings, and after centuries of regional wars the strongest kings would become emperors. Throughout these times, the arts reflect the strength, courage, and dominance of powerful ruling men. They are shown slaying enemies in battle, of course, but their godlike power is best shown in scenes of them slaying lions, which, as the most powerful and dangerous of beasts, symbolize the forces of nature.

This agrarian worldview was spread far and wide primarily by cattle and horse herders of early antiquity. Paul Shepard calls this the "Neolithic dialect"—the conflict between herders and settled farmers in the ancient civilizations.[66] With their "walking larders,"[67] herdspeople migrated around the Mediterranean into northern Africa and Europe and eastward across Asia spreading their culture along the way: Hurrians, Aryans, Hittites, Mittani, Luwians, Kassites, Achaeans, Dorians, Kurgans, and many other tribes whose names have been lost. Their "jostling readiness to kill remind us that Western civilization has a heavy heritage of pastoral thought. From the Hun and Scythian horsemen, Mediterranean goat- and ass-keepers, Semitic cattle-breeders, Persian shepherds, and Arabian camel-lovers, from them and other animal-keepers the Western world obtained its premises of a world view."[68]

As we examine the arts and culture of the ancient world, we will see their fingerprints: the misogyny of the Hebrews when they wrote Genesis around 800 BCE; the misothery of ancient Greece, whose Plato wrote in *The Republic* of "the wild beast within" the human soul; and, in contrast—perhaps as propaganda—the kindly Good Shepherd symbolism throughout Judeo-Christian-Islamic mythology. We will see human power over animals and nature and the conquest of foreign lands celebrated in violent ritual "games" before huge crowds in the arenas of ancient Rome. In Christian culture, we will see that the Antichrist is identified by the mark of the beast and that evil is personified in Satan, who is depicted with horns, tail, wings, and cloven hooves. In heraldic art, we will see the most powerful predators used as the chief symbols of aristocratic status. From ancient Mesopotamia to Europe in the Dark Ages, we will see hunting scenes, as Lord Clark puts it, as "a ritualized display of surplus energy and courage" and symbolic of the ruling classes.[69] In all of it, we will see the indelible presence of animals in the humane psyche and culture.

CHAPTER TWO

Hunting in the Ancient Mediterranean World

J. DONALD HUGHES

Hunting, the killing of other animal species for food and other uses, is the primeval way of life of human communities. Indeed, it provided sustenance to prehuman and possibly ancestral primates. *Homo erectus* ("upright man"), a species that many scientists believe to be a direct ancestor of modern humans, moved into the Mediterranean area from a probable place of origin in East Africa, where they used roughly spherical throwing stones to bring down prey. This species had a lifestyle that included gathering and hunting of animals up to the size of elephants and rhinoceroses (which still existed then in much of the Mediterranean area). They came to Europe as long ago as a million and a half years, but bone fossils date to a period between five hundred thousand and two hundred thousand years ago. Remains of *Homo erectus* have been found in Algeria, Morocco, Spain, southern France, Greece, and Israel. The Petralona skull, found near Thessaloniki in northern Greece, has been described as an intermediate form between *Homo erectus* and Neanderthal humans (*Homo sapiens neanderthalensis*).

The Neanderthals were widespread in the Mediterranean basin between about seventy thousand to thirty thousand years ago, during the ice age. Skeletal fragments have turned up in Morocco, Spain, Gibraltar, France, Italy, Israel, and Iraq. Their brains were as large as those of modern humans or larger, but their faces were characterized by heavy brow ridges, sloping foreheads, and large noses. They were stocky and muscular, and, with a finely shaped toolkit, hunted virtually every animal, large and small, in their environment. They lived in caves or shelters made of bones and skins and wore clothing of skins sewn together using bone needles and sinew. When they buried their dead, they painted the bodies with red paint made from iron oxide and manganese and made grave offerings of animal skulls, roasted meat, and flowers.

Humans of our species, *Homo sapiens sapiens* ("thinking man"), spread out of South and East Africa through western Asia and then into the southern European lands.[1] They reached Palestine perhaps one hundred thousand years ago, and Spain by forty thousand years ago. Sometimes called Cro-Magnons, they had replaced the Neanderthals by twenty-eight thousand years ago. These new inhabitants of the Mediterranean made stone tools improved beyond those of the Neanderthals and were efficient hunters who undoubtedly reduced the numbers and ranges of large mammalian species. Their material cultures were those of the Paleolithic (Old Stone Age). Some of them made convincing, energetic paintings of animals and humans on the walls and ceilings of caves. In the abundant ecosystems, they found plants to gather, fish and crustaceans to catch, and plentiful mammals to hunt. Sometimes, too, they were prey of large predators such as the lion and cave bear. They used fire to cook, to keep warm, and to drive wild animals. Using materials such as wood, antlers, bone, and stone, they fabricated spears and spear-throwers, fishhooks, and eventually bows and arrows.

They depended intimately on the prey species for their food, clothing, and shelter. The size of their groups was limited, and a natural balance, always somewhat precarious, was thus maintained between the human population and the populations of prey, along with wild vegetable foods. Individual hunters regarded themselves as integral members of communities, with the duty to provide the tribe with food, protect it against enemies both animal and human, and seek power through visions, disciplines, and repetition of rituals. Methods and rituals of hunting were preserved through oral traditions. From an ecological perspective, these traditions helped the community adapt to the local environment and use it without destroying it. Hunters had deep respect for the animals they hunted and detailed knowledge of them, as carvings and cave paintings indicate. Peoples who share a hunting and gathering way of life tend to regard the world as animated by spirits and to respect animals and plants as living beings endowed with power. Hunting, fishing, and gathering were carried out within rituals and surrounded by prohibitions developed through long generations of trial and error. Cave paintings represent shaman-like humans wearing animal skins, horns, and skulls, and dancing in movements evocative of the beasts. Stone, bone, and ivory carvings from this period represent a Lady or Lord of Wild Animals, a protecting power for the creatures, who would reward careful hunters and punish imprudent ones.

In spite of traditions that taught essential conservation, Paleolithic humans faced ecological crises, some of which they caused. The pressure of hunting drove many large animals to extinction or acted together with climatic changes to hasten their disappearance. Some of the animals that vanished from the Mediterranean area by the end of the ice age were ones that humans understandably killed because they preyed on humans, such as the cave bear and hyena, or competed with humans in hunting other animals. Then there were giant herbivores like the mammoth and rhinoceros, sources of good quantities of meat. Fire was a great force employed by the hunters, who methodically set fire to forests, brush, and grasslands in order to drive animals and to encourage the growth of new grass to feed grazing animals that were their quarry. Often, repeated fires could replace forest with grassland, so that hunters had a significant effect on the landscape. If they seriously depleted the local game, however, they might have to leave or die. Over many generations, the groups that survived learned ways that tended to preserve the landscapes within which they could live well.

EARLY CIVILIZATIONS

Hunting did not end with the invention of agriculture. It continued as a way of supplementing food supplies, of procuring skins, furs, and feathers, and of killing wild animals that preyed on domestic herds. As a young shepherd, David killed lions and bears that attacked the sheep he guarded, a practice that prepared him to kill the giant Goliath with a slingshot.[2] Dietary laws prohibited the slaughter of animals for food unless they were in captivity, however, which prevented hunting from becoming a part of traditional Jewish culture.

The hunt is a motif often encountered in ancient Egyptian art; the pharaoh is shown hunting as a demonstration of his vigor and courage.[3] In predynastic times, as petroglyphs and other works of art attest, Egypt possessed a variety of wild species as rich as that now found in East Africa, but persistent hunting by nobles and commoners alike gradually reduced this biodiversity. By the end of the Old Kingdom, elephant, rhinoceros, giraffe, and gerenuk gazelle were missing or rare north of the First Cataract, and the wild camel was extinct in North Africa. Barbary sheep, lions, and leopards were still present, but in reduced numbers. Some of this depletion may have been the result of a changing climate, since the Sahara did not dry to its present aridity until well into the Old Kingdom. But some was also caused by deliberate destruction: Amenhotep III boasted on one scarab that he had killed 102 lions with his own hand; lions were considered to be the prey of kings.[4] By the Middle Kingdom, the ranges of some antelope species had become limited and their numbers decimated.[5] Egyptian reliefs show the pharaoh hunting wild bulls. Other works of art show dogs assisting in hunts for antelope in the desert. Eventually, large wild animals almost totally disappeared from the Nile Valley, and animals captured elsewhere were increasingly imported for symbolic hunts by the nobility.[6]

Leopard skins, ostrich eggs and feathers, and countless other items secured by hunting were carried northward from the interior of Africa by boat down the Nile (see Figure 2.1).

The numbers of birds, particularly waterfowl, remained astonishing in Egypt, a "land of whirring wings,"[7] down through the New Kingdom, but their abundance was gradually reduced. Egyptian paintings show nobles hunting birds in marshes, accompanied by cats that apparently served as retrievers and were rewarded by meals of fish. Nobles of all periods enjoyed bird hunting, but fewer and fewer marshes remained as drainage proceeded.

According to inscriptions at Medinet Habu, Ramses III gave 426,395 waterfowl to temples, including his largest bequest of 9,350 per year at the Temple of Amun at Thebes alone. Some of these became part of temple flocks, while others were prepared as offerings; it should be understood that sacrifice in ancient Egypt did not consist of the ritual killing of animals and birds, but rather the presentation to the gods of food dishes already prepared and ready to be eaten. Priests consumed these delicacies after the ceremony. Bird life, diminished but not destroyed by the ancients, is today at a low ebb. The ibis is scarcely seen in

FIGURE 2.1: Fresco of African antelopes from Akrotiri on the island of Thera (Santorini), Greece. Minoan, 17th century BCE. National Archaeological Museum, Athens, Greece. Photo by author.

Egypt, and of the fourteen commonest species of duck in ancient Egyptian art, only one now breeds there.[8]

A similar fate awaited the fish of the river. Some texts indicate that they were avoided as food because of their association with the god Set, enemy of Horus, but other evidence shows that they were often caught and eaten. Some were protected; it was strictly forbidden even for the pharaoh to fish in the sacred lakes of the temples. A stela from Abydos places the following words in the mouth of Ramses IV: "I ate nothing I should not eat, I did not fish in the sacred lake, I did not hunt with the bird-net, I did not shoot a lion at the festival of Bastet."[9]

Kings of many nations engaged in hunting for recreation and as a form of royal propaganda. Even the gods in Mesopotamia are described as enjoying the hunt.[10] King Tiglath-Pileser I of Assyria boasted of killing incredible numbers of lions, elephants, and birds.[11] Palace walls often show the king of Assyria killing lions, sometimes with a sword that goes all the way through a beast, emerging from its back. Kings might have tried to reserve lions as exclusive royal prey, but this does not seem to have kept shepherds from defending their flocks. The *Epic of Gilgamesh*, perhaps the oldest extant long poem, reveals the urban Mesopotamian sense of the distinction between the tame and the wild, between civilization and wilderness, and shows a new and hitherto unfamiliar attitude of hostility toward untamed nature. Enkidu, the hairy man of the wild, first appears in the poem as a friend and protector of beasts, but he is a nuisance and even a menace for that reason, releasing animals from hunters' traps and warning them away from ambushes. When he had been tamed, his former animal friends feared him and fled. Entering the city of Uruk, he met and struggled with King Gilgamesh, who became his close friend. Together they went on a quest for cedarwood in the far mountains. The forest was a sacred grove protected by the wild giant Humbaba, and his defeat and death at the hands of the two heroes symbolized the subjugation of the wild. Gilgamesh hunted wild animals mercilessly; he is said to have killed lions simply because he saw them "glorying in life."[12]

HUNTING IN CLASSICAL TIMES

Hunting in Greece and Rome did not begin in the historical period, since along with fishing and gathering, it was the dominant occupation of ancestral people for the greater part of their existence on earth. Long before the classical period, the ancestors of the Greeks and Romans were hunters and fishers who lived in balance with the species on which they depended. The attitudes of these early hunters survived as relics in religion and folk practices, and later in doctrines such as Orphism and Pythagoreanism. In spite of this, wildlife was depleted in ancient times. Although hunting done in moderation need not reduce wildlife populations, attitudes changed, moderation was not always practiced, and other factors besides hunting affected the numbers of wild species. The Linear B tablets of Pylos in Mycenaean times identify hunters with the proto-Greek word *ku-na-ke-ta-i* (the equivalent of classical Greek *cynegetai*).[13]

The exalted view of hunting as the pastime of the gods, under the eyes of the gods as protectors of animals, is not the only or even the most prevalent concept of hunting that can be found in the surviving evidence of the Greeks and Romans. It was also regarded as a means of obtaining food and other resources, as a form of commercial gain, as a way to prepare for and support military activities, as a safeguard for agriculture and herding, and as a sport or entertainment.[14]

HUNTING FOR SUBSISTENCE

Although ancient civilization was founded on an agrarian base, and cultivated plants and domestic animals provided the bulk of the diet and materials for clothing, wildlife was still sought as a source of food, leather, furs, feathers, and so on. For many families, hunting was a direct means of support or of supplementing the diet, especially in rural areas and in earlier periods before many species had become rare or disappeared. Deer, boars, hares, and goats were among the mammalian species that were hunted for food in Homeric times and after. Turtles, frogs, and a wide variety of birds also graced the rustic table. Fishing is known from art as old as the Minoan frescoes, and seafood, including shellfish, was a major source of protein for the common people.

HUNTING AND FISHING FOR THE MARKET

Those who did not hunt for themselves could purchase animal products from a widespread trade supplied by professional hunters, who organized game drives like those seen in North African mosaics.[15] Small-scale commercial hunters also supplied the marketplaces of towns. There one could buy wild meats such as venison and many kinds of birds, from peacocks and flamingos to small songbirds.[16] The furs of beavers and other animals from distant mountains could be had, as well as ostrich feathers and various kinds of leather. Greek and Roman demand brought wild animal products even from beyond the Mediterranean basin. Ivory from African and Indian elephants was used in works of art from huge chryselephantine statues to delicate miniatures and was inlaid in furniture of every kind: writing tablets, desks, spoons, and other objects. Ivory in incredible quantities went into statues such as Phidias' forty-foot Parthenon sculpture of Athena and that of Zeus at Olympia, so large that it was one of the Seven Wonders of the World. In one day's exhibit in Ptolemaic

Alexandria, six hundred elephant tusks were shown, indicating that at the least three hundred of the mighty beasts had died to provide the exhibit.[17] Wild animal skins were worked into clothes and furnishings, and hair and feathers served as decorations on fine ladies' costumes and soldiers' uniforms.

Urban tastes supported a large fishing industry and provided work for entire villages. Fresh fish came daily to market from local fleets, and importers brought salt fish from Egypt, the Black Sea, and the Atlantic coast of Spain. Among the favorite species were red mullet, parrot wrasse, sturgeon, turbot, brill, common bass, hake, sole, and eels.[18] The Romans loved fish sauces with names such as *alec, garuum,* and *putrilago.*[19] Commercial interests not only operated fishing fleets to meet these demands, but also cultured fish in fresh and salt ponds. C. Sergius Orata ran a business on Lucrine Lake that raised fish for the tables of the elite.[20] Beds of shellfish like oysters were carefully tended and protected against competitors. Products of the sea (see Figure 2.2) were collected for purposes other than food, sponges, for example, or the murex mollusk that produced a famous purple dye for the robes of kings and the togas of Roman senators.

An example of the intentional introduction of a fish for commercial exploitation comes from Roman times.[21] Optatus Elipertius, prefect of the fleet under the emperor Tiberius, collected numbers of a fish, the brilliantly colored scarus, or parrot wrasse, from the seas between Rhodes and Crete and planted

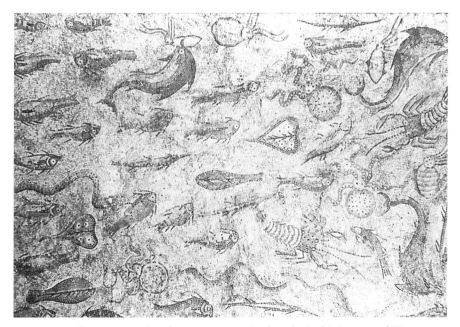

FIGURE 2.2: Roman mosaic of sea creatures, Archaeological Museum of Tarragona, Spain. Photo by author.

them along the Ostian and Campanian shores of Italy. This is reported by Pliny, who adds:

> Careful protection by land and sea rendered poaching almost impossible. For the period of five years any scarus caught in the nets had, under heavy penalties, to be returned straightway to the water. The enforcement of these wise regulations effected [a] mighty thriving of the fish...[22]

In another example, Sergius Orata planted oysters in the Lucrine Lake.[23] Others attempted to establish oyster beds on the island of Chios and near Bordeaux.[24] Wealthy Romans kept many fishponds, both fresh and salt, and we can be sure that they sought out and paid well for exotic fish distinguished by their beauty or tasty flesh.

ANIMALS AND THE MILITARY

The Roman army employed military methods in hunting to provision troops with meat. Soldiers or paid professional hunters scoured the countryside in hostile or uninhabited regions. Hunting was often regarded as a form of warfare, and art portrayed humans in battle with animals. Xenophon said, "Hunting ... is ... excellent training in the art of war."[25] His friends, the Spartans, deliberately used it in this way. Perhaps this explains the oft-told Spartan story of the boy who was carrying a stolen fox under his cloak. It was said that he met his military trainer and stood talking to him; but the fox got loose under the cloak and gnawed at the boy's abdomen, and in spite of that, the boy continued to stand without showing a sign of pain until he fell over dead.[26] The story was told to illustrate the ability of a young Spartan to bear pain and his willingness to die rather than admit he had stolen, but why he should have taken a fox can perhaps best be explained in the context of hunting as preparation for war.

Elephants were captured, trained, and used on the battlefield, resulting in a constant drain on the wild population. At the battle of Raphia in 217 BCE, 102 Indian elephants under Antiochus III of Syria defeated 73 African elephants of Ptolemy IV, collapsing the left wing of Ptolemy's battle formation, although Ptolemy managed to win the battle. Strange to say, although in modern times African elephants are known to be considerably larger than Indian elephants, the reverse was stated by every ancient author who commented on the question.[27] Perhaps this was because the African elephant then known was a smaller North African race that is now extinct. The Carthaginian elephants that invaded Italy with Hannibal in the third century BCE came from the north slope of the Atlas Mountains, but there are none there now.[28]

PREDATOR CONTROL

Ancient writers often cite the safeguarding of agriculture and herding as a reason for the destruction of wildlife, and this was doubtless a major motive both for governments and the common people. Predators were killed to protect animals on farms or herds in the countryside, while birds and herbivorous mammals were persecuted because they competed for the same vegetation as domestic animals or invaded croplands. Homer often uses the simile of lions pursued by herders in describing battle.[29] Elsewhere, relentless attempts to extirpate wolves, jackals, foxes, and bear are described. These efforts promoted hunting, but the desire to protect cropland may also have had the opposite effect—in some places, laws were enacted against hunting on horseback because the horses trampled the crops.[30]

HUNTING AND FISHING FOR PLEASURE

Hunting for its own sake as a sport, or in order to collect trophies and boast of one's own proficiency and success, is a pastime that probably developed soon after humankind began to live in urban conditions. In classical Athens, an older male lover (*erastes*) is often portrayed presenting the prey he has killed as a hunter to his young beloved (*eromenos*).[31] Plato approved of hunting to develop skill and courage in young men, but would have had his model state prohibit netting, trapping, and night hunting, as well as all forms of fishing.[32]

In art and history, hunting of various animals was portrayed as a sport of kings and heroes such as Alexander the Great.[33] In this, Alexander was following a tradition of hunting as a mark of excellence among the Macedonian nobility.[34] The Sidon sarcophagus shows Alexander and Persian nobles hunting stags, lions, and panthers.[35] The emperor Hadrian loved hunting; it is said that he killed a bear at Hadrianoutherae (a name meaning "Hadrian's beasts"), a lion in Egypt, and a boar elsewhere.[36] He, and Marcus Aurelius later, showed themselves on their coinage engaged in hunting, a valuable propaganda image. The lion was held to be royal prey, and laws often forbade anyone other than the monarch to hunt them. Julius Alexander, a Syrian of ordinary rank, was condemned to death in 189 CE for usurping the emperor's privilege by slaying a lion from horseback.[37] It was not until 414 CE that an imperial law permitted commoners to kill lions.[38] Boar hunts were also engaged in by kings, as they had been by epic heroes.[39] Kings sometimes fished for sport: Antony and Cleopatra did so, and the Egyptian queen tricked her lover by having one of her slaves attach a salted fish to his hook. Their conqueror, Augustus Caesar, also enjoyed angling.[40] Not everyone thought fishing was a royal sport, however. A character of Plutarch's, Aristotimus, disparaged it as an ignoble activity.[41]

Kings and emperors often reserved hunting lands for themselves; in the case of Greek and Roman potentates, this was in part an imitation of the Persian King of Kings and his satraps, whose parks called paradises were "full of wild beasts" to hunt.[42] Xenophon, and later Alexander, saw many of these. Since many sport hunters were affluent landowners, they too created preserves for their favored activity, as did Xenophon. There were game parks, aviaries, and large fishponds in Rome. Varro had a place near Tusculum where he fed wild boars and roe deer, but was far outdone by Quintus Hortensius, whose Laurentum estate had a game preserve of fifty jugera (thirty-five acres) surrounded by a wall. At feeding time, Hortensius had a horn blown to attract the animals, and an actor dressed like Orpheus played a lyre, as if his song were enchanting the wild beasts.[43] He gave his preserve the Greek name *therotrophion*, but there were others called in Latin *roboraria*, *vivaria*, and *leporaria*. These places preserved many animals, since common hunters were excluded, there were defenses against poachers, and the owners wanted to have large numbers to show off to their guests even when they were not hunting them.

A series of ancient handbooks, some of which have survived, purported to give advice to sport hunters. These are usually entitled *Cynegetica*, from Greek words meaning "to lead dogs," since hunters often used packs of dogs in pursuing game (see Figure 2.3). Authors of these treatises include three Greeks, Socrates' friend Xenophon and Epictetus' disciple Arrian, both of whom were avid hunters, and Oppian, who probably was not. The Latin writer Nemesianus

FIGURE 2.3: Roman mosaic of a hunter and his dogs. From the "Corridor of the Great Hunt" in the Roman villa of Casale, Piazza Armerina, Sicily, Italy. Photo by author.

of Carthage is represented by fragmentary works on hunting and bird-catching. The sport of fishing also has its literature, the *Halieutica* of the famous Latin poet Ovid, which actually contains little about fishing, and a similarly titled work by Oppian. Ausonius, writing in Gaul, devoted much of one poem to fishes and fishing.[44] All these works portray hunting or fishing as sports of the well-bred gentleman and sometimes advise him to limit his catch, spare certain animals, and avoid unworthy methods for sportsmanlike reasons.

METHODS AND TECHNOLOGY
OF HUNTING AND FISHING

Achilles outran deer, said Pindar, and caught them with his bare hands.[45] This simplest form of hunting is not unknown among primal people, but Greeks and Romans generally used assistance. Sometimes, other animals were pressed into service, such as the hunting dogs that are known from Mycenaean times, whose domestication for this purpose probably goes back to the Paleolithic era.[46] Various breeds were trained for the work; a fresco from Tiryns shows hunters with a huge hound. Hunting from horseback is not as ancient as hunting with dogs, but certainly dates from pre-Homeric times. It was widespread in classical days and is described by Xenophon and Perses.[47] Falconry, regarded as a sport of Persians and other barbarians, was practiced among the Greeks, according to Aristotle, and became popular with the last Roman aristocrats.[48] The use of prey animals as bait—for example, tethering goats to catch lions in a pitfall—was common.[49] But sportsmanlike hunters such as Xenophon denounced the use of a female animal's own young to trap her, for example, tying up a fawn to decoy a doe.[50] A repertoire of hunting implements were developed.

The idea that hunting and warfare are similar, and can use the same weapons, is much older than the classical period; a dagger from Bronze Age Mycenae shows shield-bearing warriors attacking lions with their spears, and a ring of the same period bears the design of an archer shooting a stag from a chariot.[51] Spears and javelins are often mentioned in the literature of hunting and were redesigned for use against specific prey such as boars.

Nets have been used from time immemorial; a wild bull caught in a net can be seen on one of the Vapheio cups dated to Mycenaean times. In Greece and Rome, nets of strong linen ropes were preferred. Deer and boar, as well as many other animals, were taken in nets of various designs.[52] Xenophon lists three types, purse, road, and long nets, but there were doubtless others. A purse net was a large bag with a mouth that could be closed by a noose, a road net was a rectangular one used to block game trails, and a long net was crescent-shaped with a belly and was usually set up in a forest where it could be hidden. Footsnares, devices that combined hidden nooses with wooden or iron spikes set in plaited circles of twigs, often over small pits, were also common.[53]

Birds were caught in nets, snares, and cages, or on rods or branches smeared with sticky birdlime. They were decoyed, called by clever imitators, attracted by mirrors, or lured with food as bait. As an instance of the latter, a small pit was dug and filled with berries, and two potsherds were balanced over it by a peg; when the bird dislodged the peg, the potsherds covered the hole and trapped the bird.[54] Birds were brought down with small arrows. A huge bird like the ostrich was a considerable exception; Arabian ostriches were chased on horseback.[55]

Fishing technology is a subject unto itself. Nets and spears were utilized; as Homer says of the Laestrygonians, "Like folk spearing fishes they bore home their hideous meal."[56] Not only hand-lines, but also poles of cane or light elastic woods, often six to eight feet long, were known.[57] These had fixed lines made of horsehair, flax, or a fiber called *sparton* taken from the stems of the genista shrub, a plant common on Mediterranean hills. Floats were carved of cork. Hooks were fashioned of iron or bronze and baited with real insects or with feathers and other materials to make an artificial fly.[58] Poisonous vegetable substances such as cyclamen root were used to kill fish in small bodies of water, a practice condemned by Plato.[59] Commercial fishermen erected towers to sight schools of tunny and other large fishes. At night, torches were carried on fishing boats to attract the catch.[60] Finally, it is reported that skates and other fish were attracted by music and dancing.[61]

HUNTING RIGHTS AND LEGAL POSSESSION

The ownership of game and fish in enclosures or ponds was vested in those with title to the land; outside private places, it was considered to rest in the sovereign authorities, or in those to whom they delegated it, as was the case also with unoccupied, virgin, or abandoned land.[62] Rivers, and the fish in them, were considered public property in Roman law.[63] But poaching by common people happened constantly, whether on public, private, or sacred land. The prevailing attitude was that wild animals belonged to "no one" until they were caught, and then they belonged to those who caught them. The state asserted its interest only in exceptional cases, as in protecting the animals inside a sacred *temenos*, but generally its policy was to encourage agriculture, grazing, and the reduction of the number of wild animals.

THE GODS AND HUNTING

Writers of Greco-Roman times thought that hunting might be a purer way of life that had survived from a better time. Dio Chrysostom described a family of hunters as living close to nature on Euboea, where the greed and injustice of city-dwellers had not yet corrupted them.[64] Even later hunters whose ways

FIGURE 2.4: *The Diana of Versailles*, a Hellenistic Greek marble statue of the goddess Artemis, the huntress. Museum of the Louvre, Paris, France. Photo by author.

were not so primitive believed that hunting was controlled and practiced by the gods and goddesses, Artemis in particular (see Figure 2.4).[65] The gods were protectors of game species, allowing them to be taken solely when needed and when permission had been asked and granted. Thus, a wise hunter would not heedlessly slaughter his prey, but take the gods into account. When a huge stag wandered across the path of the hungry Odysseus, he concluded that it had been sent by one of the gods, so he killed it in gratitude, but when his men slaughtered the sacred wild cattle of the sun god Helios, he knew that evil would overwhelm them.[66] As an example of the survival of earlier attitudes of reverence toward animals, an Athenian law provided that anyone who killed a wolf had to pay for its public burial.[67] Phintias, tyrant of Acragas, had a dream warning him that Artemis would send a wild sow to kill him because he had omitted her sacrifices. He immediately promised to issue coins with the goddess's head on one side and a wild boar's head on the other.[68] Arrian, the writer of a hunters' handbook, advised his readers never to ignore the gods:

> Men interested in hunting should not neglect Artemis of the wild, or Pan, or the Nymphs, or Hermes, god of the ways and pathfinder, or any other god of the mountains. If they do neglect them, needs must that their endeavors fall short of completion. Their hounds will be injured, their horses lamed, their men come to grief … One must … dedicate first-fruits of the chase no less than one must offer the spoils of war after a victory.[69]

The gods and goddesses inspired respect for animal life and enjoined practices that would make hunting less destructive, but did not forbid hunting as long as the hunters obeyed the rules that justified a human who obtained nourishment by the sacrifice of animal life. Before taking an animal, the prudent hunter would consider whether the act would offend a deity like Artemis and would have been moved to avoid killing pregnant females and young animals, thus encouraging the reproduction of game species. Xenophon says that the good hunter will spare young hares for Artemis' sake.[70] He also dedicated the first share of his kill or catch to the goddess and provided her with an altar on his hunting grounds.[71] Not only did the gods protect some animals, but they also appeared in their forms when it suited their purposes. Dionysus changed his shape to that of a lion or bull to frighten his enemies or drive them insane, and Zeus became a swan, an eagle, a bull, and countless other creatures, including an ant, usually when it suited his amorous purposes. As noted above, the appearance and movements of birds in particular were held to reveal the intentions of the gods, and there were augurs skilled in interpreting them.[72] But the protection that birds and animals might receive from their close association with the gods is problematic; John Pollard remarks concerning birds whose appearances were taken as omens: "They revered them but ate them just the same."[73]

REDUCTION AND EXTIRPATION OF WILDLIFE

An awareness of the possibility that wildlife might be totally extirpated is found in a Greek myth. According to it, the mighty hunter Orion offended Artemis, goddess of the wild, or, as some versions have it, Gaia (Gê, Mother Earth) by boasting that he would kill every wild beast in the world. In retaliation, the goddess sent a giant scorpion to sting him. Before this could happen, Zeus set both the hunter and his arachnid enemy in the sky as constellations opposite one another.[74] Mythological evidence reveals important aspects of ancient attitudes. The recognition that wildlife might be eliminated, at least from certain areas, is apparent also in the fact that many emperors, kings, and affluent landowners set aside animal preserves where only they could hunt or provision their tables, and also in the reservation of sanctuaries where wildlife was sacred to the gods and could not be killed except under carefully prescribed conditions. Poets sang about the disappearance of wild animals: "Oh distant Nasamonian lands of the Libyans, your barren plains are no longer visited by flocks of beasts of prey, you no longer tremble at the lion's roaring in the desert; for Caesar has caught a vast number of them in nets ... and the former lofty lairs of wild beasts are now pasturages."[75]

The surviving evidence gives the impression of declining populations of wildlife and the gradual extinction of certain species in one area after another. Writers often note that animals are no longer to be found where they were once abundant. Lion bones have been unearthed in archaeological sites such as the Mycenaean palace of Tiryns.[76] Herodotus reports that when the Persians invaded Greece, lions came down from the mountains to attack the camels in their baggage trains.[77] Aristotle also notes their presence in his homeland, but they were gone by the first century BCE.[78] Leopards and hyenas disappeared from Greece, and lynxes, wolves, and jackals were limited to the mountains, where they hold out today in small numbers. Bears could be found in the Peloponnesus up to 100 CE, and probably much later, since a few still exist in mountainous northern Greece.[79] Hunting reduced wild cattle, sheep, and goats to remnant herds and eliminated them from some islands in classical times. This was only one of a series of extinctions of island fauna, following the earlier disappearance, between 6000 BCE and 2000 BCE, of dwarf forms of elephants, hippopotami, antelopes, and deer; giant forms of shrews, hedgehogs, and dormice; and still other endemics.[80] Introduction of domestic species that competed with wild ones must have happened countless times, particularly on islands. The devastating effects of goats, rats, and opportunistic birds like pigeons have been observed in newly discovered lands since the fifteenth century CE; there can be no doubt that it happened in isolated places as they were visited by ships or settled by new groups of people in Greek and Roman times.

Procurement of animals for the Roman arena cleared larger mammals, reptiles, and birds from the areas most accessible to professional hunters and trappers. They exhausted the hunting grounds of North Africa, where elephant, rhinoceros, and zebra became extinct. The hippopotamus and crocodile were banished from the lower Nile to upper Nubia. By the fourth century CE, a writer could lament that there were no elephants left in Libya, no lions in Thessaly, and no hippopotami in the Nile. Lions had been extirpated from western Asia Minor, although the king of beasts persisted in Syria, where the emperor Julian hunted them, and in the Taurus Mountains; in both these areas a few could be found as late as the nineteenth century. In the Atlas Mountains there were reduced numbers, and a few lions may remain there today.[81] Distant areas felt the Roman demands; tigers disappeared from Armenia and from Hyrcania in northern Iran, the sources closest to Rome.[82] Collection of animals for the games was not the only cause of disappearance; all these creatures were hunted and killed for other reasons as well. Among the causes of the extinction of the North African form of the elephant, for example, were the use of the animal in warfare and, more importantly, the ivory trade. The Romans were persistent and efficient, could pay well, and came to dominate the commerce in animals and animal products throughout the Mediterranean basin, so the major responsibility for extinctions was theirs. Bird populations also diminished. The former richness of Mediterranean bird life can be sensed today in such relatively undisturbed areas as the Camargue near the mouth of the Rhone River in France, with its flocks of flamingos; or Coto Doñana in Las Marismas on the lower Guadalquivir River in Spain. But these are precious exceptions. The birds in Aristophanes' play berate humans for persecuting them, setting snares and lime twigs for them even on temples.[83] Ancient people devoured species that seem to have had too little meat to make the effort worthwhile, but so do some modern Greeks and Italians.

There were complaints of the depletion of fisheries. It has been suggested that the disappearance of mosquito-eating fish from Italian marshes aided the spread of malaria in the second century BCE and subsequently.[84] Increasing prices for fish on the Roman market may indicate that there were fewer left to catch than before. The finest rare fish might have sold for their weight in gold; three mullets once brought thirty thousand sesterces at Rome, and Pliny says this species rarely exceeded two pounds in weight.[85] As seas go, the Mediterranean was not particularly rich in fish, so the parts of it most accessible to the fishing fleets could have become impoverished.

The process with the most damaging effect on all forms of wildlife was, as it still is, habitat destruction. The clearing of forests, the spread of agriculture, the introduction of weeds and other exotic plant species, the overgrazing of grasslands, and the draining of lakes and wetlands all affected wildlife even more seriously than hunting. Two areas that were the objects of persistent attempts at drainage throughout antiquity may serve as examples: Lake Copais in Boeotia and the Pomptine Marshes near Rome. Although neither of these large wetlands was completely drained in antiquity, many thousands of acres of irrigable tillage land were recovered by the construction of canals and tunnels, with consequent effects on birds, fish, and other wildlife.[86] Many lakes and marshes in the Mediterranean basin were drained; in the prevailing limestone country, natural underground channels often existed that could be cleared or widened.

SANCTUARIES FOR WILDLIFE: THE SACRED GROVES

Protection within the *hiera temene*, lands set aside as sacred precincts of the gods, was given to the animals that lived there and enforced by laws of the local communities to which the shrines belonged. Hunters were forbidden to enter them with their dogs and weapons. So Xenophon noted: "As for such islands as are sacred, one cannot even disembark hounds on them."[87] On Mount Lycaeus, if a hunter saw his quarry go into the precinct of Zeus, he had to wait outside, believing that if he entered he would die within the year.[88] A cautionary tale said that the huntress Atalanta had been turned into a lioness for violating a sanctuary of Zeus.[89] In some sanctuaries there were deer or wild goats (see Figure 2.5) sacred to Persephone or Artemis, none of which could be hunted, although special permission might be given to capture a victim for sacrifice to the pertinent goddess. Sacrifices of wild animals were rare in Greek but not in

FIGURE 2.5: Goats on the island of Samos, Greece. Photo by author.

Roman times; however, most sacrifices in both periods consisted of domestic animals.[90] As a rule, wild animals in the sanctuaries were preserved as sacred to the gods, and killing them incurred punishment. Mythology, literature, and art are full of examples, such as Artemis' destruction of the hunter Actaeon by the horribly appropriate method of having his own hounds tear him to bits.[91] Although the usual version says this was because he saw her naked, that story is not found until late in Greek history.[92] If, as seems likely, in an earlier version of the myth his offense had been to hunt a deer in the goddess's sacred demesne, then his punishment truly fit the crime. He had, in any case, boasted to Artemis of his hunting prowess.[93] Bragging was also a fault of Agamemnon, the best-known literary figure to be punished for hunting in a holy place. As Sophocles says, "when taking pleasure in [Artemis'] sacred grove, he startled an antlered stag with dappled hide, shot it, and shooting made some careless boast."[94] In vengeance Artemis caused winds that prevented the sailing of the fleet against Troy until Agamemnon sacrificed his daughter "in quittance for the wild creature's life."[95] The evidence of inscriptions shows that it was not only in literature that penalties were exacted for hunting in the groves.

   To provide another example of a site where animals were given the protection of a *temenos*, tortoises were preserved on a peak in Arcadia (see Figure 2.6) where "the men of the mountain fear to catch them, and will not allow strangers to do so either, for they hold that they are sacred to Pan."[96] Similarly, the Athenians would not let anyone harm the little owls of Athena that nested on the Acropolis (see Figure 2.7) or the snake that had a den there, to which

FIGURE 2.6: Tortoises (*Testudo hermanni*) at Delphi, Greece. The shells of these tortoises were used in early times to make the sounding boxes of lyres. Tortoises were preserved on a peak in Arcadia where "the men of the mountain fear to catch them, and will not allow strangers to do so either, for they hold that they are sacred to Pan," according to Pausanias. Photo by author.

FIGURE 2.7: The little owl (*Athene noctua*), which the Athenians considered sacred to their patron goddess, Athena. Exhibit in the Goulandris Natural History Museum, Kifisia, Greece. Photo by author.

offerings of honey-cakes were made.[97] No fishing was allowed in the waters of sacred groves, under penalty of death. In some it was lawful for priests, but the priest of Poseidon at Lepcis abstained from fish, probably because they were sacred to the sea god.[98] Artemis' eels were taboo in the spring of Arethusa, and at Pharae fish sacred to Hermes could not be caught.[99]

THE BEARS OF BRAURON

An initiation into the mysteries of relationship to animals was celebrated every four years for the children of Athens. This was the *Arkteia*, a festival dedicated to Artemis at the rural sanctuary of Brauron. Little girls, and perhaps little boys too, were covered with symbolic bearskin robes and called "bears" (*ark-toi*) (see Figure 2.8). Although there were bears in Attica at least as late as the first century CE, they were rare by the Golden Age of Athens, and saffron-dyed

FIGURE 2.8: Greek marble statue of a "bear," a young girl initiate of the goddess Artemis, holding a dove, 4th century BCE. Museum at Brauron, Attica. Photo by author.

FIGURE 2.9: Columns of the Temple of Artemis, Brauron, Attica, Greece, the site of the *Arkteia*, the dedication of young maidens to Artemis, goddess of wild animals including bears, and of the hunt. Photo by author.

textile robes were substituted for the bearskins.[100] Such a festival was appropriate for Artemis, since she was believed to care for the young of both humans and animals, and myths said she sent wild animals as foster mothers to suckle infants that had been exposed.[101] Sculptures and vase paintings show children holding small animals such as hares and doves in poses of affection, even kissing them. These were not animals to be killed, since the sacrifice at Brauron was only a symbolic drop of blood from a small cut. Little girls performed a dance with slow, solemn steps imitating the movements of bears. Children sometimes wore bear masks.[102] The dominant idea of this initiation was the inculcation of respect and even love for wild creatures. A renewal of the festival was held in the city for young women near the age of marriage. The Arkteia shows that the worship of the gods had a positive side; Artemis might be seen as an early patron of environmental education (see Figure 2.9).[103]

IMITATION HUNTS IN THE AMPHITHEATERS

There were several ways in which wildlife served to entertain large numbers of people. If an animal or bird were rare and either odd or beautiful, it might simply be exhibited. Often they were tamed and taught to do tricks, as bears and lions commonly were. Small, popular shows where one animal fought another, such as cockfights or dogfights, usually involved domestic species, although sometimes wild birds or beasts were baited to combat or to devour each other. Fights were staged between partridges or quails. In a strange game called "quail-tapping," popular in Athens, a quail was put in a ring, and the owner offered bets that it would stay there even if knocked on the head.[104] But for sheer spectacle, exploitation of animals and spectators, and waste of life, nothing could surpass the Roman arena.

The shows put on first in circuses, and later in amphitheaters, for popular amusement exhausted the ingenuity of their producers. *Venationes,* or mock hunts, in which armed men on foot or horseback chased and killed animals, constituted a major part of the shows. Sometimes there were pageants or plays in which animals played a part, often involving violence or sexual perversion in addition to acrobatics. Even the rarer animals, at first exhibited as curiosities, were afterwards mutilated and killed. From at least the middle years of the Roman Republic, criminals were executed by being exposed to wild beasts that had been starved or were goaded into attacking them. The arena, so called because it had a floor covered with sand, became soaked in blood. These contests were the subject of many mosaics and paintings.

The first *venatio* in Rome was apparently held in 186 BCE by Marcus Fulvius Nobilior, conqueror of Aetolia.[105] For whatever reason, a law forbade the use of African beasts for this purpose, but Cnaeus Aufidius allowed exemptions in 170.[106] In the following year, the aediles (the magistrates responsible for the shows) exhibited sixty-three leopards, forty bears, and some elephants. Elephants had been seen in Rome for the first time in 275 BCE, when Manius Curius displayed at his triumph a number he had captured from Pyrrhus of Epirus, who had brought them to Italy for his military campaign. Romans jokingly called them "Lucanian cows," after the province where they had fought Pyrrhus. Elephants were first "hunted" in the circus in 99 BCE and were pitted against bulls twenty years later. In the late Roman Republic, the variety of wild animals and the number killed increased dramatically. Scaurus, in 58 BCE, brought crocodiles and hippopotami from the Nile. Soon afterwards, Pompey had twenty elephants and six hundred lions killed by armed Gaetulians. Caesar at various times showed a lynx from Gaul, forty elephants, and a giraffe he had received as a present from Cleopatra. Numbers continued to rise as the early emperors attempted to gain popularity by entertaining the people. Augustus held twenty-six *venationes* in which thirty-five hundred animals were killed, including tigers from India.[107] He "took especial delight in 'untold numbers and unknown shapes of beasts.'"[108] One can imagine his delight in capturing the Ptolemaic menagerie when he conquered Egypt; doubtless many of the animals killed in the excessive *venationes* at his celebrations came from that source. Claudius was not the only emperor who enjoyed watching the beast fights. Nero, in addition to his more infamous shows, flooded an arena and displayed polar bears catching seals. At the dedication of the Colosseum under

Titus, nine thousand animals were destroyed in one hundred days, and Trajan's conquest over Dacia in 107 CE was celebrated by the slaughter of eleven thousand wild animals. To these hecatombs in the city of Rome must be added the numerous *venationes* held in other towns throughout the empire.[109] The "hunters" in these sadistic spectacles were called *bestiarii* and were trained in schools like that of Domitian on the Caelian Hill.[110] Sometimes they used dogs or horses in the arena. Many of them were proud of their skill, and there were families who followed the occupation through generations.

A technology of death supported them; for example, cages were constructed under amphitheaters, complete with elevators and ramps to bring the beasts up to the arena without endangering the attendants too much. The enormous demand for a constant supply of animals was supported by an organized business for their capture and transportation. Many people found employment in this enterprise. It was far from easy, since the beasts had to be kept in good condition in pits, nets, cages, or boxes and carried or led from place to place until they were delivered. For the most part it was a private business on which the government levied an import tax of 2.5 percent.[111] Roman officials and the military amply assisted the trade, however, and soldiers were dispatched to round up the animals. Those transporting animals destined for the emperor's shows could requisition food and accommodations from towns they passed through. This was no small expense for towns on the usual routes, considering the size and number of the animals, and late imperial edicts limited the time they could stay in one city to seven days.[112] Those destined for Rome landed at wharves in the Campus Martius and were held temporarily in the enclosure for wild animals outside the Praenestine Gate.[113] There were extensive imperial menageries, including one for the elephant herd at Ardea under the care of an officer titled the *procurator ad elephantos*. A large proportion of the creatures collected for this trade must have died along the way.[114] Romans of every social level from emperor to common people attended the games, and most Romans who wrote about them approved.

PROTESTS AGAINST THE SHOW HUNTS

There were few protests against the bloody "sport" of the *venationes,* which is perhaps not surprising in light of the fact that objections to the killing of humans in the gladiatorial exhibitions were also rare. However, there was some resistance to the exploitation. In 55 BCE, the elephants in Pompey's show at the dedication of his theater gained the crowd's sympathy when, wounded by javelins, they defended themselves by snatching the shields of their attackers, attempting to break out of their enclosure, and trumpeting piteously. Cicero protested at this incident, "What pleasure can it possibly be to a man of culture, when ... a splendid beast is transfixed with a hunting-spear ... the result was a certain compassion and a kind of feeling that the huge beast has a fellowship with the human race."[115] When he governed Cilicia, Cicero refused to make his provincials collect leopards for the games; by the way, this proves the existence of the species in Asia Minor as late as the first century BCE, although he noted an extraordinary scarcity of the animals.[116] King Juba II of Mauretania objected to the destruction of African wildlife by the Romans, and his son Ptolemy, grandson of Antony and Cleopatra, closed the arenas in Mauretania, shut down the animal-port of Hippo, and enacted a conservation law to preserve animals.[117] These measures were ineffective; several species of animals including elephant, rhinoceros, and zebra became extinct in North Africa, and others declined. Marcus Aurelius, the Roman "philosopher-king," also disliked the cruelty of the games. In earlier times, a few writers voiced opposition to hunting of any kind; this was a teaching of the Pythagoreans, who refused to have anything to do with hunters, butchers, or priests who sacrificed animals. Varro was also against hunting: "There you go, chasing wild boars on the mountains with your spears, or stags, which never did any harm to you, with your javelin. What a 'splendid' art!"[118] The historian Sallust called hunting a "slavish occupation."[119] Even a confirmed hunter such as Arrian said one should not take pleasure in the sight of the kill.[120]

OPPOSITION TO HUNTING

An ancient animal rights movement, if one might call it such, existed among writers, mostly of Pythagorean bent, who honored the sanctity of all forms of life and maintained that animals possess rational souls. Ovid made Pythagoras himself a character in the *Metamorphoses* and had him advise King Numa against animal food, since it was through eating the flesh of living creatures that the Golden Age came to an end, and against animal sacrifice as making the gods into partners of mortals in wickedness.[121]

Plutarch also spoke on behalf of animals. In the dialogue *Whether Land or Sea Animals Are Cleverer*, set as a learned debate among cultured huntsmen, he argues that animals possess a degree of reason. Human beings, he adds, also have reason only to a degree; if what we wish to demonstrate is "true reason and wisdom, not even man may be said to exercise it."[122] But since animals are rational, we are unjust if we kill them when they have not injured us. Plutarch, however, does not go as far as the Pythagoreans; he would permit killing animals "in pity and sorrow," as well as eating meat as an unfortunate necessity.[123] But Plutarch's most entertaining comments on this subject are contained in a brief dialogue between Odysseus, Gryllus, and Circe. With her magic arts, Circe has changed many men into various species of animals. Odysseus won the right to have his sailors re-transformed and furthermore asked Circe to do the same for the other Greeks. Circe agreed on the condition that Odysseus had to convince a spokesman for the beasts that it was better to be a human than an animal. Chosen to speak for the beasts was Gryllus, a hog granted the power of speech by Circe. He refused the chance to return to human form because animals, he maintained, are superior to mankind in every virtue: courage, temperance, and intelligence. Besides, animal virtues are natural; humans must cultivate theirs. Odysseus, in spite of his fame as a persuasive speaker, lost the contest. Driven to use the argument that beasts cannot be rational because they have no inborn knowledge of God, he left himself open to Gryllus' riposte that Odysseus' father was Sisyphus, a notorious atheist.[124] That the dialogue was not a mere set piece is clear from Plutarch's serious objections elsewhere to hunting, animal slaughter, and the excesses of the arena. Rejecting the proposition of Hesiod and the Stoics that "human beings have no compact of justice with irrational animals," Plutarch exhibited admiration and sympathy for the myriad forms of living things and was an early defender of animal rights.[125] Unfortunately, neither in his case nor in any other known from ancient times does it seem that such ideas resulted in practical programs to help wildlife.

CHAPTER THREE

How Domestic Animals Have Shaped the Development of Human Societies

JULIET CLUTTON-BROCK

INTRODUCTION AND SOME DEFINITIONS

An animal may be said to be domestic when it has lost its fear of humans and will breed in captivity, but true domestication involves much more than this and can be defined as *the keeping of animals in captivity by a human community that maintains total control over their breeding, organization of territory, and food supply.*[1]

True domestication involves a combination of a biological and a cultural process. The biological process begins when a few animals are separated from the wild species and tamed by humans. If these animals breed, they form a founder group, which changes over successive generations both by natural selection under the new regime of the human community and its environment and by artificial selection for economic, cultural, or aesthetic reasons.

Once an animal is fully domesticated, the question arises as to what it should be called in the formal Latin nomenclature. A dog is certainly different from a wolf, so it should not be called by the name of the wolf, which is *Canis lupus*. The most parsimonious arrangement is to continue to call the dog and all other fully domesticated animals by the Latin names that Linnaeus first gave them in the eighteenth century; that system is followed here, with the name of the dog being *Canis familiaris*.[2] The end product of domestication is the breed, which may be defined as *a group of animals that has been bred by humans to possess uniform characteristics that are heritable and distinguish the group from other animals within the same species*.[3]

THE CULTURAL PROCESS OF DOMESTICATION

In order to be domesticated, animals have to be incorporated into the social structure of a human community and become objects of ownership, inheritance, purchase, and exchange. They have to be absorbed into the culture of the human owners, and in this sense the process of taming a wild animal, whether a wolf or wild goat, can be seen as changing the culture. Culture can be defined as *a way of life imposed over successive generations on a society of humans or animals by its elders. Where the society includes both humans and animals, then the humans act as the elders*.[4]

The animal is removed from the environment in which it learns from birth either to hunt or to flee on sight from any potential predator, and it is brought into a protected place where it has to learn a whole new set of social relationships as well as new feeding and reproductive strategies.

A domestic animal is a cultural artifact of human society, but it also has its own culture, which can develop, say in a cow, either as part of the society of nomadic pastoralists or as a unit in a factory farm. Domestic animals live in many of the same diverse cultures as humans and their learned behavior has to be responsive to a great range of different ways of life. In fact, so closely do many domestic animals fit with human cultures that they seem to have lost all links with their wild progenitors. The more social or gregarious in their natural behavioral patterns these progenitors are, the more versatile will be the domesticates.

As far as we know, tamed wolves, the most social of all carnivores, were the first animals to undergo the process of domestication and were thereby transformed into dogs. The archaeological record indicates that this occurred at least fifteen thousand years ago, while the ambiguous evidence from molecular biology suggesting that the split between wolves and dogs occurred much earlier has now been discounted.[5]

This chapter is concerned with the cultural history of domestication from 2500 BCE until 1000 CE, and although, on an individual basis, the interactions between people and their animals did not change much over these three and a half thousand years, the course of human history changed dramatically. For this reason, the chapter is divided into three sections, which follow the rise and fall of the world's major civilizations.

HUMANS AND THEIR DOMESTIC ANIMALS IN THE WORLD FROM 4,500 TO 3,000 YEARS AGO

By 4,500 years ago, all the main species of domestic animals present in the world today had been incorporated into human societies, and dogs were found wherever there were human habitations. It is probable, however, that people all over the world regularly tamed the young of many species of wild animals and did not distinguish clearly between the wild and the domestic, as we do today. This is shown in the art of ancient Egypt where individual animals from oryx antelopes to crocodiles are shown being handled by humans.

Western Asia

Goats, sheep, cattle, pigs, asses, and horses were first domesticated in the Fertile Crescent of western Asia, and by this period and during the ensuing thousand years they were to become the bedrock of the economies of the newly evolving city-states, such as Babylon and Nineveh. All the bovid species were probably first reared in captivity for their meat, but by this period goats and sheep were already providing milk and wool, while cattle were being used as draught animals as well as being milked.

Goats (*Capra hircus*) and sheep (*Ovis aries*) were domesticated from the locally indigenous wild species, *Capra aegagrus* and *Ovis orientalis*, probably as early as nine thousand years ago. The progenitor of cattle (*Bos taurus*) was the more widespread but also local wild aurochs (*Bos primigenius*), while the progenitor of domestic pigs (*Sus domesticus*) was the wild boar (*Sus scrofa*), which had a similar wide distribution. Cattle and pigs were domesticated about eight thousand years ago. Later on, the wild asses became a crucial part of human economies: *Equus africanus*, which inhabited North Africa and the Near East, became the donkey *Equus asinus*, while the onager, *Equus hemionus*, from western Asia was tamed and crossbred with donkeys by the ancient Sumerians and Assyrians in Mesopotamia, but never fully domesticated. The horse (*Equus caballus*) came later still, at around six thousand years ago, and was domesticated from the herds of wild horses (*Equus ferus*) that lived further north in central Asia. Among the elite of all ancient societies, horses replaced asses as soon as they became abundant, from around four thousand years ago.

The great empires of Mesopotamia and the surrounding countries that flourished for a thousand years relied on vast numbers of herd animals for their meat and milk, and the raw materials of bone, horn, hides, and wool, just as people do today. The differences to today are that they had a limited supply of metals (bronze and iron), and carts with wheels, perhaps the greatest of all inventions, were rare possessions, limited to the ruling chiefs and warlords. The earliest carts were drawn on sledges, like one that was discovered in the royal tombs at Ur (2500 BCE), but carts with solid wheels that were harnessed to oxen or asses soon replaced these. Then came the fast, horse-drawn, two-wheeled chariots that are so beautifully illustrated in the art of ancient Egypt and the Assyrian friezes. By this time, long-legged elegant greyhounds are shown as hunters' companions in both regions.

The Nile Valley

The interactions that the people of ancient Egypt had with their domestic and wild animals are better known to us than those from any other country or period before modern times. This is because of the wonderful wall paintings that have survived in the ancient tombs throughout the Nile Valley and that record every aspect of people's daily life as well as their religious ceremonies. The paintings tell us what breeds of cattle and sheep were preferred, how milking was carried out, how bees were smoked out of hives to get honey, and how some animals, such as the oryx antelope, were kept as tamed animals, even if they were not fully domesticated.

Geese, ducks, and quail are commonly depicted. A drawing of a chicken that was found on a potsherd from a tomb in the Valley of the Kings (1307–1196 BCE) is especially interesting, as chickens were domesticated from the jungle fowl of Southeast Asia, perhaps around 2500 BCE, and this drawing dates their spread westward.[6]

It is tempting to see the civilization of ancient Egypt as having a particular focus on their animal culture, but apart from their religious beliefs, which led to the mummification of thousands of cats, mongooses, monkeys, crocodiles, and other animals, which were considered to be sacred, it is doubtful that the ordinary people lived in any closer communion with their animals than the pastoral peoples of the rest of the world over the past millennia.

It is generally assumed that the cat (*Felis catus*) was first domesticated from the wild cat (*Felis silvestris*) by the ancient Egyptians, but in fact the earliest remains of a cat buried together with a human have been excavated from Cyprus and are eight thousand years old. Recent genetic evidence supports the archaeological findings that the domestic donkey is descended from two African wild asses, the Somali, *Equus africanus somaliensis*, and the Nubian, *E. africanus africanus*,[7] but as yet no evidence suggests that the one-humped camel, or dromedary, was first domesticated in the Nile Valley. The remains of the domestic dromedary (*Camelus dromedarius*) have been found in North Africa and in western Asia from 2000 BCE, but its wild ancestor is unknown.

India and Eastern Asia

By 2000 BCE zebu or humped cattle (*Bos indicus*), domesticated from the Indian aurochs (*Bos namadicus*), were the common livestock of the agricultural

FIGURE 3.1: Seal depicting a domestic zebu bull from Mohenjo Daro in the Indus Valley, Sindh province, Pakistan. Copyright J.M. Kenoyer, Courtesy Dept. of Archaeology and Museums, Govt. of Pakistan.

communities of India, along with sheep, goats, and pigs. Water buffalo (*Bubalus bubalis*) were already domesticated, and their pictures have been found on seal impressions from the ancient site of Mohenjo-Daro in the Indus Valley and from Ur in Mesopotamia (see Figure 3.1).[8] They were to become an integral partner in the rice-growing communities of China and South Asia. But less well-known species of cattle were also domesticated in Asia, although the dates are uncertain: The mithan or gayal (*Bos frontalis*) was domesticated from the wild gaur (*Bos gaurus*) of India and Southeast Asia, and Bali cattle (*Bos javanicus*) were domesticated from the wild banteng (*Bos javanicus*) of Borneo and the islands of Southeast Asia. And there is the yak (*Bos grunniens*), whose domestication from the wild yak (*Bos mutus*) enabled people to move into and live in the mountains of Tibet, Nepal, and Himalaya by providing them with transport, milk, meat, and clothing.

Nomads of Asia

It is easy to think of the human inhabitants of the world of four to three thousand years ago as settled in pockets of civilization such as ancient Egypt, the Fertile Crescent, and the Indus Valley, but in reality ever-increasing numbers of people were spreading over every continent from the Arctic to the tropics to Australasia, and they all depended on animals, either wild or domestic, for their survival.

Nomadic pastoralism, in which peoples move with their flocks and herds from one region to another, first began in central Asia at least three thousand years ago. Its impetus was probably the overgrazing of local resources by livestock herders who, as they became familiar with horse riding and wheeled carts, began to move over greater distances. The nomadic way of life is usually based on milk rather than meat; by milking their flocks the pastoralists were able to travel over great distances and yet flourish on a restricted supply of food. Not only the horses of central Asia were essential to the nomads, but also the two-humped Bactrian camels (*Camelus bactrianus*) that were domesticated from the wild species (*Camelus ferus*), probably in China around three thousand years ago. They enabled the Mongols to travel over huge distances with all their belongings and provided them with the vital resources of milk, wool, and hides. These mounted pastoralists were able to survive in the inhospitable lands of the great steppes and mountains, such as the Gobi desert and the Altai because of the very close relationship they had with their flocks, herds, and riding animals.[9]

Western Europe

In western Europe, civilization as we think of it, that is, the organization of large settled communities and the building of cities, lagged behind the East. The third millennium BCE was a transitional period from the end of the Neolithic to the beginning of the Bronze Age. Settled life and intensive agriculture were beginning to replace the hunter-gatherer communities of more ancient times. The great stone monument of Stonehenge in England was under construction, while fine pottery, known as beakers, and the use of copper for tools and weapons were spreading northward. Communities were probably organized on a tribal basis, and they would have had elaborate trading networks. Oxen and ponies may have been used for transport, the land was cultivated with a light plow, and cattle, sheep, and goats provided dairy products. Dogs proliferated and were probably used for hunting, guarding, herding the flocks, and cleaning up garbage from around the settlements.

But for a thousand years there was little indication of the fundamental changes that were to come with the invention of iron and the foundation of the Greek and Roman empires.

The Circumpolar Arctic Fringe

By four thousand years ago, hunting and fishing peoples were living across the Arctic fringe from Scandinavia through Siberia and across the North American continent.[10] They depended on their dogs for transport on sledges, and they wore fur clothing made from dog skins.

In the European and Siberian Arctic, reindeer pastoralism gradually became predominant over the hunting of wild reindeer (*Rangifer tarandus*) for meat and raw materials. The specialized breeding of domestic reindeer (also named *Rangifer tarandus*) became more efficient than hunting wild reindeer that were becoming scarce from overexploitation. Tamed reindeer could also be milked, and they could be ridden or, like dogs, harnessed to sledges.[11]

Pastoralism in Africa

By 4,500 years ago, domestic cattle, donkeys, sheep, and goats were present in North Africa and were spreading south along the margins of the Sahara, but it took a thousand years for them to reach southern Kenya and Tanzania.[12] Until this time, sub-Saharan Africa had been inhabited by hunter-gatherers who had no domestic animals other than a few dogs, perhaps, and they had no metals for making tools, nor did they even make pottery.[13] There are several fundamental reasons for this: First, the grasslands provided abundant herds of large ungulates that could be killed relatively easily whenever meat and other resources were required. Therefore, there was no need for people whose traditional and perfectly adapted culture was based on nomadic hunting to undertake the hard work of looking after animals that had to be fed, watered, and protected from the many large predators such as lions and hyenas. Second, and perhaps more important, domestic livestock are prone to a number of lethal diseases and parasite infections such as trypanosomiasis and rinderpest that are prevalent in the sub-Saharan region.

It was not until the Bantu-speaking peoples, who knew how to make pottery and forge iron, spread east and south from the Congo region and West Africa that domestic livestock began to proliferate throughout the south, and economies based on transhumant pastoralism began to replace the ancient hunter-gatherer way of life of the indigenous San and Khoisan peoples. The movement was very slow, but the spread was not restricted to the Bantu-speakers, for the earliest remains of cattle and sheep from archaeological sites in the Cape are dated to around two thousand years ago, and the owners of these livestock were Khoisan, who continued to live as nomadic pastoralists until the arrival of Europeans.[14]

The Americas

There is still no final decision on when human hunters first entered the American continents, either north or south, but by 4,500 years ago people were most probably living in all the habitable lands, and they all had dogs. It is possible that some of these dogs were descended from the American gray wolf (*Canis lupus*), but otherwise the turkey (*Meleagris gallopavo*) was the only animal that was certainly domesticated in North America—that took place in Mexico and not until several thousand years later.

In South America, the story is different, for by this period abundant remains of domestic camelids have been identified from archaeological sites in the high *puna* grasslands of the Andes in Peru. These were llamas (*Lama glama*) domesticated from the wild guanaco (*Lama guanacoe*) and alpacas (*Vicugna pacos*) domesticated from the wild vicuna (*Vicugna vicugna*).[15] Like the reindeer in a similarly harsh landscape, and the Old World camels, the llama and alpaca have been an indispensable adjunct to human survival for thousands of years. As well as transport, they provide meat, fat, hides, sinew, and, perhaps most important of all, the finest of fleeces for yarn.

It could well be that the guinea pig (*Cavia porcellus*), an endemic South American rodent, had also already been domesticated in this early period from wild species of *Cavia* in the Andes, but there is no archaeological evidence for this until much later.

Australasia

It is probable that a few people had traveled from eastern Asia to Australia and New Guinea with their dogs at least five thousand years ago. Once established in these new lands the small founder populations of dogs lived in a symbiotic relationship with the human hunters but soon spread out to breed in the wild. In Australia these dogs formed feral populations that were subject to natural selection and so evolved into what may be considered a new species of canid, the dingo.[16] Similarly in New Guinea a unique new canid evolved from the introduced domestic progenitors, the singing dog (see Figure 3.2).[17]

The first travelers to take dogs to New Guinea and to the Pacific islands (but not to Australia) also took pigs with them, and for many thousands of years pigs have provided the staple resource around which the cultural practices of these island peoples have centered.[18]

HUMANS AND THEIR DOMESTIC ANIMALS IN THE WORLD FROM 3,000 TO 2,000 YEARS AGO

Western Asia

From the first millennium BCE we have two extraordinarily complete records of the interactions between people and their domestic animals in western Asia—pictorial representations on the stone friezes of the Assyrian palaces and written accounts from the Old Testament.

The palaces of the biblical cities of Nimrud and Nineveh were inhabited by the Assyrian kings of northern Mesopotamia (now Iraq) between the ninth and the seventh centuries BCE. They were magnificent buildings whose walls were decorated with incredibly detailed, life-size stone bas-reliefs, many of which are now

FIGURE 3.2: Photo of New Guinea singing dogs, which are living relics of dogs that were introduced to the islands, many thousands of years ago. Photo Credit: Janice Koler-Matznick.

on exhibition in the British Museum.[19] Most of the friezes show scenes of battle and the hunting of lions and other wild animals. However, we can see that the asses of the Sumerian Empire have been replaced by horses drawing two-wheeled chariots, and every detail of their harness is shown in the stone engraving. These horses, like those on the ancient Egyptian wall paintings of this period, appear to have been of the slender-limbed Arab type, and they were evidently highly valued, for their tails are plaited and their necks are decorated with long tassels (see Figure 3.3).[20] Besides these magnificent horses, there are depictions of mules (hybrids between horses and donkeys) and of heavy-bodied mastiffs held on leashes by the palace eunuchs. Presumably these dogs had been bred for hunting and for guarding King Ashurbanipal, who reigned from 668–627 BCE.

Five thousand years ago, scribes began to make written records in ancient Mesopotamia, using the enormously complicated and inflexible system of cuneiform on clay tablets, while the Egyptians developed a parallel system using hieroglyphs.[21] Two thousand years later, from the tenth century BCE on, came the Semitic invention of the alphabet, which transformed the ability to write, making possible not only single records but also great works of literature; the Old Testament and Homer's *Odyssey* and *Iliad* are perhaps the best known of the oldest written works.

FIGURE 3.3: Ashurbanipal hunting in his chariot. Relief from the Palace of Ashurbanipal, Nineveh. Late Assyrian, ca. 645 BCE. Location: British Museum, London, Great Britain. Photo Credit: Werner Forman/Art Resource, NY; ART 124023.

The Old Testament contains innumerable well-known accounts, written in great detail, of how the many generations of pastoral peoples lived in ancient Palestine. Every domestic mammal found in the region today was present there three thousand years ago, with the exception of the rabbit, *Oryctolagus cuniculus* (the coney of the Bible being the wild rock hyrax, *Procavia capensis*). Not only can we learn about people's lives with their animals and management of their flocks, the appearance and coat colors of their livestock, and the plowing of the fields with oxen, but also about religious attitudes toward the animals, which are described in detail. Sheep were the most commonly sacrificed, and, as today, swine were considered the most unclean of all forbidden animals.

The domestic donkey was the common beast of transport, and mules were used for carrying burdens but were also ridden by royal persons; for example, Solomon rode on a mule when he was proclaimed king (1 Kings 1:33–34). Horses are cited in the Old Testament only in connection with war and armies, and they were not ridden but rather harnessed to chariots. The finest horses were bred by the Assyrians until the destruction of Nineveh in 612 BCE, as recorded in Nahum (chap. 2–3). As the city was besieged, Nahum tells (2:4) how "the chariots shall rage in the streets, they shall justle one against another in the broad ways." The Old Testament horses were not shod, saddle and stirrups were unknown, but, as shown on the Assyrian friezes, the harness was little different from that used today in Arabia.

The Nile Valley

The chronology of ancient Egypt is known very exactly compared to that of all other ancient empires before the Roman period. During the final thousand years BCE, it is classified into the Twenty-first to the Thirtieth Dynasties (1069–343 BCE), followed by the second Persian period (343–332 BCE), followed by the Macedonian dynasty (beginning with Alexander the Great) (332–305 BCE), followed by the Greek Ptolemaic period (305 BCE–30 CE), and finally the Roman period (30 BCE–395 CE).

Just as we have accurate dates for the different Egyptian dynasties, we also have accurate knowledge from tomb paintings concerning the animal life of all classes of society, as well as agricultural, household, and religious practices. In addition, we have the remarkable account written by the Greek Herodotus about the mid-fifth century BCE, after his journey to Egypt. It was during this late period, described in such detail by Herodotus,[22] that the domestic cat became one of the most important of all the sacred animals and the dominant animal in the mummification ritual. As is well known, thousands upon thousands, if not millions, of cat mummies have been retrieved from excavated necropolises over the past 150 years.

The tradition of burying mummified animals is a remarkable and revealing legacy of the religious practices of the ancient Egyptians, but it does little to indicate the affection with which the ordinary people as well as the pharaohs viewed their domestic animals in life. This is seen to perfection in many wonderful paintings and stone reliefs, as well as in models of pet animals, for example the famous Gayer-Anderson bronze cat of the Late Period (742–332 BCE, see Figure 3.4).

There were no wild horses in ancient Egypt and no evidence of domestic horses until the arrival of the Hyksos kings, who seized power in the Nile Delta in about 1720 BCE. They brought horses and two-wheeled chariots from western Asia for use in royal processions. After about a hundred years, the Hyksos were ousted, and the Egyptian pharaohs then adopted the horse and chariot as the noblest form of transport for royal occasions and for hunting, and so it remained throughout the Greek and Roman empires, when it was much used in war and for chariot races. As can be seen from the tomb paintings, the chariot horses looked very much like the horses on the Assyrian bas-reliefs, and all these artistic representations seem to resemble closely horses of the Arab breed today, with small heads and ears, a slender body, and fine-boned limbs. However, the few skeletons that have been retrieved from excavations in ancient Egypt are of ponies rather than horses, and the height of their withers did not exceed 150 centimeters (fourteen and a half hands).[23]

Ancient Greece

As far as is known, the use of letters in an alphabet for writing, rather than cuneiform as in the Mesopotamian civilizations or the hieroglyphs used by the Egyptians, reached Greece soon after 800 BCE, and this is believed to be around the same time that Homer's great works, the *Iliad* and the *Odyssey*, were written down in Greek. As with the Old Testament, Homer's immortal poems are full of references to agriculture and to interactions with innumerable animals, both wild and domestic. Two of these accounts are particularly well known for they are described with such poignancy that they are remembered down the centuries above all others. One, from the *Odyssey* (17, 266–339), is the account of how, when Odysseus arrived home in disguise after his nineteen years away, his old dog recognized him:

> Stretched on the ground close to where they stood talking, there lay a dog, who now pricked up his ears and raised his head. Argus was his name. Odysseus himself had owned and trained him ... but now, in his owner's absence, he lay abandoned on the heaps of dung from the mules and cattle which lay in profusion at the gate ... there full of vermin lay Argus the hound. But directly he became aware of Odysseus' presence, he

FIGURE 3.4: Bronze figure of a seated cat, from Saqqara, Egypt, Late Period, after 600 BCE. This sculpture is now known as the Gayer-Anderson cat, after its donor to the British Museum. Location: British Museum, London, Great Britain. Photo Credit: Heritage Image Partnership/Art Resource, NY; ART 187241.

wagged his tail and dropped his ears, though he lacked the strength now to come any nearer to his master. Yet Odysseus saw him out of the corner of his eye, and brushed a tear away … As for Argus, he had no sooner set eyes on Odysseus after those nineteen years than he succumbed to the black hand of Death.[24]

The second is the amazingly detailed account in the *Iliad* (23, 256–659) of the chariot race that was held at the funeral of Patroklos. The advice that Nestor gave to his son Antilochus, one of the charioteers, was surely drawn from an actual event:

> It is by skill that charioteer beats charioteer … [the turning post] is a dry stump of wood, oak or pine, standing about six feet out of the ground. The rain has not rotted it, and there are two white stones driven in on either side of it, at the place where the road narrows, and there is smooth going for horses round it … You must cut in very close as you drive your chariot and pair round the post, and let your own body, where you stand on the well-strung platform, lean a little to the left of the horses. Goad your right hand horse and shout him on, and make sure your hands give him rein; and have your left horse cut close in to the post, so that the nave of your well-built wheel seems to be just touching it—but be careful not to hit the stone, or you will damage your horses and smash the chariot, and that would delight the others and bring shame on you.[25]

About 450 years after Homer, Alexander the Great was born in 355 BCE. His father, Philip, predicted that Macedonia would never hold his son, and indeed Alexander, before he died at the age of only thirty-two, had conquered lands from Greece to Afghanistan. When Alexander was twelve years old, he gained possession of perhaps the most famous horse that has ever lived, Bucephalas (see Figure 3.5). Alexander rode Bucephalas in all his campaigns until the horse died in 326 BCE at the battle against Porus, king of India, who fought with a huge cavalry of elephants. According to the Greek writer Arrian (ca. 95–175 CE), who wrote the most authentic life we have of Alexander, Bucephalas died not from wounds, but worn out by heat and age; he was about thirty years old.[26] Bucephalas was buried with great pomp, and in his memory Alexander founded the now lost city of Bucephala, on a bank of the river Jhelum (today in Pakistan).

The most renowned ancient Greek writer on animals is Xenophon, who died at the age of seventy-four in 354 BCE, a year after Alexander was born. Xenophon wrote treatises on many subjects from advice to kings, to planting trees, to the duties of women, but his best-known essays are on horsemanship

FIGURE 3.5: The "Alexander Sarcophagus," from the Phoenician royal necropolis at Sidon, was made for Abdalonymos, King of Sidon. Battle of Issos (333 BCE). Alexander the Great on his horse, lionskin on his head, with raised spear. Late 4th century BCE; Marble, 195 × 318 × 167 cm Inv.370 T. Location: Archaeological Museum, Istanbul, Turkey. Photo Credit: Erich Lessing/Art Resource, NY; ART 104448.

and on hunting, which includes the training and management of dogs, with this advice on their equipment:

> Let the collars be soft as well as broad, that they may not wear off the dog's hair. Let the leashes have loops for the hand attached to them, but nothing else; for those who form the collars out of the leashes do not manage well for their dogs.[27]

Xenophon's chapter on horsemanship and the breaking and training of colts can hardly be improved on today and must surely be approved of by the "horse whisperers." His advice is never to approach a horse in anger and to teach him "not with harshness, but with gentleness."[28]

The Roman Empire

It was always generally accepted by ancient historians that Rome was founded in 753 BCE, probably as a trading post on the river Tiber by the Etruscans.

A regal period followed, during which the city was ruled by seven kings, until 509 BCE, when the republic was founded, the Etruscans were overthrown, and the last king was replaced by two consuls. The expansion of Rome as the ruler of Italy in about 275 BCE was followed by the Punic Wars against Carthage and then by the spread of the Roman Empire across Europe and as far as the East. The republic lasted for nearly five hundred years, but no writings survive from ancient Roman historians living before the third century BCE. Most of the significant written descriptions of the interactions between humans and their domestic animals therefore fall into the next section of this chapter.

The ox was the most common beast of burden and plow animal in Roman times. Horses were used for riding, warfare, and racing, and they were ridden with saddle and bridle, but still without stirrups. The Romans did not normally wage war from chariots. One highly important writer who gave detailed descriptions of his cavalry and other domestic animals was Julius Caesar in his *Gallic War*, probably written in 52 BCE. In his account of the first invasion of Britain in 55 BCE, he wrote that the Britons fought by driving all over the place in their chariots, inspiring terror with their horses and the noise of the wheels, while at the same time wildly throwing their javelins about.[29]

Nomads of Central Eurasia

While the Assyrians and ancient Egyptians were building elaborate temples and perfecting the chariot for warfare and hunting, the Scythians were developing into an elite society of nomads who contributed to the fall of the Assyrian Empire in the late seventh century BCE. Two hundred years later, Herodotus wrote a detailed account of the gruesome rituals that took place at the burial of a Scythian king,[30] and his descriptions have been verified by the wonderful gold ornaments and remains of sacrificed horses with all their harness and a four-wheeled carriage that have been found in the frozen tombs of Pazyryk in the Altai Mountains (see Figure 3.6).[31]

Around 44 BCE, the Greek writer Strabo also wrote about the nomads and gave this account of their strange eating habits: "In fact. Even now there are Wagon-dwellers and Nomads, so-called, who live off their herds, and on milk and cheese, and particularly on cheese made from mare's milk, and know nothing about storing up food …"[32]

HUMANS AND THEIR DOMESTIC ANIMALS IN THE WORLD FROM 2,000 TO 1,000 YEARS AGO

Two thousand years ago, people with their dogs were living in every part of the habitable world, and new empires were replacing the ancient kingdoms

FIGURE 3.6: The four-wheeled carriage from Barrow 5, Pazyryk in the Altai mountains of Siberia. Hermitage Museum.

of Mesopotamia, Egypt, and Greece. In Europe, the Romans still held power, although they were soon to lose it. China was densely populated, and the Han Empire had extended deep into central Asia. Mesoamerica was also densely populated, and the Aztec and Mayan civilizations were at their height. In Africa, the Bantu-speaking peoples had spread southward and had reached the Cape with their dogs, cattle, and sheep.

The Roman Empire

The ways in which the Romans treated and cared for their domestic animals differed little from ours of today. They gave names to their dogs, loved them, and trained them, and they wrote books on how best to feed livestock. A major difference to today is that they considered their human slaves to have the same value as their animals. A minor difference lies in their breeding of dormice for food. The Romans were responsible for spreading the European rabbit and the fallow deer around the Continent, as well as peacocks and guinea fowl.

The two great Roman writers on agriculture and the care of domestic livestock and other animals, including bees and fishes, are Columella, who lived in the first century CE, and Varro, who lived more than a hundred years earlier and died in 28 BCE. Columella's twelve "books" on agriculture are more an encyclopedia than a textbook, for they cover every aspect that an aspiring Roman farmer or landowner could possibly need to know in order to be successful in growing vines, planting trees, breeding all kinds of livestock, birds, and fishes, and training oxen for the plow. Roman farmers, of course, did not have the benefit of modern veterinary science and medicine, so their cures for diseases must often have been ineffective and even harmful, but in his attention to animal welfare, Columella far surpassed the factory farmers of today, as the following few quotations will show:[33]

> Sows indeed grow fat on cultivated ground when it is grassy and planted with fruit-trees of several kinds, so as to provide at different seasons of the year apples, plums, pears, nuts of many kinds and figs. You should not, however, on the strength of these fruits be sparing of the contents of the granary, which should often be handed out when out-door-food fails (VII, 8–9).
>
> A dog which is infested with fleas should be treated either with crushed cumin mixed in water with the same weight of hellebore and smeared on, or else with the juice of the snake-like cucumber, or if these are unobtainable, with the stale oil-lees poured over the whole body (VII, 2–3).
>
> Dogs should be called by names which are not very long, so that each may obey more quickly when he is called, but they should not have shorter names than those which are pronounced with two syllables such as "puppy" and "savage" (VII, 13).
>
> Care must be taken that it [a newly-hatched gosling] is not stung by the prickles of the nettle or sent out hungry to pasture, but that it has had its fill beforehand of chopped chicory or lettuce leaves (VIII, 8–9).

The usual picture of the ancient Romans, as learned by every schoolchild, is of a warlike people who were intensely cruel to other humans and to animals in everyday life as well as in the public spectacles of fights between gladiators and between wild animals. But this is by no means the whole story. Many Romans were repulsed by cruelty, and this is documented officially in the Theodosian Code, a compilation of the laws and decrees of the Roman emperors published from 313–438 CE. A number of these decrees laid down a law prohibiting the overloading of horse carts, as follows:[34]

> We ordain that only one thousand pounds (1 Roman pound = .72 English pound) of weight may be placed on a carriage, two hundred pounds of weight on a two-wheeled vehicle, and thirty pounds on a posthorse, for it appears that they cannot support heavier burdens.

Eight mules shall be yoked to a carriage, in the summer season, of course, but ten in winter. We judge that three mules are sufficient for a two-wheeled conveyance (8.5.8. Title 31).

We decree that provender from the fiscal storehouses shall be furnished to the Palmatian and Hermogenian horses, when they have been weakened by their lot as contestants in the chariot races, either through the uncertainty of the race or by their number of years or by some other cause (15.9.2. Title 10).

All dignitaries of high civil or military rank shall have the right always to use within Our City of most sacred name the vehicles of their rank, that is, two-horse carriages (14.11.1. Title 12).

As important as the rearing of livestock for the Romans, and perhaps exceeding in necessity all other human economic systems, was the efficient plowing of land for the cultivation of staples. The earliest plow was an enlarged digging stick that was dragged over the ground by a pair of oxen, and this is still used in arid lands. However, by Roman times, as described by the Elder Pliny in the first century CE, the wheeled heavy plow harnessed to a team of two to three pairs of oxen had been invented for heavy soils, and during the ensuing centuries its use spread to northern Europe. [35] In an evocative letter to a friend about his house and lands in Tuscany, Pliny the Younger (nephew to the Elder Pliny) wrote this:[36]

The vineyards spreading down every slope weave their uniform pattern far and wide, their lower limit bordered by a plantation of trees. Then come the meadows and cornfields, where the land can be broken up only by heavy oxen and the strongest ploughs, for the soil is so stiff it is thrown up in great clods at the first ploughing and is not thoroughly broken until it has been gone over nine times. The meadows are bright with flowers, covered with trefoil and other delicate plants.

Columella, with his usual attention to his animals' welfare, gave a detailed description of the change from yoking plow oxen by their horns to using a collar on the shoulders, as is still done today:[37]

fastening the yoke to the horns has been condemned by almost all who have written precepts for husbandmen, and not without reason. For cattle can put forth more effort with neck and shoulders than with the horns, and in this way they exert themselves with the entire bulk of the body and its whole weight; but in the other way, with their heads pulled back and faces turned upward, they are tortured, and barely scratch the surface of the ground with a very light ploughshare (II, 22–24).

The Anglo-Saxons

During the early centuries of the first millennium CE, during the final collapse of the Roman Empire, most of the Anglo-Saxon inhabitants of England,
and probably most of the people of Europe, lived in small settlements in the
countryside. Each family had a small house, a few acres of land known as a
croft, and a few cattle, sheep, pigs, a dog or so, and perhaps a cat. Manure
for spreading on tilled fields was an essential part of all farming, and it was
collected assiduously from the land and from stalled livestock. The domestic
animals were all small—the household cow would have been half the size of
modern cattle, sheep were long-legged and small-bodied, while pigs were tiny
by today's standards. Many animals would have been castrated: bullocks were
castrated to produce placid oxen for plowing and all draught purposes, while
castrated rams, or wethers, produced heavier fleeces. Castrated boars were fat-
tened to produce salted pork, and cocks were castrated to produce fat capons.
Fat was a key animal product, not only to provide food for people but also
to provide tallow for lighting. Hides and bones were essential resources for
clothing and tools, while feathers were a luxury over straw for bedding and for
making writing quills. Bees were kept for honey and provided the only sweet-
ening. Horses were not used as commonly as oxen for farm labor in Anglo-
Saxon times, but they were essential for transport.

By around the fifth century CE, the heavy plow reached the British Isles, and
this new, more powerful method of cultivating the land was instrumental in
re-shaping the social structures of communities that had previously depended
on the hard work of individual families. In order to use the new plows it was
necessary for the peasants to own teams of oxen cooperatively and to plow
the land in long strips rather than in the old, small, individual squares (see
Figure 3.7). From this new system of agriculture, the manorial system evolved
with its powerful village "head" who would settle disputes and organize the
distribution of the strips.[38]

The sharing of the oxen and of the plowed land was codified in the
Welsh Laws of Hywel Dda, dated to about 945 CE, as in the following
quotations:[39]

> Every one must bring his share for the ploughing, whether it be an ox, or
> iron, or other things that may be necessary. After every thing is brought
> by them, the ploughman and the driver ought to keep these things in
> safety, and use them as they would use their own (p. 242).
>
> The driver must yoke the oxen in such a manner that the bows of the
> yoke may not be too tight or too loose; and he must drive them so as not
> to break their hearts. If the oxen should be injured by excessive driving,
> let him pay for them (p. 242).

FIGURE 3.7: Men ploughing with oxen. ca. 1340 CE, Luttrell Psalter. Location: British Library, London. Credit: Art Resource, NY: ART 122747.

These laws not only laid down the rules and principles of shared agricultural practice but also listed the value of every animal that was owned and of every wild animal that was hunted, thereby establishing the medieval Laws of Venery. From the sums of money to be paid for the different species of domestic animals, it can be seen how they were valued by the people of Britain before the time of Domesday:[40]

The value of a pack horse is one hundred and twenty pence.

The value of a serving horse is sixty pence.

For every blemish in a horse, one third of its price must be returned, its ears and tail excepted.

If a person buy a cow, big with calf, and she suffer an abortion, the seller must produce the oaths of the herdsman and of the woman who milked her, to prove that she has not lost her qualities.

The price of a little pig, from the time it is born until it begins to burrow is one penny. When it ceases sucking, which is at the end of three months, it is worth two pence.

The price of a cat is four pence. Her qualities are to see, to hear, to kill mice, to have her claws whole, and to nurse and not devour her kittens.

The king's lap dog is worth a pound; the lap dog of a freeman, one hundred and twenty pence; that of a foreigner, four pence, and a common house dog is of the same value as the latter.

It was during this period that the metal stirrup, attached to a saddle and girth, probably reached northern Europe, having traveled as a technological invention of very great importance from China, where it is first recorded in the fourth century CE. There is no word for stirrups in ancient Greek or Latin; however, their value is listed in the Laws of Hywel Dda as:[41]

if the stirrups be gilt with gold, their price is eight pence; if with silver four pence; and if done with copper, or darkened, or stained, four pence.

This apparent gilding of stirrups implies that they were used on special occasions such as pageants or jousting, rather than in everyday transport or warfare, and their value in armed combat may not have been appreciated. The hurling of weapons while at a gallop has more force if the rider is held in the saddle by the stirrups than if he is seated by muscle and balance alone, and the lack of stirrups may explain why cavalries were never of great importance in the wars of the ancient world. Indeed, it can be argued that one reason England lost the Battle of Hastings in 1066 was that the invading Norman cavalry rode with stirrups and therefore their armed combat was much more powerful than that of the Saxons, who, although they had stirrups, dismounted and fought in the old way on foot.[42]

The Spread of Domestic Animals in Africa

Two species of guinea fowl (*Numida meleagris* and *Numida ptilorhynca*) are the only domestic animals to have originated for certain in Africa, while there is some evidence for three others, the ass, the cat, and North African cattle.[43] Mention may be made also of the elephant, which was exploited in ancient North Africa by the Carthaginians, and the eland (*Tragelaphus oryx*), which was a cornerstone of social life for the San hunter-gatherers of southern Africa, but these ungulates were never domesticated in the sense of being bred in captivity.

In the first centuries CE, the ancient Egyptian civilization collapsed and with it all the wonderful pictorial representations of the animal life, while at the same time Europe was undergoing the decline and fall of the Roman Empire and the establishment of separate nation-states across the Continent. Meanwhile, sub-Saharan Africa was being transformed by the spread of Bantu-speaking peoples with their use of iron, their cultivated cereals, and their domestic livestock and dogs.

To modern outsiders of the African world, this vast continent often appears as great expanses of endless grasslands, inhabited by exotic and beautiful "game" animals, in which herds of domestic livestock are an intrusive element. But this is very far from the true picture, for it should be realized that domestic cattle, sheep, and goats were introduced to the African continent from western Asia perhaps less than a millennium after they reached western Europe. By a thousand years ago, human pastoralism had irrevocably altered much of the landscape of sub-Saharan Africa.[44] However, the early African agriculturalists had much to contend with that was absent from Europe. What restricted the movement of people and their animals south of the Sahara were not only the physical geography but also endemic diseases that attacked the introduced but not the indigenous ungulates. Chief among these was "sleeping sickness" or trypanosomiasis caused by tsetse flies (*Glossina* spp.), which affects cattle and humans, and African horse sickness, which is a particularly virulent disease caused by orbiviruses from which very few horses survive.[45]

Before the Bantu-speaking peoples had migrated into southernmost Africa, this land was inhabited by Khoisan speakers; these were the ancestors of the more recent Khoi (Hottentots), who were traditionally pastoralists but were exterminated by European immigrants, and the San (Bushmen), who remained and remain today as hunter-gatherers. Animal remains retrieved from archaeological sites in the southwestern Cape provide evidence that the Khoi had domestic sheep, and probably also cattle, during the first millennium CE. As there were never any wild sheep or cattle (other than the African buffalo) in sub-Saharan Africa, it is certain that these domestic livestock had traveled, over many generations, from the north, either with their owners or by trade.[46] These sheep and cattle were the ancestors of the so-called "indigenous" breeds of today, the fat-tailed and Afrikaner sheep, and the Nguni and Tuli cattle.[47]

The Americas

By the first millennium CE there were probably as many different kinds of dogs in the Americas as in the all the rest of the world, and they fulfilled a multitude of different functions. This was because, until the arrival of Europeans, there were no domestic livestock in the North American continent. Dogs were used for hunting, for hauling, and for providing meat and hides, and they were also sacrificed in rituals and at funerals. Neither the Aztecs nor the Maya, despite their enormously elaborate civilizations and fully developed agricultural systems, had any domestic animals other than the dog and the turkey. Small, hairless dogs were bred by the Maya for their meat,[48] and this breed survives today as the Mexican hairless dog. The Coastal Salesh women of the Pacific Northwest kept a particular breed of dogs whose hair was shorn and woven into clothing and blankets. On the northern plains, the women harnessed dogs to travois to haul baggage, firewood, water, and provisions. The Inca Empire ruled in Andean South America, and these mountain people had dogs to herd their llamas and alpacas, on which they depended for all their natural resources.[49]

Animal Companions and the Development of Breeds

During the first millennium CE there was a great expansion in the selective breeding of domestic species in many parts of the world from Britain to China. Local breeds of livestock, as described, for example, by Columella, would have been common, and whereas in the prehistoric period the evolution of these breeds resulted from adaptation to the local climate and environment, in this later period artificial selection for favored characteristics was becoming far more widespread. The keeping of special breeds as animal companions was also becoming a worldwide phenomenon. Toy dogs, the ancestors of breeds like the Maltese in Europe and the Pekingese in China, were well established in the first century CE. In China they were known as "pai," a term applied to short-legged, short-headed dogs, "which belong under the table."[50] Goldfish (*Carassius auratus auratus*) were also first domesticated in China in the Sung dynasty at the end of the first millennium CE.[51]

CONCLUSIONS

The three and a half thousand years covered by this chapter encompass an explosive development of human civilizations. In Europe, the period ranges from Neolithic farming communities to the birth and collapse of the Greek and Roman empires and, in the north of the continent, to the rise of the Saxons, the Vikings, and the Normans, while in Asia, and particularly in China, civilization may be said to have outpaced that in Europe. However, through all the changes, and as everywhere else in the world, the patterns of human behavior remained and still remain the same to the present day. Homes had to be built and protected, food had to be produced and prepared, wars were fought, children were born and reared, myths, legends, and stories were told, and the arts were practiced. And through it all ran the dependence of every human being on domestic animals. At the most basic level this dependence was for meat and the other resources that can be obtained from a carcass: bones, leather, fur, sinew, and so on. The dead animal also fulfilled another important function in religious sacrifices and for foretelling the future, but it was the living animals that enabled elaborate civilizations with growing towns and cities to proliferate. And most of all a trio of inventions enabled the farmers, builders, warriors, and tradespeople to enlist their domestic animals to help them.

The most important of this trio was probably the wheeled vehicle harnessed to cattle, horses, or camels, for it greatly increased the power of transport, hunting, and warfare. The wheel was known in Europe and western Asia by at least 3000 BCE but not in Egypt until 2000 BCE, presumably arriving at the same time as horses were first introduced by the Hyksos. In China, too, there is no evidence for wheeled vehicles until the second millennium BCE.[52] Remarkably, the ancient Mexicans had invented a wheel that was identical in type to those of western Asia, long before Europeans reached America with their horses and cattle. The finding of an Aztec toy dog on wheels made of clay may indicate that dogs were harnessed to wheeled carts, although it is generally assumed that this object was intended as a toy (see Figure 3.8).[53]

The second invention was the combination of the horse-collar and the nailed horseshoe, which, it has been argued, played a part in the disintegration of the Roman Empire by augmenting the agricultural revolution that took place in the countries to the north between the fifth and the ninth centuries CE. According to White,[54] this revolution followed first from the widespread use of the heavy plow in conjunction with the invention of the horse-collar that differed from the yoke used on oxen, which would half-throttle a horse trying to pull a load. The horse-collar, together with the invention of the nailed horseshoe, for

FIGURE 3.8: Aztec clay models of dogs on wheels. Photo Credit: Dave Hixson.

as "Minoans." They probably emigrated from Asia Minor about 3000 BCE and used a language that was not Greek. The Minoans became a dominant sea power in the eastern Mediterranean, and their culture reached its peak about 1600–1400 BCE. Archaeologists have uncovered several large palace compounds on the island, the best known being at Cnossus (or Knossos). This palace compound, which occupies about five acres, has so many rooms and passageways that it may have seemed like a maze to visitors. Because the written documents left by the Minoans have not been deciphered, we do not know what they may have written about themselves. Although we have references to them in texts written in ancient Greek by authors who lived hundreds of years after the collapse of their civilization, for knowledge about their culture from the Minoans themselves, we must rely on information provided by their art. Fortunately, fresco paintings produced by the Minoans, as well as artifacts of metal, stone, clay, and ivory, have been found not only on Crete, but also in mainland Greece and other parts of the eastern Mediterranean world.

These physical remains reveal that a popular subject for Minoan artists was an activity that archaeologists have labeled "bull-leaping,"[1] in which young men jumped on and off the backs of bulls.[2] Because most of our evidence for bull-leaping has been located in the area of Cnossus, its occurrence as a spectacle or ritual may be peculiar to that palace compound.[3] The social status of the leapers is unknown. They may have been slaves, war captives, professional performers, or perhaps young aristocrats undergoing a rite of initiation.[4] Although the artists provide little indication about the cultural context and conventions of bull-leaping—where, when, or why the activity occurred—scholars have conjectured that it took place within the palace compounds.[5] Several different sequences of movements have been identified from the artistic depictions.[6] Sir Arthur Evans, the first excavator at Cnossus, speculated that the athlete stood facing a charging bull and grabbed its horns when it drew near. As the angry bull tossed its head upward, the athlete used the momentum to do a back flip and stand on the bull's back (see Figure 4.1). He then jumped or somersaulted over the rear end of the bull and landed on the ground. Younger, however, suggests another sequence: The athlete began from a position above the bull's head, from a platform perhaps or from the shoulders of another young man, and then dove down toward the charging bull's shoulders, doing a handspring and a back flip, and landing on the ground at the rear of the bull. Younger's theory takes into account, first, that a bull would be more likely to shake its head from side to side if its horns were grabbed than to toss it upward, and, second, that an athlete who tried to grab the horns of a charging bull had a high probability of being gored. In fact, a few of the artistic representations do seem to show athletes being gored or failing to complete the maneuver and falling to the side of the bull.[7] Clearly this activity was not for the faint of heart or slow of feet. Of course, the popularity of the event may have resided, at least

FIGURE 4.1: *Bull-Jumping*. Minoan fresco, 1500 BCE. Location: Archaeological Museum, Heraklion, Crete, Greece. Photo Credit: Erich Lessing/Art Resource, NY; ART 32424.

in part, in the spectators' anticipation of seeing a participant injured, as is true at modern bullfights and rodeo events.

These entertaining spectacles in the palace compounds may have had their origin in rural activities. Although the cattle on Crete were of domesticated stock, probably brought to the island by the Minoans from Asia Minor, they were left to graze in rugged mountainous terrain.[8] In behavior, therefore, they were essentially wild animals. Those destined for draught work were captured for castration and training when young and tractable. The bulls, however, were allowed to reach their mature physical strength and were captured only when required for a sacrifice. Separating one from the herd and transporting it to an altar in the palace compound must have been a very hazardous procedure. Artistic images depict bulls being goaded with spears, wrestled with, lassoed, hobbled, driven into nets, and trussed with ropes.[9] Perhaps one of the jobs of the "cowboys" was to confront the bull and provoke it to charge toward the net by challenging it and even grabbing its horns. The "cowboys" would vie with one another to display their fearlessness and skill in these extremely risky situations. The formalized, but still daring performances of bull-leaping at the palace may have evolved from these rural activities, even as modern rodeo events like steer-wrestling evolved from competition among cowboys doing ranch work.

One piece of evidence suggests that bull-leaping was, indeed, a competitive exhibition of athletic skill. A *rhyton* (drinking cup) from Hagia Triada (see note 7) provides scenes of bull-leaping alongside scenes of boxing and wrestling. In the latter events, pairs of human contestants are matched in an event whose climax is the victory of one of them. Seen in this context, bull-leaping may have been a competition in which human athletes contended with one another for the title of "best leaper." However, the presence of the bull sets the activity apart from boxing and wrestling contests. Some scholars have proposed that the bull is not the adversary of the leaper, but rather the "platform" on which athletes display their courage and gymnastic skills. It has even been suggested that the bulls were trained, or at least tamed, for the performance.[10] It is more likely, however, that the bull was perceived by both performers and spectators as the primary opponent, and that the purpose of the activity was, like modern bullfights and rodeo events, to demonstrate the ability of humans to overcome hostile nature. Humans may compete with one another to be the best matador or bull rider or bull-leaper, but in all these activities, the true opponent is the nonhuman, the "other." The victor in these contests is the human who most successfully prevails over the forces of nature.

Even long before they were domesticated, bulls were seen as symbols of immense strength, frightening savagery, and prodigious, uncontrollable sexuality. Human fascination with bulls can be traced back to the cave paintings of Paleolithic hunters who produced images of aurochs, the ancestors of our domesticated cattle.[11] The Minoans apparently brought with them to Crete not just their cattle, but also rituals in which bulls played a prominent role, and some scholars contend that bull-leaping may have had a religious component.[12] In addition to images of bull-leaping, the popularity of bulls' heads and horns as an artistic motif in Minoan art suggests the cultural importance of this animal.[13] Unfortunately, we do not have available Minoan literary evidence that might guide our interpretations of the artistic evidence.

Bulls and the threats they pose to humans figure conspicuously in the myths that later Greeks told about the people of Crete, particularly the residents of Cnossus. In one myth, Zeus, the king of the gods, seduced a Phoenician princess named Europa by appearing to her in the form of a handsome bull. Europa was persuaded by its unusual gentleness to sit on its back, at which point it leapt into the air and carried her across the sea to Crete. As a result of the rape, a son was born to Zeus and Europa. This son, named Minos (hence the name chosen by Sir Arthur Evans for the civilization he discovered at Cnossus: the Minoans), became a powerful king.[14] Poseidon, the god of the sea, sent him a pure white bull to confirm his legitimacy as the king of Crete. The god expected that Minos would sacrifice this bull in thanksgiving for his support, but Minos substituted another bull. In retaliation, the angry god caused Minos' wife, Pasiphae, to become sexually obsessed with the white bull. To satisfy her lust, she had a master craftsman, Daedalus, construct a hollow cow in which she concealed herself, so that the bull would mate with her. The offspring of this unnatural union was a monster with the body of a human and the head of a bull, a creature called the Minotaur ("the bull of Minos"). In order to confine the monster, Minos had Daedalus construct a prison for him.

In another myth, Minos' son, Androgeos, who had won all the contests at the Panathenaic festival in Athens (discussed below), was killed by jealous Athenian youths. To avenge his murder, Minos forced the Athenians to agree to send to Crete, at regular intervals (perhaps every three or nine years), seven young men and seven young women to be placed in the labyrinth and devoured by the Minotaur.[15] One year, the Greek hero Theseus volunteered to be one of the fourteen young people. Minos' daughter, Ariadne, fell in love with him and gave him a long thread to enable him to find his way out of the labyrinth. He confronted and killed the Minotaur and rescued the other youths. This was not Theseus' only victory over a monstrous Cretan animal. Hercules (or Herakles), as one of his famous twelve labors, had captured a ferocious bull that was wreaking havoc on Crete. He took it back to mainland Greece and released it. When the bull began to terrorize the region of Marathon (near Athens), Theseus killed it.

The mythical Minotaur was imprisoned in a maze called the labyrinth.[16] The confusing design of passageways at the real palace compound at Cnossus may have given rise to a story about the existence of a maze. And the myth may reflect an actual occurrence when a bull, captured in the mountains and brought to the palace for sacrifice,[17] perhaps escaped from its captors and ran furiously through the maze of streets, attacking anyone in its path. Or perhaps, as at modern Pamplona, it was goaded to run through the maze, to remind spectators of the dangers that bulls pose, but also to allow them to torment this symbol of savage nature, to test their own skills at escaping its horns, and thus to participate in the victory over nature.

Because we lack literary evidence from Minoan Crete and because our pictorial evidence is often fragmentary, we can only speculate about the significance of bulls in Cretan culture and about the meaning of the myths and the bull-leaping activities. The monstrous Minotaur was the horrifying consequence of the copulation of a human and an animal. The myth is a cautionary tale, warning that passions of irrational, "bullish" proportions may result in the loss of human identity. It reflects a human fear that yielding to animal instincts can erase the achievements of human culture and plunge humans into a bestial existence. The handsome white bull, the object of Pasiphae's lust, represents the attractiveness of animal strength, but also the destructiveness of animal passion. In a sense, the bull symbolizes both the danger without—the antagonistic forces of nature—and the danger within the human soul—the potential to sink into bestiality. The product of Pasiphae's lust was a beast of enormous strength that demonstrated its lack of humanity by indulging an insatiable appetite for human flesh and blood.

In the ancient world, humans were fascinated by the strength, courage, and fertility of bulls, but also determined to prove that they could prevail over these savage creatures and therefore control their own destinies. It is notable that the list of exploits for two of the greatest heroes of Greek mythology, Hercules and Theseus, included the defeat of a bull. In the performances of bull-leaping in Crete, the outmaneuvering of the bulls was ritually repeated again and again and represented the triumph of human culture over adversarial nature.

The Greek world produced other types of spectacles of humans dominating bulls. Roman authors report, for example, that the Thessalians of northern Greece developed an activity in which men riding horses chased wild bulls across an arena until they exhausted them. A rider then positioned his horse alongside a bull, jumped on it, grabbed its horns, and wrestled it to the ground. One report states that the rider killed the bull by twisting its neck.[18] This activity seems very close to the steer-wrestling practiced in modern rodeo arenas, although the object of the modern event is to subdue, not kill the animal. A relief from Smyrna, a Greek city in Asia Minor, which depicts riders leaping from horses to bulls and holding onto bulls' horns, may represent a similar activity.[19] Bullfighting was also practiced in ancient Italy. An inscription from the town of Pompeii advertises an exhibition of bulls and bullfighters, although it provides no details about the event.[20] The abuse of bulls in Roman arenas will be discussed later in this chapter.

COCKFIGHTS

The popularity of watching cockfights as a leisure activity in ancient Greece is attested to by both written and pictorial sources (see Figure 4.2).[21] It is a natural behavior of male chickens to fight with one another in order to determine which of them will occupy the dominant position in the flock, and the bloody, often lethal skirmishes of cocks must have been a familiar sight in Greek farmyards. Although chickens are constructed in modern metaphors as cowardly, in reality cocks are ferocious combatants that will fight to the death. As is true of many cultures, men in Greece frequently pitted cocks against one another as a source of entertainment. So enamored were Greek men of cockfighting that Columella, a first century CE Roman author, remarked that, in contrast to the Romans, whose breeding programs were governed by practical considerations of productivity, the Greeks desired birds that were unyielding in combats and therefore bred them to be as fierce as possible (*De re rustica* 8.2.4,5).

The pleasure of watching a cockfight undoubtedly arose from the antithetical sentiments that Geertz noted at Balinese cockfights.[22] On the one hand, a cockfight was a display of the animal savagery that caused anxiety in humans, but also reassured them that humans were indeed very different from beasts. The behavior of the animal combatants was a "rage untrammeled,"[23]

FIGURE 4.2: *Cockfight*. Menelaos Painter (5th century BCE). Red-figured krater Attic. Around 440 BCE. Location: National Museum, Warsaw, Poland. Photo Credit: Erich Lessing/Art Resource, NY; ART30788.

a violence unfettered by the social and moral concerns that cause humans to restrain themselves. It was a frightening reminder of what humans would be like if not bound by social conventions. On the other hand, the spectators identified with the cocks and perhaps even envied their capacity to indulge their rage. The owner of the winning bird, moreover, would feel a pride of accomplishment; the owner of the losing bird would suffer the humiliation of having misjudged the abilities of his cock and of himself.[24] In addition, cockfights may have functioned as "playful" enactments of human hostilities, providing a riveting display of anger, violence, and death, but at no risk to human life. Like Greek tragedies, cockfights permitted powerful emotions to be expressed within socially permitted boundaries.

Cockfights acquired additional significance at Athens. Although most were privately sponsored entertainments, we have reports of state-funded exhibitions where the tenacity of fighting cocks was utilized as an object lesson for soldiers. Several authors mention an annual display of cockfighting, which was probably held in the Theater of Dionysus, on the slopes of the Acropolis in Athens.[25] The third century CE writer Aelian records that there was a law in Athens that, on one day each year, cocks were to fight in the theater (*Variae historiae* 2.28). He attributes this injunction to Themistocles, the general responsible for the Athenian victory at the Battle of Salamis in 480 BCE. According to Aelian, Themistocles ordered his soldiers to observe that fighting cocks were so determined not to be defeated that they were willing to endure grievous injuries. Themistocles' words inspired his soldiers to fight with similar courage and intensity. The first century CE author, Philo, provides a different version of the origin of the public cockfight, stating that the Athenian general Miltiades, who led the army to victory at Marathon in 490 BCE, ordered his soldiers to watch cockfights and maintained that viewing this spectacle would stimulate them to bravery more than any words could (*Quod omnis probus liber sit* 131–133). Philo adds that nothing produces a greater incentive to improve one's own behavior than seeing a lowly creature reach a height of achievement beyond even our own aspirations. A third author, Lucian, who wrote in the second century CE, assigns to the Athenian legislator Solon (ca. 640–ca. 558 BCE) the statement that, by law, all men of military age were required to assemble and watch birds fight to the utmost limit of exhaustion (*Anacharsis* 37). By viewing this spectacle, says Solon, the souls of men acquire an appetite for danger because they do not wish to appear less courageous than cocks.

Whatever the genesis of the annual public cockfight in Athens may be, the stories concur that it was provided at public expense because it served as an edifying lesson in martial valor and reinforced the conviction that the Greek hoplite (heavy-armed infantryman) must never yield in battle. Chrysippus, the third century BCE Stoic philosopher, remarked on the utility of fighting cocks "to incite soldiers to war and instill an appetite for courage."[26] Philo quotes the fifth-century BCE Greek tragedian Ion as saying that "battered in body and blind in each eye, the fighting cock rallies his courage and, though faint, he still crows, for he prefers death to slavery" (*Quod omnis* 133).

The Greek word for "cock," *alektryon,* may be cognate with the verb *alekzo,* "to defend."[27] In myth, the bellicose cock was associated with the god of war, Ares. Greeks thought that the cock's crest resembled a military helmet and that the bronze points that were fastened to the spurs of the fighting cock, to make it more lethal, resembled the spears of a Greek hoplite.[28] Vase paintings indicate that the cock was so closely associated with combative behavior that it became a common motif on shield blazons (Figure 4.3).

Fighting cocks were also associated with the warrior goddess, Athena. Pausanias remarked that the image of a cock that appeared on the helmet of one statue of Athena was appropriate because cocks are so eager for battle (6.26.3). Victors at the athletic competitions that accompanied the Panathenaic festival (see below) were presented with vases that depicted Athena, defender of the city named after her, flanked by two columns on which cocks are perched.[29] The cock was an artistic metaphor for the competitive spirit necessary for athletes, who engage in activities that prepare them for war. Attic vase paintings also juxtapose fighting cocks and battle scenes, and cocks depicted on vases were sometimes given the names of Homeric heroes.[30] In addition, Attic vases pro-

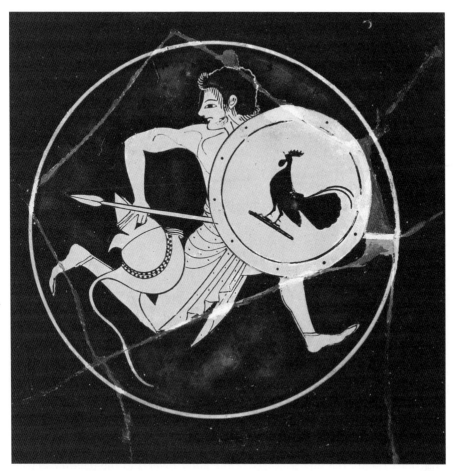

FIGURE 4.3: *Running hoplite* (heavily armed Greek infantryman), with shield, spear, and helmet. Skythos Painter (5th century BCE). Interior of a red-figured cup from Tanagra. 520–510 BCE. Inv. CA 1527. Location: Louvre, Paris, France. Photo Credit: Erich Lessing/ Art Resource, NY; ART13903.

vide examples of decorative parallels between cocks and mythological fighters, such as Herakles, and between cocks and soldiers.[31] Fighting cocks were thus visually linked to heroes and to men who performed heroically.

Cocks were, however, also associated with Aphrodite, the goddess of sexual activity, and thought to be lecherous creatures who copulated anytime and anywhere.[32] Birds, in general, were associated with lustfulness, and therefore Aphrodite is often depicted as riding on a bird such as a cock, swan, or goose, or being drawn in a chariot pulled by birds such as sparrows. So closely were birds associated with salaciousness that Greek artists produced images of *phalli* with wings and of birds portrayed as *phalli*, that is, having the legs, body, and wings of a bird, but a head and neck resembling a *phallus*.[33] And in many vase depictions, the phallic bird is a cock.

The cock's crest and its crow provide overt signals of its sexual activity. When the cock is sexually aroused, its crest, like erectile tissue, becomes rigid and red, and it crows. The first century CE Roman author Pliny noted that a castrated bird does not crow (*NH* 10.25.50). The crest and crow are also, however, indications of the cock's combativeness. The crest becomes erect and red during combat, and, when it triumphs, the cock crows over the dead body of its opponent.[34] The cock's behavior was, then, the same at the climax of either combative or sexual performance, and the crest and the crow were indications of its endowment and proficiency in both pursuits. As Csapo remarks, the cock was hypermasculine. "It has all the essential characteristics of a 'real man' in Greek society: an ideal hoplite and an assiduous lover. It excels at both poles of the masculine domain."[35] In contrast, the defeated cock, if it lived, never crowed again, and forever after followed the victor obsequiously; indeed, the phrase "like a beaten cock" was a metaphor for slavish behavior.[36] Thus one object lesson for the spectators was that defeat in battle meant not just a loss of virility, but also reduction to slavery.

Perhaps because the fighting cock was a paradigm of virility, it was the most common courtship gift in male homosexual relationships.[37] In ancient Athens, male homosexual relationships were often asymmetrical in terms of age and therefore of power. The lover was an adult, the beloved was a youth. Attic vase paintings portray the presentation of cocks by older men to younger men as part of the pederastic seduction process (see Figure 4.4).[38] Or, sometimes a depiction of a cockfight appears directly below a scene of pederastic courtship, visually linking cocks to homosexual lovers in the same way that, on other vases, cocks are visually linked to warriors.[39] There are several possible explanations for the appearance of cocks in these contexts. A cockfight scene on a vase may represent the virile combativeness of homosexual eroticism. In addition, the gift cock may signify the salaciousness of the adult lover and the tenacity that he will need to win over the object of his affection. Or perhaps the cock is intended to inspire lustiness in the beloved or, alternately, to suggest that he make the pursuit interesting by not yielding too soon.[40]

Exhibitions of cockfighting did not hold the same appeal for the ancient Romans. As noted above, Columella observed that the Romans did not share the zeal of the Greeks for breeding cocks to be as fierce in combat as possible. When skirmishes between cocks are mentioned by Roman writers, it is usually in the context of farmyard behavior, rather than in the context of matches staged by humans. Morgan contrasts the "deafening silence of so many Roman writers" with the ubiquity of references to cockfights in Greek writers.[41] There are, moreover, far fewer images of fighting cocks in Roman art, and these images do not present the paradigm of homoerotic courtship.

THE PERFORMANCE OF ANIMAL SACRIFICE

Animal sacrifices were a common spectacle in the ancient Greek and Roman worlds. The Latin word *sacrificere* means "to make (something) a gift to the

FIGURE 4.4: *A youth offering a rooster to another young man; a leopard and a dog.* Greek vase painting, 5th century BCE. Location: Chateau-Musee, Boulogne-sur-Mer, France. Photo Credit: Erich Lessing/Art Resource, NY; ART29976.

gods." The petitioners might be requesting help from the gods, or thanking them for help that was given. Sometimes, sacrifices were made to appease gods who had been offended by an inappropriate human action or to avert harm or disaster. The religions of the ancient Greeks and Romans were polytheistic, and thus there were many gods who required gifts. Sacrifices were central to the ritual of worship, and members of the community were expected to attend or else risk dishonoring the gods. The "community" might be as large as a state or city, on whose behalf the sacrifice was performed by a priest or political leader, or as small as a family, for whom the male head of the household performed the sacrifice. Not all sacrifices took the life of an animal. On some occasions, and particularly in small communities, the sacrificial offering might be biscuits, flowers, wine, fruits, cheese, or honey. Our focus here, however, will be on the performance of sacrifice as a spectacle during which community members witnessed the killing of an animal.

The animals killed at the sacrifices were domesticated animals: sheep, goats, pigs, and cattle. As opposed to wild animals, with which humans were always "at war,"[42] domesticated animals had value, when alive, to humans. Sheep and goats produced milk and wool, and cattle were used for draught labor (rarely for milk). Even pigs played an important role on farms; they cleaned up organic refuse, and they "cleared" land for the cultivation of crops by eating the seeds and roots of wild trees. Dedicating these animals to the gods was thus truly a "sacrifice" in the modern sense of the word: a relinquishment of something valuable.

Sheep and goats were the livestock with the largest populations in the rocky, arid regions of the Mediterranean, and, not surprisingly, they were the animals most frequently sacrificed. Nonetheless, in both literary and pictorial representations of sacrifices, the animals most often depicted are cattle.[43] Pliny the Elder noted that bulls were "splendid sacrificial animals" and a "very sumptuous appeasement of the gods" (NH 8.70.183). A sacrifice of cattle was considered particularly honorific, perhaps because oxen, when alive, were so valuable to humans. Pliny, Varro, and Columella all declared that the ox was the partner of humans in their farm labor. Columella adds that because the ox was our hardest-working partner, "it ought to surpass all other farm animals in honor." And all three authors report that, among the ancient Romans, it was as much a capital crime to have killed an ox as a human.[44]

The most lavish sacrifice was the hecatomb, a slaughter of one hundred cattle.[45] When Athens was at the height of its imperial power in the fifth century BCE, a hecatomb was offered to the city's protective deity, Athena, at the Greater Panathenaic ("All Athens") festival.[46] However, Attica (Athens and the countryside around it) was not a region where large numbers of cattle could be pastured, and the hundred cattle for the sacrifice were therefore obtained mainly by compelling areas under Athenian control to send cattle as tribute payments.[47] The fact that Athens could acquire cattle from its far-flung imperial possessions was a testament to the strength of its military. The grand sacrifice thus provided an opportunity for Athens to flaunt its prosperity and to proclaim its military might.

The Latin word for sacrificial animal is *victima*. The ideal "victim" was young and unblemished, and white or light in color, although dark-colored animals were sacrificed to the gods of the underworld. The ideal victim was also an animal that had never been used for work. Indeed, Aelian writes of a prohibition in Attica against the sacrifice of working cattle (VH 5.14). However, although an individual with no scars, deformities, or injuries was desirable, at some sacrifices, particularly in small communities, the victims may well have been animals that were sick, injured, unproductive, or old. From a strictly economic point of view, it seems likely that the Greeks and Romans sometimes sacrificed animals that could no longer work.[48]

The prelude to the spectacle of the sacrifice was a festive procession in which the victims were led to the altar by a joyful community. The animals were often decorated with flowers and ribbons, and some may have had their horns gilded to increase the perception that they were costly gifts to the gods.

A frieze that was created to adorn the Parthenon, the temple of Athena on the Acropolis, portrays a procession during the Panathenaic festival.[49] This festival was celebrated every year, on the summer day considered to be the birthday of the goddess Athena. Every fourth year, however, it was expanded and hence called the Greater Panathenaic festival. The grand procession through the streets of the city and up to Athena's temple on the Acropolis included, as the frieze reveals, townspeople, priests, their attendants, and the many animals that were to be sacrificed.

A very important aspect of the sacrifice was that the animals appear willing to be dedicated to the gods. Ideally they would walk quietly and approach the altar without hesitation. Pliny noted that "the gods are not propitiated by a victim that is lame or pulls itself away from the altar" (*NH* 8.70.183). Again, the reality may often have been quite different. The animals were sometimes reluctant performers in these spectacles. In one image, a bull is tethered to a ring at the foot of the altar, presumably to keep it from running away.[50] The Parthenon frieze reveals that the cattle in the Greater Panathenaic procession were led, or dragged, by ropes. In one segment of the frieze, one man struggles to keep hold of a fractious bull, while another man shortens his lead rope to gain better control over a straining bull (see Figure 4.5).[51]

FIGURE 4.5: *Youths leading a sacrificial cow*. Phidias (ca. 490–430 BCE). From the north frieze of the Parthenon in Athens, ca. 445–438 BCE. Location: Acropolis Museum, Athens, Greece. Photo Credit: Nimatallah/Art Resource, NY; ART11149.

At the altar, the performance continued. Willing or not, the victim was, in some way, made to signal its agreement to be sacrificed by nodding its head. The human participants sprinkled the victim with water and grain kernels, an action that may have caused the animal to toss its head and thus "nod its assent." The priest or presiding official uttered a prayer, and the animal was then killed, its throat slit or stabbed with a knife. (Larger animals were first stunned with a blow from an ax; see Figure 4.6). As the spectators looked on, blood from the animal's throat was caught in a vessel and poured on the altar. The organs, particularly the liver and heart, that contained much blood and thus much "vitality," were removed from the dead victim and carefully examined. Healthy entrails signified a successful sacrifice and indicated that the gods had accepted the gift and were well-disposed. Unhealthy entrails might be a portent of misfortune.[52] Among the ancient Greeks, the entrails were then roasted and eaten by participants.[53]

There are few pictorial representations of the killing of a victim. The Parthenon frieze, for example, shows the procession of the animals, but not their slaughter. Perhaps artists and their patrons preferred not to commemorate a process that, even when carried out efficiently, was a bloody mess. The stabbing or throat-slitting caused a massive hemorrhage that, in turn, must have sprayed blood on the people close to the altar. If the blow did not immediately

FIGURE 4.6: *Altar of Vespasian*, Temple of Vespasian (69–79 CE), Pompeii. The relief shows a sacrificial scene: The sacrificer and his aide bring the sacrificial bull, while the priest, a veil over his head, pours the libation over a tripod. Location: Pompeii, Italy. Photo Credit: Erich Lessing/Art Resource, NY; ART78500.

render the animal unconscious, it would bellow in pain and struggle to escape, spattering even more blood. "Actual sacrifices were presumably chaotic and unpredictable affairs. ... Moreover there were disgusting aspects to them: the guts of the animals (and in state sacrifices there were often dozens of animals) to be disposed of, the flies to brush away, the smell of blood and raw meat. Art could dispense with all these realities and provide prescriptive images."[54] The images of the Parthenon frieze, for example, present an idealized atmosphere of order and piety that was probably not present at the actual event.

For most sacrifice participants, any sympathy they may have felt for the animals would have been tempered by their anticipation of the next part of the event: the communal feast. The dead animal was butchered, and part of it was served to the gods. This process was an important component of the sacrifice because it provided an opportunity for gods and humans to dine together. However a Greek myth explains that because of a trick that Prometheus played on Zeus, the gods forever after received that part of the animal that humans did not desire: the bones and the fat.[55] Thus, the thigh bones were cut out of the victim, wrapped in fat, and burned on the altar. Wine and sometimes incense were then poured on the altar, perhaps to mask the smell of burning animal matter. The pungent smoke wafted to heaven and, it was believed, satisfied the gods. The rest of the animal was then butchered, cooked, and eaten by community members.[56] Sacrifice was a practice that emphasized the possibility of communication between humans and gods, while, at the same time, it underscored the distinction between humans and animals, who did not worship the gods and who ate raw meat. The feast signified that the human condition is closer to the divine than the bestial.

The communal feast was a key element of ancient society. In contrast to American diets, which emphasize meat, the diet of the ancient Greeks and Romans consisted largely of cereals, legumes, and cheese. In rural areas, people might eat wild animals, but almost all the meat that the ancient Greeks and Romans ate, particularly in urban areas, was derived from the sacrifice of domesticated animals. One theory about the origins of the practice of sacrifice posits that the ritual legitimized the killing of a domesticated animal in order to eat it.[57] By constructing the taking of animal life as an action necessary to maintain the good will of the gods, humans explained to themselves why they would kill for food an animal that was an ally and more valuable alive. The guilt for killing was thus resolved by placing responsibility for it on religious obligation.

Nonetheless, some people in the ancient world were troubled by the practice of sacrificing domesticated animals. In his epic poem, *Metamorphoses*, the first century Roman poet Ovid assigns a criticism of this practice to Pythagoras, the sixth-century BCE Greek philosopher and advocate of vegetarianism (15.103–142). Ovid's words suggest that Pythagoras opposed animal sacrifices because he believed that humans should respect the lives of the animals on which our very survival depends. Ovid's Pythagoras notes that sheep supply us with milk and wool, and thus benefit us more when alive than dead (116–119). Of cattle, Ovid's Pythagoras comments that he is an ungrateful man who has been able to slaughter the ox that had just pulled the plough in his fields and to strike with an ax the neck of the ox with whose help he had so often worked the hard ground and produced so many harvests (122–126). Pythagoras continues:

> Men believe that the gods find pleasure in the slaughter of the toil-enduring ox. A victim without blemish and of the most outstanding beauty … is decorated with ribbons and gold and led to the altar. It hears the priest's prayer, but does not understand. It sees grain being placed on its forehead, between its horns, grain which it helped to produce. It is struck, and it stains the knives with blood. … At once, men tear out the entrails from its still living chest and scrutinize them and detect in them the will of the gods. (129–137) … When you give the flesh of slaughtered cattle to your palate, know and understand that you are chewing your own fellow laborers. (141–142)

Despite the misgivings expressed by Ovid's Pythagoras, most people considered the sharing in the sacrificial feast to be an essential element of one's role as a community member. Heath observes that "in contrast to the perfunctory fast-food frenzy of today, meat-eating for the Greeks was consistently linked with the social and civic functions of animal sacrifice: vegetarianism and cannibalism were equally freakish perversities that meant the rejection of human community and civilization itself."[58] The animals slaughtered at public sacrifices were purchased with public funds or acquired through tribute payments. Rosivach comments that the distribution of meat at public sacrifices in Athens can be viewed as "a significant system of resource redistribution" whereby the Athenian state transformed its income into nourishment for all its citizens.[59] And, because participation in the shared feast was usually limited to members of the community, public sacrifices also served to define the community and contribute to its cohesiveness.

SPECTACULAR PROCESSIONS

One of the most extravagant displays of animals in the ancient Mediterranean world was a procession that was staged in Alexandria, Egypt, about 275 BCE, during the reign of Ptolemy II (also known as Ptolemy Philadelphus).[60] The Ptolemy family came from Macedonia, an area in the northern part of mainland Greece. The Ptolemies who ruled Egypt carefully retained their Greek names, language, and customs. Indeed, the famous Cleopatra (a Greek name), who was the daughter of Ptolemy XII and queen of Egypt until her suicide with Mark Antony in 30 BCE, may have been the only member of the Ptolemy family to have learned the language of her Egyptian subjects.[61] Ptolemy (later called Ptolemy I, or Ptolemy Soter) was born in Macedonia about 367 BCE and became an officer in the army of Alexander the Great, who was also Macedonian. In 331, Alexander captured Egypt and initiated the building of a city on the Mediterranean coast that was named after him: Alexandria. Alexander soon proceeded eastward on his tour of conquest in Asia, but Ptolemy remained behind to govern Egypt. He died in 283, and was succeeded by his son, also named Ptolemy (309–246).

About 275 BCE,[62] Ptolemy II Philadelphus commissioned a procession of gigantic proportions through the streets of Alexandria, a procession that served both to ingratiate him with residents of the city and to demonstrate his might to the Greek world. An account of this procession, preserved by Athenaeus,[63] relates that it was composed of several segments, each one very long, and that it began at sunrise and ended at sunset. Scholars have conjectured, however, that it may have taken several days for all the segments to pass one reviewing site.[64] The greater part of Athenaeus' account is a description of just the one segment that honored the Greek god Dionysus, but apparently the entire procession was an unbridled display of opulence.

The participants were adorned with gold and jewels and dressed in expensive purple and red robes, many of them gold-embroidered and gem-encrusted. They carried gold objects associated with the worship of Dionysus, and gold containers of rare spices like frankincense and myrrh. There were numerous large carts, some pulled by as many as six hundred men, carrying statues of Dionysus, gold altars and tables, jewel-encrusted wine basins and cups, and silver wine presses. The wine presses celebrated Dionysus' role as the god of wine, and the grape juice from the wine presses flowed onto the streets of Alexandria, perhaps to be scooped up by the jostling crowds. Another cart, pulled by five hundred men, held a cleverly constructed artificial cave, from which gushed forth two streams, one of milk and one of wine (again perhaps collected by spectators). There flew out from the cave pigeons and doves, but their feet were fastened with ribbons and they were therefore easily caught by spectators who took them home to cook and eat. The birds were a token of the pharaoh-king's munificence, and the spectators would have been delighted to receive from their monarch the enjoyable gift of both a parade and a good dinner.

These floats formed but a small part of the lavish displays. However, our focus in this chapter is on the animals that were exhibited in the Grand Procession. One cart displayed a scene of Dionysus' triumphant return from India. It bore an eighteen-foot-high statue of Dionysus, wearing a purple robe and gold crown and reclining on an elephant. The elephant was used here as a symbol of India. Its submission to being ridden signified that India had submitted to Dionysus. In a later section of the Grand Procession, there appeared a gold statue of Alexander the Great in a chariot drawn by four live elephants. Here, similarly, the harnessed elephants reminded spectators that Alexander, like Dionysus, had reached India. He had, moreover, gained control of the elephants that had been used, unsuccessfully, in battle against him, and he had subjugated the people of the East. The Latin verb *subjugare*, from which we obtain the English verb "to subjugate," means literally "to put under (*sub*) a yoke (*jugum*)." The people of the East had been harnessed to Alexander's will as surely as the elephants that pulled his chariot. Indeed, among the people marching in the Dionysiac segment of the procession were Indian women, displayed as prisoners of war.

Historians of Alexander were fond of making the analogy between the eastern triumphs of Alexander and those of Dionysus.[65] In turn, Ptolemy II was eager to emphasize the parallels between his accomplishments and those of the god and the military genius to whom he claimed to be related.[66] Ptolemy II had not embarked on any wars of conquest in India. He did, however, by presenting animals from India in his Grand Procession, encourage favorable comparisons of himself to his "ancestors," Dionysus and Alexander. The procession demonstrated that he, too, had the power to bring the resources of the East to the Mediterranean world. Thus, a parade ostensibly in honor of Dionysus became an occasion to celebrate Ptolemy and promote him as a strong and legitimate ruler. And by stressing the link between himself and Alexander, Ptolemy suggested that he was a champion of Greek causes. As Coleman comments, the Grand Procession "was, at least in formal terms, a religious event, but it was exploited as an occasion for a powerful public statement about the nature of Ptolemaic rule."[67]

In the Dionysiac segment of the procession alone, there were many different species of animals, many of which were not native to Egypt.[68] There were chariots pulled by 96 elephants, 120 goats, 24 saiga antelope (from the area north of the Black Sea), 14 oryxes, 30 hartebeest, 16 ostriches, 14 onelaphoi (wild asses), 8 wild asses of another type, 16 horses, and 12 camels. Each chariot was driven by a small boy and held a small girl as a passenger. Perhaps the animals had been tamed sufficiently to be managed by a child, but it is more likely that an adult walked at the front of the chariot to control them. Nonetheless, the harnessing of animals is a demonstration of humans' ability to gain control over their environment and to exploit nature. By exhibiting children as drivers, the producers of the procession may have intended to emphasize that the abilities of humans are so remarkable that they can train wild animals to obey even children. Perhaps they even intended to suggest a favorable comparison of the human with the divine. Dionysus was often depicted as riding on wild animals like leopards, or in vehicles pulled by wild animals. His domination of these fierce beasts was evidence of his power to tame nature and, in turn, to introduce civilization to humans. The display of children driving chariots may have signaled the success of the god's lessons to humankind.

In addition to the chariots drawn by wild animals, there were also carts pulled by donkeys and mules, and camels carrying enormous quantities of spices such as frankincense, myrrh, saffron, cassia, and cinnamon. Camels were native to India and may have been introduced to Egypt by Ptolemy II.[69] Their appearance reminded spectators that Ptolemy had brought to Egypt not just the expensive spices of India, but even exotic Indian beasts of burden that would now serve the people of Egypt. Men from Ethiopia carried six hundred elephant tusks in the procession, evidence certainly of Ptolemy's wealth, but also of his ability to kill these massive beasts. Diodorus notes that Ptolemy was passionately fond of hunting wild elephants (3.36.3). In this case, the killing of elephants represented not a triumph over the military might of Eastern civilizations, but a triumph over hostile nature.

There also appeared 2,400 hunting dogs from several different geographic regions, including India. One group of 150 men carried trees to which were attached a variety of animals and birds, while another group carried cages in which were situated birds from India and Ethiopia. Then there appeared 130 Ethiopian sheep, 300 Arabian sheep, and 20 Euboean (Greek) sheep, 26 white Indian cows and 8 cows from Ethiopia, 1 large white bear (probably not a polar bear, but an albino or light-colored bear from the area north of Greece),[70] 14 leopards, 16 cheetahs, 4 lynxes, 3 cheetah cubs, 1 giraffe, and 1 Ethiopian rhinoceros. At the end of the Dionysiac section of the procession 24 extremely large lions were exhibited, and then 2,000 bulls with gilded horns and gold harness. The 2,000 bulls were probably destined to be slaughtered at the sacrifice that, following Greek practice, would provide the community with a feast. Perhaps the sheep were also intended for sacrifice. In any case, the 2,000 bulls—and these were just the bulls in the Dionysiac segment—would provide substantial amounts of meat for the spectators.

The animals not slaughtered when the procession finally ended probably went (or went back) to Ptolemy's large private zoo or *paradeisos*. The word *paradeisos* (English "paradise") was imported into the Greek language from the Near East. It refers to the large parks in which Persian kings kept animals of many species, primarily for the purpose of hunting them. The area where the old kingdom of Persia had been located was one of the territories captured by Alexander the Great. At his death, control of this part of Alexander's empire was taken over by one of his Macedonian generals, Seleucus, who founded the Seleucid dynasty. The Seleucids, who were rivals of the Ptolemies in the claim to be the legitimate heirs of Alexander, had continued the Persian tradition of "paradises." In establishing his animal park, Ptolemy II may have been striving to surpass the "paradises" of his Seleucid rivals. Or perhaps, as several ancient

authors suggest, he was genuinely interested in collecting exotic species. Diodorus records that Ptolemy II spent enormous amounts of money to pay for the
capture and maintenance of wild animals, and that he therefore brought to the
attention of the Greeks animals that they had never seen before.[71] Of course,
the animals served a propaganda function. The ability to display exotic novel-
ties served as evidence of the magnitude of Ptolemy's influence in the foreign
lands from which he had acquired the animals, having received them as gifts
or tribute.

   The Grand Procession provided residents of Alexandria—both native Egyptians and Greek overlords—with a lavish civic event that could inspire pride in
their young city. It demonstrated, moreover, that the Ptolemies venerated Greek
gods. And at the very end there appeared a formidable display of 57,600 infan-
trymen and 23,200 cavalrymen. This exhibition of military might suggests that
Ptolemy also intended the Grand Procession to serve as an advertisement to
the world outside Egypt of the power of the Ptolemaic kingdom.[72] People visiting Alexandria at the time of the procession would report home that this new
city and new regime had produced a remarkably impressive display both of its
capabilities and of its affiliations with the Hellenistic world. The spectacle of
animals was a key element in Ptolemy II Philadelphus' strategy to secure the
confidence of his Egyptian subjects and the admiration of his fellow Greeks.

ANIMALS IN ROMAN ARENAS

The ancient Romans, like other humans, regarded civilization as a triumph of
rationality over the chaos of the natural world. Rationality enabled humans
to exploit those animal species that provided food and labor and to eradicate
those species that threatened human survival. And, like other societies, the Romans devised spectacles that made manifest the ability of humans to create a
secure environment for themselves.[73] These spectacles included displays of humans killing animals and of animals killing other animals. The former offered
proof of the superiority of humans; the latter were demonstrations of the savage and irrational violence of nature. These exhibitions reminded spectators
that they were fortunate to belong to the human community, whose members
protected one another from the brutality of animals.

   The enactments of domination over animals were an important element of
Roman life. In 80 CE, for example, to celebrate the dedication of the Flavian
amphitheater in Rome (later known as the Colosseum), nine thousand animals
were killed over a period of one hundred days.[74] The first-century CE Roman
poet Martial recorded the agonizing deaths of some of these animals. His descriptions reveal that the Roman crowd enjoyed watching animals respond to
the torment in novel ways. He relates, for example, that when a pregnant sow
was stabbed with a spear, a piglet emerged from her lacerated womb. "Nor did

the piglet lie still; instead, as its mother fell, it ran away. ... At one and the same time, the sow lost life and gave life. ... By her fatal wound, she became a mother. O, how ingenious are sudden and unexpected events" (*De spectaculis* 14 (12), 15 (13), and 16 (14)). Martial also recounts that a tame tigress, confronted by a wild lion, "savagely tore at the lion with frenzied fang—a new and strange occurrence, unknown at any other time" (*De spect.* 21 (18)). The events of 80 CE also included the sight of a rhinoceros killing a bear and an elephant killing a bull (*De spect.* 20 (17), 22 (19), and 26 (22)).

The carnage at the spectacles of 80 CE was surpassed in 107 CE, when the emperor Trajan celebrated his military victory in Dacia (modern Hungary and Romania) with 120 days of spectacles during which eleven thousand animals were killed.[75] The Romans were not unusual in their enthusiasm for spectacles in which animals were tortured and slaughtered. Even today, for example, bull-fights and cockfights attract large crowds of people eager to be entertained by violence against and between animals. What is unparalleled about the spectacles in the ancient Roman world is, first, their scale and, second, the significant role they played in defining Roman culture and influencing public affairs. These spectacles, as Brown remarks, "were not merely an entertainment, but virtually a requirement of Imperial Roman social and political life."[76] Displays of animal slaughter had been a familiar aspect of Roman culture for many centuries before Trajan sponsored the killing of eleven thousand beasts. And in his use of the displays to consolidate popular support for his policies, Trajan was simply following a pattern that had been established by Roman aristocrats of a much earlier period. And not just in Rome, but also in small towns throughout the Roman Empire, animals were regularly abused and killed in exhibitions sponsored by municipal officials. Even far from the great capital, a man who aspired to political authority felt the obligation to arrange such entertainments, albeit on a much more modest scale, for local residents. For example, in 249 CE, at Minturnae, a town south of Rome, a four-day event consisted of the display and killing of ten bears and several herbivores.[77] In fourth-century Syria, the animal slaughters were so popular that people gathered early in the cold air to secure seats, as if the stone of the arena was softer than their beds.[78] The exhibitions of animal slaughter provided pleasure for spectators, but also served to gather them together for a communal event sponsored by officials who were advocates of the Roman state. At its greatest extent, the Roman Empire stretched from Britain in the northwest to Syria in the southeast and encompassed people of many different cultures and traditions. The production of the spectacles was utilized as a means of promoting Roman values in even the most remote regions of the empire.

One well-known story about an ambitious politician's eagerness to provide extravagant animal shows for the populace in Rome concerns Marcus Caelius Rufus, a friend of the famous statesman Marcus Tullius Cicero. In 51 and 50 BCE,

Cicero was governor of the Roman province of Cilicia, in southern Asia Minor, and Caelius was in Rome, preparing to serve a term in the elected public office of *curule aedile*. The aediles were the magistrates to whom fell the task of organizing public entertainments in Rome, and Caelius was anxious that the animal shows he produced should outdo those of his political rivals. He therefore wrote numerous letters to Cicero in Cilicia, pestering him to order the residents of his province to capture leopards to be sent to Rome. Cicero was reluctant to impose this burden on the people he governed. With some exasperation, he finally replied to Caelius: "About the leopards: the matter is being handled with diligence by men who are skillful hunters. But there is a remarkable scarcity of leopards. And I am told that the few leopards left are complaining bitterly that they are the only animals in my province for whom traps are set. And therefore they have decided, or so the rumor goes, to leave Cilicia" (*Ad familiares* 2.11.2).[79]

The exchange of letters between Cicero and Caelius reveals that politicians took advantage of every connection they had to acquire crowd-pleasing animals for their shows. Caelius undoubtedly pestered other friends in other provinces, and Cicero probably received requests from other acquaintances. Cicero's remark about the scarcity of leopards also reveals the enormous impact that the collection of animals had on local environments. In 55 BCE, Pompey produced spectacles at which he exhibited about four hundred leopards, six hundred lions (far exceeding the previous record of one hundred set by Sulla[80]), twenty elephants, and a rhinoceros, the first seen in Rome.[81] And in 46 BCE, Julius Caesar sponsored shows at which four hundred lions and, for the first time in Rome, a giraffe were displayed.[82] Strabo, writing a few decades after Caesar's shows, remarked that the Roman fondness for killing animals had encouraged agriculture in the North African province of Numidia (2.5.33). Nomads who had previously not been able to survive as settlers because of the large number of wild animals were now farming and hunting. Strabo's comment suggests that the Numidians were trapping and selling to the Romans the large African cats that had threatened farmers in the past. A poem in the *Greek Anthology* (7.626) applauds a similar situation in Libya, where countless numbers of lions were captured to be killed in arenas. "The mountains which were once the habitat of wild beasts are now pastures for the domesticated animals of men."

The development at Rome of the slaughter of animals as a public spectacle can be traced back to activities in rural areas. In agricultural communities, people routinely killed animals that were their competitors, that is, animals that preyed on their livestock or consumed their food plants. And several times a year, rural residents congregated at festivals where they celebrated their community's success in producing abundant food. At some of the festivals, celebrants watched as large numbers of pest species, such as rabbits and foxes, were killed.[83] The purpose of these "re-enactments" of the eradication of pests was to remind celebrants that humans were, with divine help, capable of subduing hostile elements of their environment. These festivals were observed also in urban areas, and, although very few town-dwellers had personal knowledge of the damage done by rabbits and foxes, they understood the symbolic significance of the killings. The publicly witnessed destruction of pest species served to reassure them that the rational and orderly civilization that the Romans had created could confront an irrational, unpredictable, and therefore dangerous nature—and defeat it. Spectators took pleasure in the pain of the animals because the animals were "enemies"; their suffering was the penalty they paid for threatening human life. As Brown remarks, they were considered "legitimate victims of institutionalized violence."[84]

The development of urban spectacles of violence toward animals is also linked to the sport hunting enjoyed by upper-class men, many of whom held positions of power in the state. They advocated hunting as an activity that fostered the physical stamina and moral courage necessary in a leader.[85] In addition, they promoted the killing of dangerous or devouring animals as a public service that made the entire community safer. Of course, few town-dwellers had the opportunity to hunt; only the wealthy could afford to travel to rural areas and arrange costly hunting parties. However, men who were vying for the endorsement of lower-class voters brought the hunting experience to the town in the form of staged hunts. We have already noted the frantic attempts of Cicero's ambitious friend, Caelius, to obtain exotic animals to be displayed at the staged hunts he was producing as aedile. Shows like these permitted even the poorest of town-dwellers to take part, at least as spectators, in an activity that was otherwise well beyond their means. Thus, the destruction of animals in urban arenas became a popular entertainment that was exploited by upper-class men for their political purposes. And the Latin word *venatio* (plural *venationes*), usually translated as "hunt," came to mean both a pursuit of animals in the countryside and an urban display of killing animals that people attended as spectators.

To the modern mind, a rural hunt and an urban display seem to have little in common, even if both involve the killing of animals. However, a passage from Varro's book about agriculture explains the similarities (*DRR* 3.13.1–3). Varro describes a country estate whose absentee owner wanted wild animals readily available to kill when he visited. The estate staff therefore trained the animals to appear when required by placing food in the same location every day as, simultaneously, a man dressed up as the mythical figure Orpheus played a trumpet. The mythical Orpheus was such a skillful musician that he charmed even wild animals, who were attracted by his music and approached him without fear or aggression (see Figure 4.7). His story signifies the civilizing power of music, which is able to pacify even beasts. It also suggests that humans can live in harmony with other animals. On the estate that Varro describes, the animals associated food with the trumpet music of "Orpheus" and "flooded around so that the sight seemed as beautiful as the hunts staged in the Circus Maximus in Rome." Of course, in contrast to the myth of Orpheus, the sole purpose of training the animals to trust humans was to make them easy to kill. When Varro compares the estate to the Circus Maximus and describes circus hunts as "beautiful," he reveals the nature of the hunting parties of the elite. For upper-class Romans, most hunts in the countryside were, in fact, carefully staged events, where the so-called "hunters" simply waited for the animals to be summoned or driven toward them.[86] The thrill of the hunt thus lay not in the pursuit, but in the kill. The urban "hunts" were therefore similar to their rural counterparts in their focus on killing animals. For Varro and his readers, moreover, the corresponding element in each location was the sight of a large number of wild animals that had been assembled through the cleverness of humans and that would be killed by ingenious humans. Both the estate and the circus offered opportunities to demonstrate the superiority of humans over nature.

As the Romans expanded their imperial territory, they began to import to Italy exotic animals from the most remote regions of their empire: lions, tigers, and leopards from Asia Minor, elephants from North Africa, even the occasional crocodile and hippopotamus from Egypt. These foreign species were

FIGURE 4.7: *Orpheus charming the animals.* Mosaic from Blanzy. Roman, 4th century CE. Location: Musee Municipal, Laon, France. Photo Credit: Bridgeman-Giraudon/Art Resource, NY; ART21265.

exhibited and killed before appreciative crowds of city residents in spectacles that served several functions. For example, the animals were considered part of the spoils of war taken from the vanquished enemy. Their exhibition in Rome therefore provided concrete proof that the wars had been successful and that Rome was able to subdue any force that resisted it. The spectacle also established that the upper-class politician who sponsored it was attentive to popular wishes, had the military and political connections needed to obtain animals from foreign lands, and was thus worthy of holding a position of great authority.

The display and slaughter of animals continued to symbolize human domination over nature, but now also signified Roman supremacy over the rest of the world. Capturing large and fierce animals and transporting them over great distances involved considerable risk, careful planning, and much expense (see Figure 4.8). Thus, the fact that the Romans were able, with apparent ease, to bring vast numbers of animals to their city, and then simply destroy them, was verification that their state was powerful and prosperous and could afford the costs of providing pleasure for the urban masses.[87] For the masses, the destruction of exotic animals was an entertaining reward for supporting the state's military campaigns; but it was also an opportunity to witness the process of imposing Roman justice on a barbarian world. The animals were viewed as representatives of the regions from which they had been imported, and their slaughter in the arena dramatically reenacted the triumph of the Roman military in battles with fierce, but ultimately weaker humans. The slaughter of leopards, for example, symbolized the defeat of the people of Asia Minor. Similarly, the slaughter of elephants, which had been used as war machines against the Romans by the army of African Carthage, represented the crushing of that army.[88] Most human prisoners of war were not killed, but rather sold as slaves, a process that enriched the state treasury. Thus, the torment and execution of animals from areas of Roman conquest served, in part, as a substitute for the torment and execution of the vanquished humans. The gathering together of the Roman people was an important element of these spectacles because it reaffirmed their existence as a community, united by their ability to gain control over menacing elements of the environment, by their self-proclaimed responsibility to impose order on the rest of the world, and by their right to enjoy the profits of their state's military ventures.

The men who killed the animals were called *venatores* ("hunters") and *bestiarii* ("beast-fighters") (see Figure 4.9). They were skilled athletes who trained hard to perform successfully, that is, to kill animals and escape injury. Like other performers, such as actors, chariot drivers, and gladiators, the *venatores* and *bestiarii* were often slaves or former slaves, and they therefore occupied the lowest rank of the rigid social hierarchy. However, they were accorded the admiration of the spectators for bravery in their performances on the arena floor.

FIGURE 4.8: Stags and ostriches are brought aboard a ship. Detail of the *Big Game Hunt*. Roman mosaic, 3rd–4th century CE. Location: Villa del Casale, Piazza Armerina, Sicily, Italy. Photo Credit: Erich Lessing/Art Resource, NY; ART94486.

Although fighting animals was clearly a very hazardous activity, it is likely that most *venatores* and *bestiarii* were the victors in these encounters. It was, after all, the intention of the producers to present a display of human dominance over animals. In any case, the animals were sometimes too traumatized by the injury, illness, and stress that resulted from their capture and transport to put up much of a fight. Martial records that a bull had to be prodded with fire to confront an elephant (*De spect.* 22 (19)) and a rhinoceros had to be goaded to attack a bear (*De spect.* 26 (22)). Another author reports that during the spectacles sponsored by the emperor Probus in 281 CE, one hundred lions were brought into the Circus Maximus, but they were unwilling to leave their cages and were therefore slaughtered right at the doors of their cages, "providing no great entertainment" (*Historia Augusta, Probus* 19).[89] In 393 CE, Symmachus was disappointed when the bears he had ordered for a spectacle finally arrived

FIGURE 4.9: *Mosaic with circus scene: fight with leopards.* Location: Galleria Borghese, Rome, Italy. Photo Credit: Scala/Art Resource, NY; ART79542.

in Rome: He received only a few bear cubs, and they were very weak from starvation and stress (*Letter* 2.76.2).

In addition to the spectacles in which animals killed animals or humans killed animals, there were spectacles in which animals killed humans. These events were executions. The people who were placed on the arena floor with the animals were not trained "hunters," and they had no weapons or protective equipment (see Figure 4.10). They did not leave the arena alive. They were people who had been judged guilty of a capital crime, and they were accordingly condemned to a capital punishment. Like crucifixion and burning alive, *condemnatio ad bestias* was a very painful and very public method of execution, intended not just to satisfy the community's demand for vengeance, but also to warn potential wrongdoers of the hideous fate that awaited them.

People "condemned to the beasts" became "legitimate victims of institutionalized violence" because they had refused to abide by the laws that the rational community had established to constrain bestial behavior in humans. By choosing to act like predatory animals and to harm community members, they were considered to have forfeited the protection that human society offers and thus to have made themselves liable to the same type of destruction that was imposed on menacing animals. The condemned person was exposed on the arena floor to suffer the consequences of his preference for the chaos of nature. He became a beast vulnerable to attack by other beasts, and his death was an exhibition of the savagery of the natural world in which he had chosen, by his lawlessness, to live. *Condemnatio ad bestias* was an expensive form of execution because of the costs related to trapping, shipping, and maintaining the animals, but it was, for the audience, a particularly satisfying method of execution because it allowed the forces of nature to deal with one of their own. Moreover, the mauling to death by a "fellow" animal completed the

FIGURE 4.10: *A condemned prisoner offered up to the wild animals.* Detail of a Roman mosaic from the Domus Sollertiana. End 3rd century CE. This is the only Tunisian mosaic depicting this Roman tradition. Location: Musee Archeologique, El Jemm (Thysdrus), Tunisia. Photo Credit: Gilles Mermet/Art Resource, NY; ART159494.

dehumanization of the condemned, whose voice was reduced to nonverbal, animallike shrieks. These inarticulate utterances confirmed for the audience that the condemned had, in fact, been a beast all along. In the final process of reduction to the category of animal, the condemned was eaten by the animals and thus converted to bestial flesh. Spectators could watch the torment with the same detachment and even amusement with which they watched their animal enemies being abused. Indeed, entertaining the public by their suffering was part of the penalty that the condemned paid for their lawlessness. In turn, laughing at their enemy's plight helped to defuse any fear of injury that the crimes had caused community members to experience.

By the first century CE, executions were embellished to make them more attractive to spectators who craved novelty.[90] Martial (*De spect.* 24 (21)), for example, describes a *condemnatio ad bestias* for which the scenery on the arena floor resembled a forest. Animals of several species were placed in the forest, and also a condemned man, costumed as the mythical Orpheus. He was soon mauled to death by a bear. The audience was thus doubly satisfied, to see the execution of someone who had threatened their society and to be entertained by a novel inversion of a traditional myth. Unlike the mythical Orpheus, who was able to live peaceably with animals, the arena "Orpheus" was killed by them. The "snuff play" in the arena instructed spectators that humans cannot coexist with wild beasts; because they are not members of the human moral community, beasts must be dealt with ruthlessly.

The frequent appearance on art objects throughout the Roman Empire of scenes depicting the capture and display of animals attests to widespread interest in these activities. For example, animal slaughters and human executions were popular themes in a large number of the colorful mosaics found in North Africa. And these mosaics were prominently located in the center of dining-room floors, so that people could enjoy the gruesome scenes while dining. The intent of the homeowner was to remind viewers that the man who had sponsored the spectacles was generous to the community and could be entrusted with maintaining its security. A third century CE mosaic from Tunisia shows the killing of leopards by *bestiarii*, but the most prominent place in the mosaic is occupied by the bags of coins that the *editor* (sponsor), a man named Magerius, expended on the *venatio* (see Figure 4.11).[91] And on each side of the money bags is an inscription lauding Magerius' gift to the community. The mosaic thus commemorates the sponsor's munificence and the audience's appreciation for it. There is no sympathetic concern for the animals or humans being executed.

FIGURE 4.11: *The Magerius mosaic*. Hunting scenes in celebration of venationes offered by Magerius, 3rd century CE, from Smirat, Tunisia. Location: Museum, Sousse, Tunisia. Photo Credit: Vanni/Art Resource, NY; ART93729.

The arena was a human construction that brought into sharp relief the boundaries between order and chaos, culture and nature, human and animal. It was a place where the community gathered to witness and celebrate the elimination of threats to its security. The spectacles of the torment and death of animals and bestial humans provided the audience with the assurance that their state could triumph over the menacing chaos of nature.

The Observation and Use of Animals in the Development of Scientific Thought in the Ancient World with Especial Reference to Egypt[1]

ANDREW H. GORDON

Observation of the natural world by predynastic ancestors of the ancient Egyptians and the possible domestication of cattle as early as 9000 BCE at Nabta Playa in the western desert led to the development of a cattle cult. This focus on and obsession with cattle led the precursors of the ancient Egyptians and the ancient Egyptians themselves to keenly observe every aspect of the life cycle of their prized and beloved animals. Because of the Egyptians' religious and economic need for the animals, they were concerned with keeping the cattle in health, which led to the development of early biomedical theories regarding both animals and humans. This progressed to the development of an early comparative medicine.

The predynastic domestication of cattle, their care by healers and priests, and the ritual sacrifice of cattle observed by priests and the elite led to the development of an understanding of comparative anatomy and physiology. These findings were also applied to humans. At least two original theories came from these observations: the male's role in reproduction and life as movement, especially as seen in the fasciolations of excised limbs, the so-called "living flesh." Egyptians saw the ka (usually translated as "life force") as an animating force, which explains why they held an excised bull's foreleg to the mouth of a deceased person to reanimate him or her. While their first theory, regarding reproduction, is incorrect, it did apparently influence the later Greeks and possibly the ancient Hebrews and the surrounding ancient Near East. Ancient Egyptians' observation of the animal world indicates that comparative animal medicine profoundly influenced the development of human medicine, and not the other way around.

When people think about the development of science in the ancient world, they most likely recall the Greeks as the start of a rationally based science. When they consider the origin of medicine, they again think of the Greeks. They see Hippocrates and his oath and perhaps the physicians of Alexandria. What they do not see is that the development of science, including medicine, goes back at least to the origin of the Egyptian civilization, if not further, and that the observation of animals led to the development of medicine. The Greeks, such as Herodotus, praised Egyptian science, including medicine, and considered it an important influence on their own research. The working conditions and the subsequent prejudices of nineteenth- and twentieth-century historians and scientists have obscured this development.

SCHOLARLY BIASES AND THE ORIGIN OF EGYPTIAN MEDICINE[2]

Until recently, the usual explanation for the origin of ancient Egyptian medicine, especially regarding anatomy and physiology, is that it arose in the treatment of battlefield wounds or during the process of mummification. Physicians or those working closely with them have promoted these ideas. Few scholars have suggested the possibility that medicine may have arisen through the maintaining in health of domestic animals destined for ritual slaughter or for food. Sigerist only reluctantly suggested that the chief sources for anatomical knowledge were the cult and the kitchen.[3] Most physicians and their nonmedical associates believed that veterinary medicine was derivative from and secondary to the study of human medicine. In addition, since all but one of the extant medical papyri refer to human rather than to animal medicine, these scholars felt justified in their approach. They did not see that references to animal anatomy abound in the religious texts, such as the Pyramid Texts and the tomb scenes and texts. Also, it did not occur to most of them that modern biology might provide insight into ancient religious or apparently irrational practices.

Further, they failed to realize that practices of modern Nilotic tribes might also point the way to an understanding of ancient practices.

That twentieth-century researchers believed the treatment of battlefield wounds would lead to some advances in anatomy and physiology is not surprising. But on the battlefield, where time is of the essence, detailed observation of either anatomical or physiological human processes would be difficult, if not impossible. In addition, given the Egyptians' and many other ancient peoples' taboo against autopsy and vivisection, at least except for a short time in Ptolemaic Alexandria, detailed knowledge of interior anatomy and physiology had to have come from animals, where no such taboo existed. The Edwin Smith Surgical Papyrus from the late Second Intermediate period (ca. 1600 BCE), but dated on physical and grammatical grounds to several hundred years earlier,[4] does show a scientific knowledge of how to treat wounds from war or construction accidents. However, even so it is later in date than the Kahun Veterinary Papyrus, which is dated to the Middle Kingdom (ca. 1875 BCE), but was probably originally composed during the Old Kingdom (2625–2200 BCE).[5] Warren Dawson, a pioneer in the study of Egyptian medicine, credited the Edwin Smith Surgical Papyrus with being the "earliest known scientific book,"[6] even though the Kahun Veterinary Papyrus was evidently older. According to Dawson, surgery originated "in the attempt to repair the ravages of man."[7]

With regard to mummification, Smith and Dawson stated, "Mummification had a great influence on the development of the science of anatomy, and in fact on medicine in general."[8] They also indicated that the process of mummification would have given the Egyptians a good knowledge of anatomy and physiology, but at the same time said there was little evidence that they actually had this knowledge. Dawson noted further that mummification would have been the first opportunity for comparative anatomy, but he neglected to consider the Kahun Veterinary Papyrus, which deals with the diseases of an indeterminate number of different animals. Although the wrapping of a body in linen strips with a resinous substance may have begun as early as the Badarian period (4500–4100 BCE), the first evidence of the extraction of internal organs does not occur until the beginning of the Fourth Dynasty (ca. 2600 BCE). Also, as acknowledged by Harris, "contrary to common belief, the process of mummification would have afforded little opportunity for the study of internal anatomy, the viscera being roughly drawn out of the abdominal and thoracic cavities through a ventral incision with no concern for finesse."[9] It is generally thought that embalmers did not enjoy an elevated position in Egyptian society because handling the dead would have made them unclean. However, a very few instances exist in which a healer (*swnw*) was related to an embalmer. Because of this, it has been suggested that the two professions shared similar technical training.[10] It seems much more likely, however, that the relative absence of evidence is an indication of what really existed, that is, that few healers would have had embalmers in their families.

With regard to the earlier downgrading of Egyptian medicine relative to Greek medicine, Gaston Maspero, one of the most important Egyptologists of the late nineteenth and early twentieth centuries, perhaps said it best when he opined that the Egyptian physicians knew so little, but they knew it thirty centuries before our time.[11] More recently, scholars have downgraded veterinary medicine. James Henry Breasted, one of the foremost Egyptologists of the first part of the twentieth century, wrote about the temple cult in his study of Egyptian religion: "I have not undertaken the problem of origins ... like that of sacred animals so prominent in Egypt."[12] Or, "In the age discussed these two highest gods [Re and Osiris] were altogether human and highly spiritualized, though the thought of Re displays occasional relapses, as it were, in the current allusions to the falcon, with which he was so early associated. Another subject passed by is the concept of sacrifice, which I have not discussed at all."[13]

In Dawson's pioneering study of ancient Egyptian medicine, he relegated the Kahun Veterinary Papyrus to an "Other Documents" section following the section on medical papyri. This "Other Documents" section contained literary and magical texts. In modern times, John Nunn fails to list the Kahun Veterinary Papyrus in the medical papyri chapter of his important work on Egyptian medicine.[14] Halioua and Ziskind follow Nunn's example.[15] In fact, many papyri fragments were discovered at Kahun, including parts of a veterinary and a gynecological papyrus, which their original decipherer, F. Ll. Griffith, clearly designated as separate, as they were found seven months apart, presumably in different areas.[16] Examining the Kahun Veterinary Papyrus, Grapow initially suggested, but quickly rejected, the idea that "the forms of the [Egyptian] physician's language were developed in veterinary medicine and only from that transferred to human medicine."[17] He then concluded that because of the similarity of the Veterinary Papyrus to [other] medical papyri, it must have been based on a [lost] book of human medicine. Ghalioungui agreed, but added that the veterinarian was so well trained that he must have been a human doctor as well. He did not consider that the study of animal and human medicine may have not been divided, even though it is today. But even he indicated that with regard to anatomy, the study of animals preceded that of human beings.

In another example of anti-veterinary bias, Alan Gardiner, one of the foremost Egyptologists of the first half of the twentieth century, referred to the temple personnel who sacrificed bulls as "butchers" and the product of the sacrifice as "meat" or "joints." While the slaughter of animals may be for food, the tomb scenes show priests and sometimes healers (swnw) officiating. Clearly, there is a ritualistic aspect to these scenes. Gardiner also initially referred to a list of anatomical terms in the Ramesseum Onomasticon, dated to the late Middle Kingdom (1800 BCE), as those of people and only later realized that the list referred to the anatomy of a bull. Gardiner thought that the papyrus may have come from the tomb of a "doctor or magician."[18] He wrote that "this indicates that the scribe was here writing with an eye to the butcher, rather than to the surgeon or medical practitioner."[19] And further, "Thus it can barely be disputed that the lists of objects … are concerned solely with sacrificial joints."[20]

While several words referred to ancient Egyptian healers, the most common was *swnw*, usually translated by Egyptologists and/or modern physicians as "doctor" or "physician." Since those who study the ancient medical texts have almost always been physicians, or Egyptologists who collaborated with physicians, it is hardly surprising that they referred to *swnw* as "physicians." These researchers regarded the study of animals as a lower form of practice. The word "physician," originally meaning "natural philosopher," first connoted a medical practitioner in eleventh-century Europe. The apparent absence of an ancient Egyptian word for "veterinarian" may, in fact, imply that *swnw* referred to both human and animal healers.[21] Modern researchers have seen human and veterinary medicine as two distinct fields, with veterinary medicine occupying an inferior and secondary role. But if one looks at the history of medicine, human and animal medicine were united for most of it. It was quite clear to the Egyptians as well as to the Greeks that man is an animal, a fact also underpinning modern biomedicine.[22] Schwabe has noted that it is precisely when animal and human medicine were united as comparative medicine that the greatest scientific advances were made. In essence, veterinary medicine was the driving force in the progress of human medicine.

Other evidence for the origin of human medicine in veterinary medicine is that most, if not all, the hieroglyphs for internal organs are those of animals other than man, chiefly cattle. Thus, the origin of the hieroglyph for "heart" (*ib*) is that of a bull, the word for "throat" (*xx*) depicts the head and trachea of a bull, the hieroglyph for "jaw" is the lower jawbone of a bull, the hieroglyph for "tongue" is likely that of a bull or cow, and the word for "womb" (*idt*) is the bicornuate uterus of a cow.[23] In addition, the hieroglyph for "ear" is a mammalian ear, probably a bovine, and the hieroglyph for "tooth" is a mammalian tusk. The hieroglyphs for "backbone," "ribs," and "intestines" also come from mammalian anatomy. That the representations of internal organs were those of animals other than humans indicates clearly where the Egyptians received their earliest knowledge of anatomy and physiology.

In an example that may be related to veterinary medicine, Manetho, an Egyptian priest of the third century BCE who wrote in Greek, stated in *Aegyptiaca*, a chronology of the Egyptian kings, that the second king of the First Dynasty, Athothis, was a physician whose works on anatomy still existed during Manetho's time. Unless he was personally dissecting criminals or conquered enemies, Athothis was most likely taking part in the sacrifice of animals, such as bulls, during which he would have acquired a good knowledge of anatomy.

The name of the king appears to come from the God Thoth,[24] the inventor of writing, patron of doctors, and supervisor of the *Per Ankh,* the House of Life, in which medical works were written and/or stored.[25]

Besides Egyptological sources of evidence for the idea that ancient Egyptian medicine began with the maintaining in health and sacrifice of large animals such as bulls, biological evidence from tomb scenes and their sometimes enigmatic texts suggests that Egyptians developed a theory of life based on movement, especially as seen in the fasciolations of limbs excised during sacrifice, an event frequently attended by the elite, healers, and priests. Many times the same people occupied all three positions. In addition, evidence may be adduced through the performance of modern sacrificial experiments to see what the Egyptians would have observed. These observations may then be used to elucidate the ancient scenes and texts.

Regarding ethnographic evidence, a few Egyptologists and anthropologists have noted that modern Nilotic tribes have beliefs and practices that may resemble those of the ancient Egyptians. The two are not necessarily related but similar environments may yield similar responses, a process that in paleontology is called "convergence."

To fully understand the importance of animals in the development of medicine, one must acknowledge that predynastic and dynastic Egypt was a cattle culture. The fertile, powerful bull and the milk-producing, life-giving cow occupied a prominent position in the Egyptians' minds and psyches. The Egyptian king portrayed himself as a powerful bull with his ka name, the first of his five official names, often mentioning the bull, such as Amenhotep III's ka name of "Strong Bull arising in Truth." More than five thousand years ago, Narmer portrayed himself as a bull trampling his enemies and as a human with a bull's tail. Egyptian texts record that the kings often hunted wild bulls to show their prowess. Other texts also state that the king is a strong bull and that the queen mother was the cow that birthed the bull; the gods are also called bulls, while the sun is "the bull of heaven," and the sky is a large cow. The king was depicted sucking from the teats of Hathor, the cow goddess. Humans are called "the cattle of god." Bull and cow cults were extremely important. All in all, cattle were deeply embedded in the psyche of the Egyptians. The Egyptians were keen observers of their environment, and their religion included the integration of nature and society.

THE KAHUN VETERINARY PAPYRUS

Animals played a very important role in the development of ancient medicine, and it could not have been any other way. Because of the conditions of preservation in ancient Egypt, with its hot, dry climate, we have a few remains, including the oldest known medical papyrus, which point to the importance of animals in the development of science. Two of the oldest papyri, the Kahun and the Edwin Smith, are very rationally based. The first deals with comparative veterinary medicine and the second with surgery, introducing the idea of triage.

The Kahun Veterinary Papyrus is one of the oldest known papyri to deal with animal or human medicine (see Figure 5.1). The papyrus is a fragment of a much greater corpus, probably devoted to eye diseases of animals. While it may contain model case histories,[26] it may also be a healer priest's manual. It was found at the village of Kahun (really Lahun) in the Fayum area, which had been constructed *ex nihilo* by King Sesostris II for the workers building his funerary complex. Also found in the workers' village was a gynecological papyrus; a mathematical fragment; and judicial, accounting, and temple archive fragments. The layout of the town clearly indicates the highly structured and bureaucratic nature of the king's administration. Thus, this papyrus among others may have been part of this administration. While the veterinary papyrus's time of use may be dated to about 1875 BCE, the condition and style of writing more likely indicate an Old Kingdom date (2686–2125 BCE). The fact that the back of the first column of the papyrus was repaired with papyrus fragments suggests both its age and its frequency of use. Unlike all other papyri, except Papyrus Ramesseum V, it was written in cursive hieroglyphs, not in hieratic. The title was written horizontally with the case history; the description, prognosis, and

FIGURE 5.1: *The Kahun Veterinary Papyrus,* the oldest Egyptian medical document. Plate VII of the plate volume of F. Ll. Griffith, *Hieratic Papyri from Kahun and Gurob* (London: Bernard Quaritch, 1898). Image provided by ETANA (http://www.etana.org/).

treatment were written vertically underneath, as in the Ramesseum Papyrus. The vertical lines are read in a retrograde fashion, much as in certain religious texts. It was written uniquely in the first person, using somewhat archaic grammar. All these factors indicate that this papyrus is the oldest known medical papyrus not only by age but also by the date of its original composition. Both the Kahun and Ramesseum papyri resemble the archives of King Neferirkare (ca. 2450 BCE) of the Fifth Dynasty, found in his pyramid complex at Abusir.

The fragmentary cases that survive all appear to refer to the eyes of various animals, including cows, dogs, geese, and fish. This is the earliest known example of comparative medicine. The presence of a gynecological papyrus also found in the same area may indicate that the pharaoh was interested in keeping both his animals and his harem healthy.

The structure and wording of the papyrus are quite rational, without the magic of some later papyri. After a descriptive heading, the healer notes the symptoms of the animal, names the disease, discusses the symptoms, prescribes treatment, gives a prognosis, and occasionally even discusses how to make the animal more comfortable. In case the treatment does not work, the healer sometimes suggests further examination and treatment. The examination, diagnosis, and treatment sound modern and scientific, and not almost four thousand years old. Walker[27] has discerned the following pattern in the text: (1) title, (2) symptoms, (3) admonition ("What is to be read for it"), (4) treatment, (5) prognosis, (6) progress, (7) re-inspection and fresh symptoms, and (8) additional treatment. He finds the cases highly organized and disciplined.

Evidence from Egyptology, biology, anthropology, and ethnography suggests that the ancient Egyptians' observation and use of animals led to an early scientific understanding of medicine, that their priests and healers developed a comparative understanding of animals as well as humans, and that sometimes this understanding was valid, and sometimes not, but was always based on sound observational principles. For modern observers and scholars, it has been difficult to study the ancient Egyptians because of our own biases and prejudices. Most have lived far from the farms and outdoor environment of our ancestors. They have looked at veterinary medicine, if at all, as a subordinate offshoot of human medicine, rather than as a comparative medicine of all animals, including humans. But until recently (even the term "physician" is relatively recent), the healer who treated animals might also treat humans. Veterinary healers were also able to observe their charges more closely, and because of the ability to dissect could get a far better idea of animal anatomy and physiology than could someone who exclusively healed humans.

The domestication of large animals, especially cattle, led the prehistoric Africans and predynastic Egyptians to an understanding of the nature of disease as well as a knowledge of anatomy, physiology, and pharmacology. Their relationship with bulls in the ritual hunting of the wild aurochs bull and the use of the milk of another species was entwined with their religion and culture. Cattle were not just meat and joints, but a significant part of their sacred landscape. As it was extremely important to keep their cattle in good health before use or ritual sacrifice, their priests and healers observed them with extreme care and transmitted, first orally and later in writing, their symptoms and the treatment necessary to make or keep them well.

It is not surprising then that one of the earliest medical documents of the ancient Egyptians, the Kahun Veterinary Papyrus, relates to animals and is not loaded with magic or incantations but is very scientific. While later papyri on human medicine may contain a lot of magic and incantation, this early document would not be out of place in the nineteenth century. In sum, its importance is that (1) it is the only medical papyrus written in the first person while all other medical papyri were written in the third person, (2) it and only one other papyrus take the form of a religious/priestly document, (3) it deals with several species, and (4) it is logical.

EGYPT AS A CATTLE CULTURE[28]

Evidence indicates that ancient Egypt had much in common with modern East African cattle cultures, including the centrality of the bull and the cow, the bull's use in ritual sacrifice, the use of "living flesh," real or imitation bulls' horns on funerary monuments, the emphasis on the power and fertility of the bull, the awe in which the bull was held, the fixation on the bull in the bull cults of the dynastic period, the deforming of the horns, the drinking of another species's milk, and so on. A few Egyptologists and anthropologists have indicated that a better understanding of the ancient Egyptian mind-set might be obtained by studying the people and cultures of the modern Nile Valley. As Evans-Pritchard said with regard to the Nilotic Nuer pastoralists, "Most of their social activities concern cattle and *cherchez la vache* is the best advice that can be given to those who desire to understand Nuer behaviour."[29] Even their relationships with other tribes are influenced by their love of cattle and their desire to acquire more by any means necessary. They seem obsessed with cattle, and "their social idiom is a bovine idiom."[30]

The wild aurochs bull seems to have been adored from Paleolithic times. The Paleolithic Qadan culture, which flourished from 12,000–10,000 BCE on the east bank of the Nile north of Wadi Halfa, has human burials with bulls' horns found in the vicinity. Whether these horns were meant to be with the burials or whether their presence is accidental is unclear. In either case, the evidence indicates bulls were important to Qadan culture.

As early as 9000 BCE,[31] cattle may have been independently domesticated in eastern Africa. The upland areas on either side of the Nile were savannahs rather than desert at that time. Excavation at Nabta Playa, in what is now the western desert of Egypt, indicates a complex Neolithic cattle culture from approximately 9000 to 4000 BCE. From about 8800 to 6900 BCE, pastoralists apparently moved herds, possibly from the area of the First and Second Cataracts, to Nabta Playa during the dry season. These migrations would have provided the pastoralists with a mobile source of food in milk and blood, and flesh if killed. A relative lack of bones may indicate little actual sacrifice. From about 7100 to 6900 BCE, human activity was more intense. Deep wells and storage pits for food may indicate larger groups. Incidentally, Grivetti has noted that the penning of large animals at night after their having grazed during the day may yield food plants after the seeds have passed from the animals' feces to the ground. Thus, plant domestication may be encouraged by the herding and penning of animals, such as goats and cattle. By the Middle Neolithic (6300–5600 BCE), large numbers of cattle bones found at a ceremonial center may imply sacrifice. By the Late Neolithic (5500–4200 BCE), a large ceremonial center existed with stone tumuli under which partial or complete cattle burials were located. When Nabta Playa was abandoned about 4200 BCE due to worsening climatic conditions, the inhabitants may have settled permanently in the Nile Valley. Thus, with its increasing complexity, Nabta Playa may have been important not only to the origin of the African cattle complex but also to the development of the Egyptian state.

During the Naqada I period (4000–3500 BCE), cattle were buried next to humans and using similar burial treatments.[32] Vessels in the shape of bulls' horns and bulls' testicles indicate the power and virility of the bull.[33] Vessels also depict cattle,[34] and a pottery bull or cow model was found, as well as bull amulets and bulls' horns on cosmetic palettes and hair brushes. According to Wilkinson, "a full thousand years before Narmer and his ceremonial palette, the imagery of the bull was central in Egyptian art and culture."[35] This cattle-centric culture continues into and through dynastic times.

In a recent tantalizing article, Gifford-Gonzalez has suggested that for sub-Saharan Africa it may have taken as much as a thousand years from the start of domestication until the emergence of cattle-based cultures because of the need to deal with diseases in new environments. That is, as cattle are brought together from different areas and, as grazing enters new areas, diseases are introduced that are difficult to deal with. Thus, the need for healers who can at least mitigate the effects of these diseases is extremely important for both economic and religious reasons. This is in turn a good reason why the origin of Egyptian medicine may be more in animal than in human medicine.

If one looks at the records of ancient civilizations, very little direct evidence exists for the use of animals in the development of medicine and medical ideas.

And many modern researchers downplay the importance of animals in the development of religion, magic, or science. These two factors taken together yield an apparent dearth of information on veterinary medicine and its role in the development of human medicine and medicine in general. In Egypt, the earliest specific reference to an animal healer is the healer Ahanakht, "who knows bulls," in the Twelfth Dynasty (1985–1773 BCE), while in Mesopotamia the earliest reference appears to be to the healer Urlugaledenna from about 2200 BCE. Two of the earliest known rational papyri refer to animals rather than humans. The first, the Kahun Veterinary Papyrus, dated to roughly 1875 BCE, deals with comparative medicine among various animal species, while the Ramesseum Onomasticon (a catalog of objects grouped according to similar characteristics), dated to the latter part of Dynasty 12, about 1800 BCE, lists the parts of a bull (originally thought by Gardiner to be parts of a human), descriptions of bulls with special markings, and lists of birds, fish, and mammals.

THE RAMESSEUM ONOMASTICON

The Ramesseum Onomasticon (Papyrus Berlin 10495), dated to the latter part of Dynasty 12 (ca. 1800 BCE), is a catalog of objects arranged by their kinds.[36] The papyrus was found in the bottom of a shaft of an Egyptian tomb of late Middle Kingdom date. It was found in a box that included reed pens, papyri fragments in a bad state of preservation, and fragments of four so-called "magic wands."[37] The "magic wands," common in burials of this period, were amuletic devices for the protection of people.[38] Portrayed on the wands are protective deities with knives in hand to ward off evil spirits.[39] This oldest known Onomasticon includes a list of the parts of cattle,[40] including the foreleg, which was one of the first parts to be removed from a sacrificial bull, and parts of the neck and back. Other sections of this early Onomasticon include a list of the varieties of cattle and lists of birds, fish, and four-footed mammals.

AN EGYPTIAN EXPLANATION FOR THE MALE'S ROLE IN REPRODUCTION[41]

With the ritual sacrifice and dissection of temple bulls, observed by the elite, including the nobles, priests, and healers, an explanation arose for the male's role in reproduction. When the bull is dissected after slaughter, one can observe that the muscles surrounding the bull's phallus are connected to the spine (see Figure 5.2). That is, the two retractor penis muscles arise on the ventral surface of the first two coccygeal (tail) vertebrae, generating a theory that semen arose in the spine, especially the marrow or spinal column, and then flowed through the spine and out the phallus. While only late Egyptian texts explicitly state this, early texts such as the Pyramid Texts imply it, and one condition commented on by the Edwin Smith Surgical Papyrus seems to cement this view. Even though the spine and the penis are not connected in man, the taboo against the dissection of humans evidently prevented not only the Egyptians, but also the Greeks and Romans (with one or two exceptions) and Europeans until the Renaissance from observing that there was no such connection.

In the Pyramid Texts (ca. 2375–2181 BCE) and in the Coffin Texts (ca. 2181–1773 BCE) equivalences and puns between marrow and semen as well as between milk and water and semen are found. In Case 31 of the Edwin Smith Surgical Papyrus relating to the dislocation of cervical vertebrae, the healer notes that a dislocation of a vertebra of the neck of a male patient, which extends to his backbone, will yield paralysis and an erection from which urine dribbles. If it is a dislocation of the middle cervical vertebra, a seminal emission or at least an erection occurs.[42] Thus it appears that a dislocation of the neck at the top of the spine causes at least an erection if not a spontaneous seminal emission. Although the papyrus is dated to the late Second Intermediate period (ca. 1600–1550 BCE), Allen postulated an origin of several hundred years earlier.[43] Thus the observation of the dissection of bulls and the observation of the dislocation of a cervical vertebra in humans would lead the ancient Egyptians to conclude that the cervical vertebrae, which were connected to the thoracic and lumbar vertebrae, must be connected to the penis because it caused an erection when injured, a very rational though invalid hypothesis.

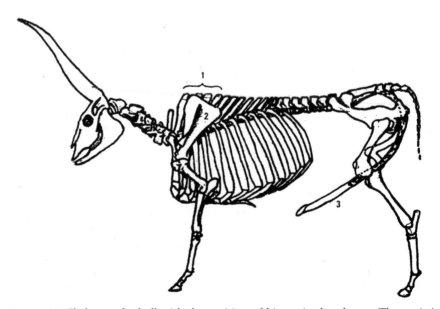

FIGURE 5.2: Skeleton of a bull with the position of his penis also shown. The penis is connected to the bull's first coccygeal vertebrae by its white retractor penis muscles. Previously published in Andrew H. Gordon and Calvin W. Schwabe, *The Quick and the Dead: Biomedical Theory in Ancient Egypt* (Leiden: Brill-Styx, 2004).

The Egyptians were unaware that it was the spinal cord, not the vertebrae, that caused an erection or spontaneous seminal emission.

In ancient Egyptian religious texts, such as the Pyramid Texts, Coffin Texts, Book of the Dead, and the much later texts on the walls of Greco-Roman temples numerous references, some direct and many more indirect, are found to Egyptian beliefs concerning the spine and its role in reproduction. Surprisingly, many of the most obscure references become clearer when examined from the point of view of the Egyptians' understanding of the bull's anatomy. Many mortuary texts are concerned with the revivification of the deceased. Texts may discuss the reassemblage of the body parts of the deceased, including the backbone and the phallus, identification of these body parts with various gods, and marrow as a source of life. Pyramid Text 828a–c states, "She [Nut] will protect you, she will protect you from lacking [having any missing parts], she will give you your head, she will reassemble your bones for you, she will join together your members for you, she will bring your heart into your body for you."[44] Pyramid Texts 1308c and 1313c (ca. 2300 BCE) state, "My spine is [that of] the Wild Bull ... My phallus is [that of] Apis.[45] Pyramid Text 116a–d states, "Hail to you Incense! Hail to you brother of the God! Hail to you Marrow (*Mn wr*) which is in the limbs of Horus! Be great, my father, extend your self in your name of 'Pellet."[46] The Egyptians loved to pun and in this text, the words for "incense" and "brother of the god" are puns, as are the words "extend" and "pellet." The word for "marrow," literally "great firmness," may be a pun on an erect phallus, while the word for "extend" may further that image. If bone marrow was regarded as congealed or "firmed" semen, then "incense" may be a euphemism for "semen." The words "incense" and "marrow" may also be synonymous and may also stand for "semen." Coffin Text Spell 530 of the Middle Kingdom (ca. 2155–1733 BCE) enlightens the previous text somewhat. "You are made strong by means of incense ... the incense comes ... the ear of corn comes; there comes the spinal cord, which issued from the backbone of Osiris, there comes the marrow."[47] In Pyramid Text 502a and 2128b, the phallus and the spine are associated. The former states, "The Phallus of Babi is drawn back (*sTA*), the doors of the sky are opened."[48] According to Faulkner, the phallus is figuratively used for a "door bolt." The word *sTA* may also mean "to flow." The latter text states, "Your spine is the door bolt of the god." This shows that the spine and the penis were closely associated. Book of the Dead Spell 155 (ca. 1550–1295 BCE) mentions the vertebrae, backbone, and *djed*, which has elsewhere been linked to the sacral and lumbar spine.

In the Late period (664–332 BCE) and Greco-Roman Egyptian texts, some of the most explicit references to marrow and semen originating in the bones of the back and exiting the penis are found. At least some of these texts were composed hundreds, if not thousands, of years before they were written on the temple walls. The Egyptians' theory of the male's role in reproduction is that bones, especially those of the spine and their marrow were the source of semen. The semen created the white parts of the fetus, including its bones. Sauneron and Yoyotte were the first to collect these texts. Sauneron's thesis is that from Dynasty 27, the so-called Persian period, starting when Cambyses conquered Egypt (525 BCE), the Egyptians postulated that the bones were reservoirs in which semen was made. This idea was first expressed on the walls of the Temple of Hibis in the Kharga oasis and later reproduced on the walls of the Greco-Roman temples of Edfu, Philae, Dendara, and Esna. Three examples are:

> [Khnum] who creates the egg, who makes the chick grow, and who creates sperm in the bones in the body [or "and in the belly"]. Temple of Philae (unedited).[49]
>
> [The king is] the charitable god, the heir of Khnum. It is he who effects the fixing of his semen in the bones in the body [or "and in the belly"]. Temple of Edfu 3.114.7.[50]
>
> You fertilize women by means of the semen [coming] from the bones. Edfu 4.298.3–4.[51]

Yoyotte adds that the fetus receives the semen from the marrow of the male and the flesh from the female. Specifically, in Papyrus Jumilhac, dated to the Late Ptolemaic period, the male contributes the white semen from his bones to form the white parts of the fetus, while the female contributes her red menstrual blood to form the red parts of the fetus. The Egyptian priests also thought that the phallus and the backbone were functionally connected, an idea one could get from their observation of the sacrifice and dissection of bulls or other large mammals. Importantly, Yoyotte points to the primacy of these ideas among the Egyptians rather than the Greeks. He sees these ideas going back almost one thousand years to the Eighteenth Dynasty of Egypt and believes the ideas are recycled. The earlier mortuary texts cited in this chapter, however, imply that these ideas may extend at least an additional one thousand years if not more.

Spanning more than two millennia from the Old Kingdom to the end of the Ptolemaic period, these religious texts, when taken together, give evidence of some Egyptian ideas on anatomy and physiology. The importance of bones, especially spinal bones, to ideas of procreation and revivification is clear and indicates that the Egyptians were keen observers of their environment. In the religious and magical world in which they operated, they were still able to construct a theory that, although incorrect, was rationally based.

The connection between the early Greek schools of medicine and ancient Egypt can no longer be denied, while the emergence of the Alexandrian school of medicine in Egypt during the third century BCE is certainly not fortuitous. When the Greeks, such as Herodotus, tell us they learned medicine in Egypt, they were telling the truth as they knew it. The Egyptian medical papyri, some quite rational in character, represent a pittance of the medical knowledge that the Egyptians once possessed. When Clement of Alexandria, a second-century CE Christian theologian and scholar, says that, of the forty-two books of ancient Egyptian wisdom, six dealt with medicine,[52] it seems likely he was correct.

The Greeks had a theory for the origin of semen similar to the Egyptian theory, and it is tempting to consider that this theory was passed down from the Egyptians. Homer, who must be placed at least before 700 BCE, regarded Egyptian medicine as preeminent. The "wall of the Milesians," a fortified trading post found in the Egyptian Delta and dated to the eighth century BCE, gives evidence of Greek-Egyptian trading relations. Ionian mercenaries from Ionia and Caria, who helped Psamtek I take power in Egypt in 664 BCE, were rewarded with a settlement in the delta. Another Greek trade settlement, Naukratis, also in the Egyptian Delta, became a center of cultural and intellectual exchange. Amid all this cultural interaction, visiting Egypt, and learning in the temples and "Houses of Life" (*Per Ankhs*), where at least some medical papyri would have been kept, there should have been some influence. As Sauneron has stated so well, "The ancient Greek texts leave no doubt that Egypt was seen as the cradle of all science and wisdom ... The most celebrated Hellenic scholars and philosophers crossed the sea to seek initiation in new sciences by its priests ... And [even] if they did not go there, their biographers hastened to include this voyage—now regarded as something both traditional and necessary—among the episodes of their lives."[53] When the Greeks hastened to give Egypt credit for the development of the sciences, perhaps they were correct. Even with all the cross-fertilization going on between Egypt and Greece, the former appears to have been the senior partner.

The Greeks and Egyptians held similar beliefs about the relationship between bones, the spine, and semen, at least by the fourth century BCE if not earlier. Alcmaeon, Hippon, and Diocles, as well as the Hippocratic writers of *On Seed* and *Airs, Waters and Places*, were proponents. Plato called semen "a soft flow from the spine" and seemed slightly scandalized that the gods had connected the spinal marrow (i.e., the spinal cord) to the urethra of the phallus, through which the semen could emerge. Aristotle believed that semen was the product of surplus blood. It was not until the third century CE that Galen identified the true source of semen as the testes.

The belief that semen arose in the bones, especially of the spine, is also found in other civilizations. In Jewish writings, the Torah, or Bible, says that Eve was made from a rib or thoracic bone (Genesis 2:21–32). The important point here is these are the bones where semen was supposed to originate. In Ginzberg's *Legends of the Jews*, he states that at the end of the coccygeal vertebrae is the *luz* or almond bone, which is indestructible and which, at the resurrection, will furnish the human material that will become alive. Tehillim

11, 102 states that the soul is attached to the spine.[54] In another legend, the celestial dew from being in God's presence filled Jacob's bones with marrow.[55] The Talmud also states that the male supplies the "white" (semen), which forms the bones, brain, sinews, nails, and ocular sclerae (i.e., the white parts of the body), while the female supplies the "red" (menstrual blood) for the skin, flesh, hair, and ocular corneas (i.e., the colored parts of the body). Since there was constant contact between the Egyptians and Israelites, it is probable that these ideas filtered through from Egypt to Israel.

In the Zoroastrian tradition, the relationship of marrow to semen continued with the added idea that the marrow and semen of an ox or bull made the grains and healing plants and domestic animals. The cosmological work *Budahishn* states:

> It is said in the religion: When the sole created ox passed away, there where it sent forth its marrow, the fifty-five species of grain grew up, and the twelve species of healing plants ... The semen of the ox was borne up to the moon station. There, they purified it, and he [Ohrmazd] created domestic animals of all species [from it].[56]

Likewise, the Sanskrit *Garbha Upanishad* states that from bones comes into being "marrow (*majja*), and from the marrow semen (*sukra*)."[57] The treatise *Aitareya Aranyaka* states that "the woman contributes the skin, blood and flesh, whereas the man contributes the fat, bone, and marrow parts of the fetus."[58]

The use of similar examples from modern-day African Nilotic pastoralists may at first glance seem beyond the pale, but this type of anthropological approach has been suggested by Frankfort, Seligman, Childe, Aldred, and others. Schwabe has noted that among these Nilotic cattle-culture peoples, the practices of animal husbandry, healing, and religion are inextricably mixed, just as they were for the ancient Egyptians. Childe noted that the Dinka preserved cultural practices and a social structure similar to those of the predynastic Egyptians. The Dinka believe that the sire and the dam create all parts of the fetus equally. They also believe that semen originates in the brain and spinal cord. from whence it passes through the spinal cord and down to the testes where it is stored. Dinka sometimes use the word *aciek* (creator) for cattle. For the Nuer who are closely related to the Dinka, the word *jok*, frequently translated "ghost" or "spirit," may also mean "back" and bones of the neck (i.e., cervical vertebrae).[59] Among non-Nilotic African peoples, Ashanti, Venda, and Congolese all believe that the bones of a fetus come from the male contribution, and that this power originally may have come from a sacred bull.

Concerning the male's role in reproduction, it appears clear that the earliest evidence comes from Egypt. The source of this evidence seems to come from Africa and is prehistoric in date. Egyptian, Greek, Judaic, Iranian, Indian, and modern African concepts seem to come from the same cultural center. As Schwabe has stated,

> These rationally derived, albeit erroneous, physiological notions about reproduction in vertebrate animals, namely, the production of sperm in bones, its presence in marrow, its collection as the spinal cord and its passage thence to the urethra—inextricably related to the analagous acts of creation and of re-birth after death—persisted more or less intact for some time.[60]

LIFE AS MOVEMENT[61]

The ancient Egyptians were very concerned with death and the dead as well as life and the living. As opposite ends of the same idea, they were interested in what infused the body to make the organism alive. The ultimate medical treatment would be the revivification of the dead. The Egyptians were therefore concerned with the "magic of life." Egyptologists have postulated that the ka, the "life force," was the animating principle. Frankfort thought the ka was an impersonal "vital force," while Morenz called it the "hyper-physical vital force." This force is not confined to humans but is found in nature and in the gods. The king receives the life force from the gods and distributes it to his subjects. With regard to the ka of the king, the issue is more complex, but Frankford states that the ka never entirely lost its original meaning of "vital force." Bell speculated that the king becomes so infused with the universal vital energy of the ka that the distinction between both is blurred. Pyramid Text 149c–d seems to corroborate this interpretation. This energy not only revitalizes the king but can be passed down to his descendents. While every organism may contain this vital energy, the king's body contains more of it because he represents the gods and the natural order or *maat*. The ka has been compared to the Hebrew *ruah* or *nephesh*, the life-spirit which returns to God after death, the "genius" of the Romans, and the beliefs of several modern African tribes. The Egyptians were keen observers of their environment and would have noticed an energy or biological force that appeared to animate matter. They would have focused their idea through the prism of their religion and society.

In hieroglyphic writing, the ka is represented as a pair of arms extended or raised, perhaps in imitation of the horns of a bull, followed by a vertical stroke. Modern Nilotic tribes, such as the Nuer and the Dinka, may dance with upraised arms in imitation of the horns of the bull. In fact, it is not surprising that the hieroglyphic word for bull is also ka, many times written with the ka sign followed by an erect phallus followed by a bull. The bull represented vitality and virility to the Egyptians. The vagina, the place from which new life emerges, was called *kat,* a pregnant woman *bkat,* and work or construction resulting in the formation of something new *kat.* The ka energy was present in both men and women, and the interaction between the two resulted in creation or rebirth. The word for food or nourishment is *kaw,* the plural of *ka,* depicted as a *ka* sign with a stroke followed by the bread sign with plural strokes. The relationship between the life force and food or nourishment is obvious.

The question is whether the Egyptians were able to see some biological function that to them would be the ka energy or life force. In the ritual sacrifice of animals, such as bulls with their vitality and virility, was there a real process going on that the Egyptians would have recognized? If motion is a sign of life, then the motion or contractibility of muscle tissues with their ability to respond to stimuli even after the death of the animal would have fascinated the Egyptian priests and healers. They would have observed, pondered, and then attempted to apply the observations that bundles of muscle fibers or "flesh" would continue to contract for a period after the death of the animal and even after the animal's dissection. Today, while this phenomenon is not commonly known to the layman, the veterinarian and even the butcher are familiar with it.

One of the most important religious ceremonies for the ancient Egyptians was the Opening-of-the-Mouth ritual, in which the priest attempted to revivify the deceased. In the ceremony, a bull's foreleg or even an adze was presented to the mouth of the pharaoh or noble to open it so he could breathe and talk again (see Figure 5.3a). If we understand that recently severed bulls' forelegs have spontaneous postmortem fasciolations that can be reinduced by hitting

FIGURE 5.3a: New Kingdom Opening-of-the-Mouth ritual showing the amputated forelimb of a sacrificed bull being presented to the statue of the deceased noble. Previously published in Andrew H. Gordon and Calvin W. Schwabe, *The Quick and the Dead: Biomedical Theory in Ancient Egypt* (Leiden: Brill-Styx, 2004).

the muscle with a hard object, but that these fasciolations eventually stop, then we can see that it would appear to the Egyptians as if the magic of life from a vital animal such as a bull was being transferred to the king or noble. When the muscle movement stopped, the magic was all transferred.

During the sacrifice of bulls, the foreleg appears to have been almost always the first part cut off (see Figure 5.3b). Frequently, it is shown being removed before any other parts. The bulls are frequently shown on their backs with the other three legs tied together. The mechanical reason for the forelimb being chosen for the reanimation of the deceased in the Opening-of-the-Mouth ritual is that it is the only musculoskeletal assemblage that can be removed easily from the body with one or two cuts of a sharp knife. If one wishes to kill a bull quickly, full body restraint is not necessary. The Nilotic Dinka fully restrain bulls only when doing the vivisection surgery called castration. When killing a bull, the Dinka use only a neck harness and spear the heart, while the kosher slaughterer uses only a manual head restraint to slit the neck. Therefore, the question is why the ancient Egyptians would have used an unnecessary full body restraint if all they wished to do was to kill the bull quickly?

To test these ideas, a simulated bull sacrifice at an ambient temperature found in Egypt (22 degrees Celsius) was performed at the Muscle Physiology Laboratory of the University of California at Davis. At the death of the bull, the front forelimb was amputated by means of a sharp knife passed through the axila between the scapula, the rib cage, and the thoracic spine, during which process a number of robust muscles were cut. The motor units of these muscles exhibited intermittent spontaneous tremors or fasciolations for more than fifteen minutes. Afterwards, they were mechanically restimulated. Moreover,

FIGURE 5.3b: Old Kingdom Egyptian bull sacrifice showing the amputation of a forelimb of a bull. The forelimb was generally the first part removed. Previously published in Andrew H. Gordon and Calvin W. Schwabe, *The Quick and the Dead: Biomedical Theory in Ancient Egypt* (Leiden: Brill-Styx, 2004).

contractions of whole muscles were also induced by mechanical stimulation. This was done in four ways. First, a muscle was stabbed with a thin-bladed knife, second with a garden hoe sharpened to resemble an Egyptian adze, third it was prodded with a knife, and fourth with a finger. The "adze" had the second greatest result after the stabbing by a knife. In all instances, the gross muscle contractions were of the whole limb, not just of the specific muscle stabbed. Both types of responses could still be mechanically induced two hours after the death of the bull.

In modern scientific terms, what the Egyptians would have seen in the excision of the foreleg was the loss of contractility and extensibility caused by the disappearance of adenosine triphosphate, or ATP. Even after excision, muscles may produce ATP as long as there is glycogen left in the muscles. When glycogen is depleted and ATP can no longer be produced, rigor mortis sets in. The higher the temperature, the faster rigor sets in. In Egypt's hot, dry climate, it would have been imperative for the Egyptians to get the foreleg to the deceased quickly if the fasciolations were to still be active. The Opening-of-the-Mouth ritual was in modern terms an often-repeated physiological experiment with the therapeutic objective of translating the ka energy, or life force, of the fasciolations from the foreleg to the mouth of the deceased. The Greek Praxagoras would much later induce fasciolations of excised muscle tissue, but apparently not the more dramatic muscle and joint movement of the foreleg.

If the ancient Egyptians, namely the priests and the elite, did notice the spontaneous muscle fibrillations of excised forelimbs, then there should be an indication that forelimbs were important to the Egyptian afterlife. This indication is found mainly in the texts and pictures in the ancient Egyptian tombs that were concerned with the revivification of the deceased in the next world. The depiction of the removal of the foreleg may first be seen in a rock drawing from southern Libya dated to approximately 3500 BCE, followed by a possible appearance in a late Gerzean tomb painting from about 3200 BCE. From the Early Dynastic period (3100–2700 BCE) there are an ivory spoon in the shape of a gazelle's foreleg, First-Dynasty (3100–2900 BCE) ivory furniture bases in the form of bulls' legs, and the first hieroglyphic representation of the foreleg from a stela found in the ceiling of a tomb of a Second-Dynasty princess (2900–2700 BCE).[62]

Papyrus Ramesseum E was found, along with the Ramesseum Onomasticon, in a late Middle Kingdom tomb (ca. 1700 BCE), but its origin may be as early as Dynasty 3 (2700–2625 BCE). This mortuary papyrus is written in cursive hieroglyphs, is read in a retrograde fashion, and has horizontal headings just like the Kahun Veterinary Papyrus. It refers to trussed and untrussed bulls, forty of which are to be sacrificed. Bearers of forelegs are summoned, the forelegs and hearts are removed and sent to "the Mansions of the [proph]ets of many Westerners." The bearers of forelegs are then ushered into the place of embalmment. Dealing with royal burial, the papyrus details the importance of forelegs to this process. One question that needs to be asked is why the bearers of forelegs apparently have to be summoned before the forelegs are removed. Because the royal burial takes place at a *mastaba*, a tomb consisting of subterranean rooms beneath a mud brick or stone superstructure, rather than a pyramid, this presumes the burial would have taken place before the end of the Third Dynasty, when step pyramids, composed of a series of superimposed mastabas, were replaced by true pyramids.

The earliest tombs to show the sacrifice of bulls in any detail were from the Old Kingdom (2625–2200 BCE). A few early Fourth-Dynasty (2625–2510 BCE) tombs may show either a bull on its back with the foreleg extended by a sacrificer just before he cuts it off or offering bearers with forelegs. Study of these scenes indicates that they relate to the nourishment of the deceased in the funerary cult. Later Fourth-Dynasty tombs as well as Fifth- and Sixth-Dynasty ones almost always have scenes of bull sacrifice in which the foreleg is apparently the first part removed and taken away before other incisions are made. In a classic modern study Eggebrecht, as well as Junker before him, states that the removal of the foreleg was the focus of the sacrifice. The importance of these scenes is underscored by their near ubiquity and by the similarity of details. From a study of Fourth-Dynasty tomb scenes Junker inferred that living bulls might have the foreleg amputated, a type of vivisection. During the New Kingdom (1552–1069 BCE), a number of tomb scenes and papyri depict a young calf with a foreleg partially or entirely amputated as part of the funeral rites. These scenes are usually close to those involving the presentation of the foreleg to the deceased.

Texts above sacrificial scenes frequently state that the offering is for the ka, that is, the life force or animating force of the deceased. In some Sixth-Dynasty (2460–2200 BCE) scenes of foreleg removal, the texts indicate that speed is important. In perhaps the most developed of them from the tomb of Mereruka, the first of the two lines of hieroglyphs reads, as usually translated, "Hurry comrades! The lector priest is performing a ceremony. Bring the choicest offerings. Hurry as quickly as you can." Or, if one translates the second part of the line more literally, "Bring the choicest of forelegs. Hurry! Go speedily with the life."[63] The second line of texts mentions the bringing of long-horned cattle and the choicest of forelegs for the ka of the deceased.

The Opening-of-the-Mouth ritual is found in Pyramid Texts of the Sixth Dynasty (2460–2400 BCE). Pyramid Text Utterance 20 states in part, "O king, I have come in search of you, for I am Horus [i.e., your son]. I have struck your mouth for you … I have split open your mouth for you … [I have adjusted your mouth] to your bones … [Offering] one foreleg."[64] Here it is clear that the foreleg is used to open the mouth of the deceased. In the following text, Pyramid Text Utterance 21, it is the iron adze of Wepwawet that opens the mouth of the deceased. In the Opening-of-the-Mouth ritual during the New Kingdom (1552–1069 BCE) as well, either the foreleg or the adze may be presented to the mouth of the deceased. The word for adze is also the name for the constellation of the Big Dipper. The constellation was alternatively considered either an adze or a forelimb by the Egyptians. In the Pyramid Texts, the constellation is written with the adze determinative, a hieroglyphic sign at the end of a word that determines the meaning of the word. By the start of the Middle Kingdom (2040–1674 BCE), the constellation was drawn as a foreleg but labeled an adze. In the late Ptolemaic Papyrus Jumilhac, the God Horus cut off the foreleg of his uncle Seth, who is often described as a bull, and threw it into the sky where it became the Big Dipper constellation, written in hieroglyphs as "adze." It appears that many chthonic, or underworld, beliefs of cattle-culture peoples may be transferred to the heavens. Wainwright has suggested that the constellation may have appeared to the Egyptians like an adze when high in the northern sky and like a foreleg when standing upright in the eastern skies. In any case, it is clear that the foreleg and the adze are closely connected, as they are in Pyramid Texts 20 and 21. In the Pyramid Texts, the verb *stp* "to cut up" an animal or "to cut off" limbs always has an adze determinative, and it is always used in the sense of cutting off limbs.

In several medical papyri of the New Kingdom (1552–1069 BCE) are two prescription ingredients called "fresh flesh" or "raw flesh," and "live flesh" (the latter written with the *ankh* sign). Although the two terms were considered synonymous, a recent study by Buchheim indicates that the two terms must be translated literally and that they were considered magical remedies useful in life-threatening conditions or those not responsive to other remedies. "What is closer to the primitive way of thinking than to refresh the patient by visible 'medication' with another material which contains strong life power?"[65] She considered it likely but did not explore further the ramifications of animal vivisection with regard to the revivification of the dead. Regarding the amputation of a live calf's leg during the New Kingdom and its probable use in the Opening-of-the-Mouth ritual, Majno notes that the focus "was precisely a matter of infusing life into mummies or statues."[66]

The sign for the bull's leg, transliterated *wHm,* and usually translated as "repeating," as in "repeating life," *wHm ankh,* when considered in regard to the rituals with the bull's foreleg, may perhaps be better translated as "renewal of life." *WHm msw* or "repeater of births" or "repetition of births" may perhaps be better translated "renewal of life" or "rebirth."

Returning now to the idea of the ka or "life force" or "animating principle," there were apparently three types of ka transfer to the dead and the living. The first was to reanimate the mouth of the deceased with the ka energy from the fasciolating bull's forelimb placed at his mouth. This act had to be done quickly because the energy transfer lasted only an hour or two. The fact that the ka energy came from a bull also called *ka* would not have escaped the Egyptians' notice, especially as they liked to pun. Once the mouth was reanimated, the second type of transfer was through food offerings called *kau*, to sustain the animating force. The third type involved cutting fasciolating flesh from a living bovine animal and using it to raise the ka energy of an ill person. This was a medical application of a physiological theory about the life-transferring properties of muscle tissue.

Starting with James Bruce, who was in North Africa from 1768 to 1772 CE, travelers and scholars have noted that some tribes in the Nile basin had a practice of excising live flesh from the hindquarters of a bovine and eating it. Cattle muscle vivisection has been noted elsewhere in Africa as well. The Nilotic Dinka believe that flesh is divine and has spiritual force. Muscle quivering may be an indication of this spiritual force, especially in the sacrifice of cattle. They believe that although the bull has been sacrificed, its divine flesh is still alive. After sacrifice, a piece of quivering muscle may be swallowed by the priest to replenish this animating force. Before sacrifice, the Dinka may run a bull until exhaustion, perhaps to induce spontaneous muscle fasciolations.

Regarding the Greeks, the Hippocratic Collection of medical texts from the fifth to fourth centuries BCE seems to have little regard for muscles. Spontaneous muscle fasciolations were thought to be caused by obstructions in the blood vessels or by the arterial pulse. Flesh was thought to be the passive support and packing between the bones and skin. Anaxagoras of the fifth century BCE thought there were seeds in flesh and that these were also found in food. Plato used this idea to envision the soul as the origin of movement, while Anaximenes of the fifth century BCE thought it was the life force. Praxagoras of Cos of the third century BCE thought a force in the arteries caused the movement when a piece of flesh cut from a live animal and thrown to the ground fasciolated. While the Egyptian healers and priests had the advantage of direct observation of sacrifices and the ability to postulate medical interventions based on their observations, the Greek healers and philosophers seem somewhat removed from the sacrifices, such as the Dionysian rites, and had to postulate based on secondhand knowledge. Some Greeks, including Herodotus, thought Dionysus originally came from Egypt and was originally a bull. Plutarch quotes a women's hymn that says of him, "Come hither Dionysus, to thy holy temple by the sea ... rushing with bull's foot, O goodly bull." The worshippers of Dionysus would tear apart an animal and eat the raw flesh to receive the power of the god. The frenzied dancing of the worshippers would have led to involuntary muscle trembling or fasciolations. It was not until Herophilus (third century BCE in Alexandrian Egypt) that the Greeks began to believe that muscles were responsible for muscular movement. According to him, muscular convulsions, tremors, and palpitations came from the muscles themselves rather than the arterial pulse. While Herophilus or Galen of the second century CE is usually credited with the first theory of muscle physiology, the Egyptian priests and healers who long preceded them seemed not only to have reached similar conclusions but also to have used them in healing the sick with "live flesh." Both the Egyptians and Greeks based some of their theories on their observations of animals other than humans.

CONCLUSION

While many general texts still credit the Greeks with the origin of a science of medicine, it is clear that the rational origin of scientific medicine is far more complex. An early step in its development was the domestication of animals, especially in seeing which animals could be domesticated and which could not and why. Regarding Egypt, the origin of medicine appears to stem from the husbandry and sacrifice of large animals, especially the bull. The necessity of keeping animals in good health prior to sacrifice, and the observations of the healer priests before, during, and after the sacrifice led to a rudimentary understanding of anatomy and physiology and an ability to posit theories. This led to the development of a rationally based medicine whose results were transferred to other animals, including *Homo sapiens*. Thus, it appears that the origin of scientific medicine was in veterinary medicine.

CHAPTER SIX

Animals in Ancient Philosophy

Conceptions and Misconceptions

STEPHEN T. NEWMYER

In his work *Pan's Travail: Environmental Problems of the Ancient Greeks and Romans,* historian J. Donald Hughes, with obvious enthusiasm for the seemingly advanced ideas of certain classical authors, claimed that "an ancient animal rights movement, if so one might term it, existed among writers, mostly of Pythagorean bent,"[1] and he further identified the biographer and ethical philosopher Plutarch (ca. 50–120 CE) as "an early defender of animal rights."[2] Along similar lines and also with reference to Plutarch, Liliane Bodson had somewhat earlier argued that even this "most open-minded among the ancient philosophers and moralists" was never able to raise the "question of animal rights" above a merely speculative level or to influence the actual treatment of animals in ancient society.[3] In his magisterial work *Animal Minds and Human Morals: The Origins of the Western Debate,* philosopher of mind Richard Sorabji, in a carefully argued examination of the question of whether ancient philosophers countenanced the notion of "animal rights," concluded, in contradiction to the assertions of Hughes and Bodson, that ancient discussions of such issues as the potential kinship between humans and nonhuman species were in fact attempts to define the nature of justice toward animals rather than arguments for the existence of any "rights" owed to nonhuman animals by human beings. For Sorabji, what is at issue in ancient discussions of human kinship with other animals is the isolation of what constitutes human duty toward those animals and not, as in the case of true discussion of animal rights, a definition of the nature of the animals themselves.[4] In Sorabji's view, it is anachronistic to speak of "animal rights" at all in the case of ancient discussions of the moral status of animals.

An even more striking divergence of opinion, hinted at in the assertion of Hughes on Pythagoras cited above, can be traced in interpretations of what is generally accepted to be the one universally acknowledged fact of ancient animal philosophy, namely, the commitment of Pythagoras and his followers to a vegetarian lifestyle. Little scholarly agreement exists at all, however, on the issue of what motivated Pythagoras' stance. Ethical philosopher Peter Singer, one of the prime movers in the modern crusade to accord "rights" to animals, associates Pythagoras' abstention with his doctrine of metempsychosis, or transmigration of souls, observing, "Pythagoras … was a vegetarian and encouraged his followers to treat animals with respect, apparently because he believed that the souls of dead men migrated to animals."[5] Animal rights advocate and chronicler of history's atrocities against animals Richard D. Ryder, while mentioning Pythagoras' belief in transmigration of souls, emphasizes Pythagoras' apparent kindliness as a motivating factor in his call for abstention when he claims, "Pythagoras certainly regarded kindness to animals as a fundamental good …"[6] It is noteworthy that although Singer makes more direct reference to Pythagoras' doctrine of metempsychosis as a factor contributing to his advocacy of abstention, both Singer and Ryder see as well a certain animal-friendliness behind Pythagoras' philosophical position.

Even the contribution of Aristotle himself to later attitudes toward the treatment of animals has been the subject of widely divergent interpretations. Much of Sorabji's treatise is devoted to an exposition of his thesis that Aristotle's denial of a capacity for reason and belief in nonhuman species led to a crisis when post-Aristotelian thinkers, in particular the Stoics, moralized their great predecessor's denial of reason to animals into a denial of kinship between humans and nonhuman animals, in consequence of which humans were judged to have no obligation to include animals in the sphere of their moral concern.[7] Yet others have viewed Aristotle's contribution to subsequent philosophical thought on animals in a considerably rosier light, as is observable in the assertion of Rod Preece and Lorna Chamberlain that "Aristotle was among those who took the initial steps to diminish the exploitation of both humans and animals and to recognize that humans share a great deal with the animal realm."[8]

As is clear from the above examples, the conclusions of some modern scholars who allude to ancient discussions of the moral status of animals, including philosophers active in the modern animal rights movement, appear at times to rely on decades, if not centuries, of widely accepted opinions, views in some instances colored by sensibilities and preoccupations of relatively recent

provenance and foreign to classical thought. Current beliefs relating to the ancient philosophical stance on such issues of fundamental importance as the nature of animalkind vis-à-vis that of humankind, the intellectual and emotional
worlds of nonhuman animals, the existence and makeup of the animal soul,
and the justifications for advocating or rejecting a commitment to a vegetarian
lifestyle, do not always suggest close engagement with extant Greek and Roman
sources. As a result, the classical view of humans' fellow creatures is frequently
presented to us, both in more popular historical accounts of the history of humans' relation with other animal species and in sober and closely reasoned
treatises by philosophers of the modern animal rights movement, as either more
cruel and benighted or more sympathetic and enlightened than ancient texts
allow. This study offers a chronological survey of ideas set forth in extant Greek
and Roman philosophical texts from the pre-Socratics to the Neoplatonists, and
in ancient testimonies relating to these thinkers, on the intellectual and moral
dimensions of nonhuman animals, in an attempt to arrive at an appreciation of
the complexity and range of ancient speculation on nonhuman animals.

The earliest philosophical reflection on the nature of animalkind in Greek
literature antedates the development of philosophy among the Greeks by more
than a century. Although the *Iliad* and *Odyssey* make frequent mention of animals, the interest that Homer (eighth century BCE) shows in animals is limited
to their appearance in epic similes in which the poet may liken the strength,
endurance, or courage of a warrior to that of a lion, tiger, or bull. The didactic
poet Hesiod, generally considered roughly contemporary with Homer, offers,
in contrast, clear evidence that the Greeks had begun to speculate even at this
early date on the moral dimension of animals. In *Works and Days*, his poetic
catalog of instructions to farmers on activities proper to particular days in the
month, Hesiod observes that Zeus accorded an understanding of justice to humans but not to animals, which, according to Hesiod, is proven by the fact that
animals eat each other (*Works and Days* 276–280). Hesiod does not develop
his observation further, which is made in the context of his attempt to convince
his dishonest brother to abide by the dictates of justice, a relation that is di-
vinely ordained by heaven in the case of humans, but not of animals. Hesiod's
mention of animals is incidental, but it is intriguing to find speculation at this
early date on the possibility of a juridical relationship between animal species.

Although random pronouncements on the capacities of animals are trace-
able in moralizing authors like Hesiod and in occasional fables embedded in the
fragments of Greek lyric poetry, it is with the dawning of formal philosophical
thought among the pre-Socratics that we begin to detect serious speculation
on the content of animal intellect and on humans' proper moral stance toward
other species. The term pre-Socratics is applied, in its simplest sense, to those
Greek philosophers whose lives fell for the most part before that of Socrates
(ca. 469–399 BCE), although the term is often used of that class of early think-

ers who displayed a stronger interest in natural science than did Socrates.[9] In a famous remark in the *Apology* of Plato, in which the pre-Socratics and their philosophical preoccupations are alluded to, Socrates himself complains that in his comedy *Clouds*, the poet Aristophanes falsely portrayed him as an eager student of all things in the heavens and beneath the earth (*Apology* 18b), things of which, he shortly afterward protests (*Apology* 19c), he knows nothing at all. It is not surprising, then, to find that philosophers who took as their subject all things in nature included animals in their philosophical purview.

Unfortunately, the works of the pre-Socratics are poorly preserved at best, and the most intriguing of the group, from the point of view of students of ancient philosophical attitudes toward animals, Pythagoras himself, is represented by no extant writings at all, a circumstance that has encouraged a proliferation of interpretations on his teachings relating to animals.[10] Although the religious and philosophical doctrine of metempsychosis, or transmigration of souls, according to which the souls of animals, including humans, pass upon death into other animals, is popularly identified with Pythagoras, he is not the only pre-Socratic to advocate the notion. Plutarch (*On the Eating of Flesh* 997E) recounts that Empedocles (ca. 492–432 BCE) joined Pythagoras in discouraging the consumption of flesh both from his belief that one might consume one's own relatives and also because he sought to accustom humans to acting more justly toward other living creatures. Similarly, the Neoplatonist Porphyry (234–ca. 305 CE), author of the most extensive philosophical defense of vegetarianism to survive from antiquity, cites (*On Abstinence from Animal Flesh* 2.31) two verses from Empedocles' poem *Purifications* in which the pre-Socratic bewails the day on which he first committed terrible crimes by touching animal flesh to his lips.[11] Furthermore, Cicero tells us (*Republic* 3.19) that both Pythagoras and Empedocles declared that the same principles of justice applied to all living creatures, and that sure punishment came to those who hurt an animal.

Although Empedocles enjoys considerably greater renown, the physician Alcmaeon of Croton (fifth century BCE), if we may judge from the few surviving fragments and testimonies relating to his scientific work, seems to have developed rather forward-looking theories on the nature of animal intellect. Theophrastus, the botanist and follower of Aristotle, reports (*On Senses* 28) that Alcmaeon taught that humans are unique among animal species in having understanding, while other animals have merely perception. The pre-Socratic offers here an early formulation of a subtle argument that would exercise philosophers from Aristotle to Plutarch who attempted to differentiate functions of the mind from the operation of the senses and who sought to isolate those qualities that in general distinguish humans from other animals. It is possible to see in Alcmaeon's observation a foreshadowing of Aristotle's doctrine of *synecheia*, "biological gradualism, continuity," an idea set forth by Aristotle at *History of Animals* 588b5, *Parts of Animals* 681a12–15, and elsewhere, according to which living creatures advance naturally from less intellectually developed species to humans themselves, who, in Aristotle's view, alone possess reason.

The contribution of Pythagoras (sixth century BCE) (see Figure 6.1) to the ancient philosophical debate on human–animal relations is likely to strike the modern reader as unambiguous, due in part to his place as something of a

2

PYTHAGORAS CLAR OLYMP. 64

Pythagoras samius laudasse silentia fertur
Pythagoræ uera est numquit imago tacet

FIGURE 6.1: *Portrait of Pythagoras*. Woodcut. Location not indicated. Photo Credit: Image Select/Art Resource, NY; ART82902.

hero in popular studies of the history of vegetarian thought. It is important, in discussion of classical pronouncements on abstention from animal flesh, to distinguish between arguments based on concern for animals as suffering creatures, a type of appeal that figures prominently in modern vegetarian philosophy, and what might be called the more self-interested motivations of ancient spirituality that may have influenced the position of Pythagoras. Enjoining humans to refrain from eating animal flesh on the grounds that devouring an animal might entail ingesting one's own relatives might reasonably be considered a more anthropocentric motivation than the kindliness toward animals that Ryder postulates as a leading factor in Pythagorean abstention. Not even the ancients themselves agreed on Pythagoras' teachings. In a recent study of vegetarian philosophy in Pythagoras and Plutarch, Damianos Tsekourakis commented on this problem, "If one tries to find out which of the Pythagorean doctrines can be attributed to the founder himself, one is confounded with insuperable difficulties. The main reasons for this are the complete secrecy shrouding the teaching of the school till the second half of the 5th century B.C. ...."[12] There seems at least to have been general consensus in antiquity that Pythagoras and his followers believed that a soul passed into another being at the death of its current body and that a soul that had inhabited a human body could pass into an animal or apparently even into a plant. Diogenes Laertius (*Lives and Opinions of Eminent Philosophers* 8.36) quotes some verses in which Pythagoras enjoins a companion to refrain from abusing a dog because he recognized it as a former kinsman. Although commitment to a vegetarian regimen would seem a natural consequence of such a belief, it is not clear to what extent Pythagoras' posture toward animals reflects concern for animals themselves.

When Plutarch reports (*On the Cleverness of Animals* 964C) that Pythagoras taught that humans could make use of animals and even punish and slay unsociable ones without committing injustice, he implies that the earlier philosopher's intention was to foster virtuous behavior in humans rather than to avoid hurtful actions toward nonhuman animals. Earlier in that treatise, Plutarch stated that Pythagoras enjoined kindness toward animals in order to make people more humane and compassionate in themselves (*On the Cleverness of Animals* 959F). Plutarch adopts here what would now be classified as an indirect duty view toward human–animal relations, according to which harming animals may indirectly lead to harming humans if such conduct leads humans to act cruelly toward humans, while kindness toward animals may encourage kindness toward humans. Diogenes Laertius, in his life of Pythagoras (8.13), maintains that the "real reason" why Pythagoras forbade the eating of animal flesh was to accustom humans to a simple lifestyle based on easily attainable foods, preferably uncooked, which contribute to a healthy body and sharp mind. Tsekourakis is certainly correct in concluding, "... The main reason for the avoidance of animal flesh by Pythagoras and his followers was

their belief in transmigration of souls and consequently their motives for abstinence were above all religious and hygienic."[13] The only unequivocal ancient
statement that Pythagoras advocated abstention on grounds of concern for
the suffering of animals is found in the speech that the Roman poet Ovid
puts into the mouth of Pythagoras (*Metamorphoses* 15.75–142), which may
in fact reflect Ovid's own attitudes toward animal suffering. Ovid's Pythagoras
laments that innocent beasts like sheep and oxen that have done nothing to
deserve their fate are cruelly slaughtered and devoured by humans (*Metamorphoses* 15.117–126). Yet even in Ovid, the philosopher ends his plea for better
treatment for animals with a reminder (15.139–142) that when humans eat
animals, they are actually eating their fellow workers. If we may judge by surviving testimony on Pythagoras' teachings, the spiritual and hygienic welfare
of humans regularly takes precedence over concern for other species, and modern claims that Pythagoras argued prominently from a position of sympathy
for the sufferings of animals are poorly supported by ancient sources.

Another figure of interest in early Greek philosophical speculation on animals
who is generally included among the pre-Socratics although he outlived Socrates
is Democritus of Abdera (ca. 460–357 BCE), a thinker remembered principally
for his contributions to Greek atomism, but noteworthy as well for pronouncements on the moral relationship between humans and other species. Democritus
argued that humans have the right to kill any animals that "act unjustly" or
"seek to act unjustly" (Democritus fr. 257DK) and that humans have an obligation to kill all creatures that "cause injury contrary to justice" (Democritus fr.
258DK).[14] Intriguing here is Democritus' suggestion that animals bear moral
responsibility for their actions, which renders them liable to punishment at the
hands of humans whom they injure. The issue of whether animals can be morally
liable for their actions, especially if they are assumed to be irrational, would take
on increased importance in later Greek philosophical discussion on animals.

A fundamental philosophical goal of the pre-Socratics was the identification of the substance or substances that constitute the physical world: Was the
kosmos, or "world-order," made up of one substance, despite the apparent diversity of life forms, or might several elements contribute to that order? The
early pre-Socratic Thales (sixth century BCE) claimed that water was the *archē,*
or "first principle," of all things, while Empedocles isolated four elements—air,
earth, fire and water—that in combination and recombination constitute the
world order. If the texts of the pre-Socratics were better preserved, we might
have found that these philosophers who endeavored to identify the fundamental principle of life concluded that there was after all no substantive difference
between human and nonhuman animals and that all species shared the same
archē. Despite the state of the texts, we can see that some of the central issues raised in later Greek speculation on animals were at least adumbrated in
pre-Socratic thought, including that of the nature of the animal soul and of

the possibility of a relationship of justice between species. We see foreshadowed as well the question that would take center stage in subsequent Greek philosophical and scientific thought on the nature of animals, namely whether nonhuman animals possess any traces of rationality, a circumstance that might earn them a place in the sphere of human moral concern. Porphyry (*On Abstinence from Animal Flesh* 3.6) makes the tantalizing comment that "Aristotle, Plato, Empedocles, Pythagoras, Democritus, and all others who were concerned with ascertaining the truth about animals, recognized that they share in *logos*." Since *logos* may mean "reason" but also "speech," it is impossible to determine Porphyry's exact meaning, and if he means "reason," his assertion is not strictly correct in the case of all of the philosophers whom he names here. In any case, it is noteworthy that the Neoplatonist acknowledges the abiding interest of Greek philosophy in determining the components of animal intellect, whether they manifest themselves in some sort of thought process or in vocalization.

It was the task of the Greek philosophical schools of the fourth and third centuries BCE to refine and focus the random observations on animal psychology set forth by the pre-Socratics. Debate on the nature of animal intellect focused on several interrelated issues, and the answers offered by those thinkers whose ideas ultimately prevailed have ramifications that are still felt both in formal philosophic discourse on animal rights and in our everyday attitudes and behaviors toward animals. Unfortunately for animals, preoccupation with the question of animal rationality in fourth- and third-century Greek philosophy led not to reaffirmation of the pre-Socratic conclusion that human and nonhuman animals are fundamentally akin but rather to categorization of the ways in which they differ. The eventual triumph of Aristotelian animal psychology, with its subsequent moralization by the Stoics that would survive in Christian teaching on the place of animals in the scheme of creation, has helped to foster a permanent moral alienation between the species as perceived differences are used to supply justifications for the manifold atrocities that humans still visit on other species. Creatures that were viewed in fourth-century philosophy to be irrational were judged to be incapable of sensation and feelings as well, so that apparent evidences of pain or anxiety in animals were declared to have no relevance to human conduct toward them. Perhaps the most significant manifestation of irrationality in animals that fourth- and third-century Greek philosophers identified was their apparent lack of a capacity for meaningful language, in consequence of which animals were judged to be incapable of expressing a desire for consideration and respect at the hands of human beings. Greek speculation on animals would come full circle in the fourth and third centuries, and an atmosphere at once less animal-friendly and more rigorously anthropocentric would emerge.

Although it is sometimes difficult to assess the position of Socrates and his great pupil Plato (ca. 429–347 BCE) on animal psychology because of contradictions in Plato's pronouncements and his metaphorical manner of expression in referring to animals, the Academic school of philosophy clearly contributed to the tendency of post-Socratic philosophy to stress differences between the species rather than similarities. Since he left no writings, we depend on his students to form a judgment on Socrates' position on animal psychology. Despite the often-mentioned asceticism of Socrates, he was apparently not inspired to adopt a vegetarian lifestyle. Porphyry (*On Abstinence from Animal Flesh* 1.15) portrays an opponent of abstention claiming that Socrates himself, that wisest of persons, did not refrain from eating meat. In his history of ancient philosophical teaching on vegetarianism, Daniel A. Dombrowski maintains that "Socrates seems to have had *some* degree of sympathy for animals themselves,"[15] but statements by Socrates' pupil Xenophon (ca. 430–355 BCE) on his master's views suggest a different picture. In his *Memorabilia,* four books in which he recorded his recollections of Socrates' teachings, Xenophon reports (1.4.11) that Socrates maintained that the gods gave humans the advantage over animals in according them upright posture, hands, and articulate speech that enabled them to designate objects with appropriate names.[16] Even if the gods had given humans the strength of a steer, he continues (1.4.14), they would still need reason to be able to accomplish anything. Thus, he concludes, humans, unlike other animals, live like gods because of their natural constitution, body and soul (1.4.14). Xenophon's recollections of Socrates' views on other species suggests a distinctly anthropocentric thrust that belies Dombrowski's assertions.

In Plato, the designation "animal" sometimes appears as a disparaging term for what he views as the baser aspects of human psychology and conduct. Those things that are deemed honorable and fine, if not actually divine, cause the "animal" in us to become subject to our human side (*Republic* 589D), while chastisement is said to cause the "animal" element in humans to be tamed and quieted, leading to the liberation of the soul (*Republic* 591B). Although the souls of animals have "courageous" and "appetitive" elements, they do not have the "rational" element that the human soul possesses (*Republic* 441B). In a highly metaphorical discussion of the derivation of various sorts of animal species from certain classes of intellectually deficient humans, Plato claims (*Timaeus* 90E–92C) that four-footed animals and those with many feet were formed so by god in imitation of more earthbound humans whose foolish intellects drew them closer to earth, and so that foolish creatures like animals would have more support in this less desirable posture. In his *Laws,* however, Plato allows animals "mind (*nous*) along with the finest sensations," which he declares to be, taken together, "the salvation of every creature" (*Laws* 961D). Since this treatise is Plato's last work, it is tempting to surmise from this passage that the philosopher had reconsidered his earlier strictures on the intellectual capacities of animals, but the evidence from the *Laws* is probably too slight to warrant such a conclusion. Sorabji observes that Plato wavered in his position on animal intellect, at times denying them reason and at other times, as in *Laws,* conceding it to them, but since the philosopher held that even the nonrational parts of a soul (*psychē*) are capable of exercising belief (*doxa*), Plato, in allowing nonrational elements to the animal soul, necessarily attributed belief to animals.[17]

However intriguing Plato's observations on animals may be, it was his pupil Aristotle (384–322 BCE) (see Figure 6.2) and Aristotle's own pupil and successor as head of the Peripatetic school, Theophrastus (ca. 370–287 BCE), who placed Greek speculation on animal psychology on a firmer and more scientific footing. Aristotle brought to the study of nonhuman species that element notably lacking in Plato, namely a deep commitment to natural science. Ironically, the findings of Aristotle the naturalist were at times at odds with those of Aristotle the political and ethical philosopher, and the tension that arose enabled Stoic moralists to employ Aristotelian zoology as scientific justification for their exclusion of nonhuman species from the sphere of human morality. The text of Aristotle suggests that he fluctuated in his estimation of the intellectual capacities of animals, attributing to them more highly developed mental faculties in his narrowly zoological treatises while stressing their intellectual inferiority to humans in his more anthropocentric works.

In his nonzoological works, Aristotle frequently argued from the position that animals are creatures whose intellect and behaviors are best understood in their differences from human norms rather than in their similarities. He thereby contributed substantially to the thoroughly Greek view that humans alone of animals possessed one or another positive attribute.[18] Only humans, he claimed, are capable of experiencing true happiness based on mutual affection with others of their own species (*Eudemian Ethics* 1236b1–6); only humans can contemplate the divine (*Nicomachean Ethics* 1178b21–28);[19] only humans have a language through which they can impart information and communicate ethical values to others, although other animal species can use such voices as they have to communicate their pain or pleasure to others of their species (*Politics* 1253a10–19). Furthermore, only humans have technological skill (*technē*), so that while human conduct reflects a combination of "reasoning and skill," animals live solely by "impressions and memories" (*Metaphysics* 980b26–28). In his mention here of "reason" (*logismos*), Aristotle touches on the attribute that, in his system, most clearly distinguishes humans from other animals. "Man lives by reason (*logōi*)," Aristotle declares (*Politics* 1332b5–6), "for he alone of animals possesses reason." Animals, in contrast, are said in this passage to live "for the most part by nature (*physei*), but to some degree by their habits as well" (*Politics* 1332b3–5), perhaps a glimpse toward a theory of what modern zoologists often term "instinct." At the very least, Aristotle seems to suggest that, however purposeful and artful animal actions like nest building, the construction of elaborate dens, and the designing of intricate webs may appear, they do not issue from reason.[20]

Aristotle refined and elaborated his position on the makeup of animal intellect in his zoological treatises, but in these works he acknowledged a kind

FIGURE 6.2: *Bust of Aristotle*. Bronze. Location: Museo Archeologico Nazionale, Naples, Italy. Photo Credit: Scala/Art Resource, NY; ART113199.

of kinship between human and animal intellect, whereby differences were viewed not so much as proof of shortcomings in other species but as evidence of quantitative differentiations between analogous mental processes. This view is inherent in Aristotle's doctrine of *synecheia*, "biological gradualism, continuity."[21] According to this doctrine, which the philosopher sets forth at *History of Animals* 588b5 and *Parts of Animals* 681a12–15, species advance in complexity of structure and intellectual ability from the lowliest species to humankind, so that observed differences between species are largely quantitative rather than qualitative in nature. The souls (*psychai*) of at least some animal species resemble those of humans in having *synesis*, "comprehension" (*History of Animals* 588a18–22). Nevertheless, Aristotle reserves that higher faculty that he terms *phronēsis*, "deliberative capacity," for humankind alone. In his treatise *Movement of Animals*, Aristotle comes close to acknowledging the presence of a rational faculty in nonhuman species. While discussing syllogistic reasoning, the philosopher observes that when people see water, they think that they are thirsty and therefore seek the water. He allows that animals are impelled by a similar desire that arises in them through "sensation, imagination, or thought" (*Movement of Animals* 701a33–36).

It is noteworthy that even in those passages from the zoological treatises cited above in which he seems to come closest to arguing for a rational component in animal psychology, Aristotle always stops short of a direct avowal of that conclusion. In *History of Animals*, for example, we find repeated assertions that animals exhibit "traces" (*ichnē*) of human characteristics" (588a20), that they betray only "resemblances of intelligence" (588a23–24), and that they demonstrate merely "some sort of similar natural capacity" (588a30–31). The philosopher speaks of analogy and similarity, not of identity of faculties. Nor does Aristotle's doctrine of *synecheia*, "biological gradualism," in the final analysis argue for rationality in animals, for the doctrine allows for a break between humans and other animals in the matter of intellectual capacity, leaving an uncrossable gulf between the species. Animals may in important respects be *like* human beings, but, in Aristotle's view, they will never be *equal* to humans because of the fundamental absence of reason in animals. This absence had important consequences. In his *Nicomachean Ethics*, the philosopher sets forth a theory of friendship in which likeness of status forms a ground for that ethical relationship. A king cannot be a friend to a subject because of their difference in station, and likewise a human cannot be a friend to an inanimate object or to an animal nor stand in a relation of justice toward such classes (*Nicomachean Ethics* 1161b2–9). In the *Politics*, Aristotle argues that since nature does nothing without purpose, she has clearly made animals "for the sake of man" (1256b22), suggesting that humans have no obligations to animals.

It would be an exaggeration, however, to conclude from such statements as these from the *Ethics* and *Politics* that Aristotle intended his zoological theories to serve as the basis for a comprehensive ethical system governing human conduct toward other species. Sorabji is correct in observing, "Aristotle, I believe, was driven almost entirely by scientific interest in reaching his decision that animals lack reason."[22] It was the Stoics and, to a lesser extent, the Epicureans who imparted a moral dimension to Aristotle's zoology by focusing on his denial of reason to nonhuman species and by concluding therefrom that because only humans are rational, other species are so alien to them that they can have nothing in common with humans. The irrationality of animals, which denies them a meaningful language, makes them incapable, in Stoic teaching, of sharing in that sense of relationship, belonging, and kinship that the Stoics termed *oikeiōsis* and that formed perhaps the centerpiece of Stoic ethical philosophy.[23] Humans participate in this relationship with other humans, as do animals with other animals, but humans can never participate in this relationship with animals because they are intellectually alien to animals. Consequently, animals fall outside the purview of human morality.

The contribution to Greek speculation on human–animal kinship made by Aristotle's pupil and successor Theophrastus has been unjustly overshadowed by the enormous influence of Stoic ethical philosophy. Although he is remembered today primarily for his work in botany, Theophrastus deserves mention for his challenge to Aristotle's pronouncements on animal psychology and his attribution of considerably greater intellectual faculties to nonhuman species than his predecessor allowed. In his life of Theophrastus, Diogenes Laertius tells us (5.49) that the philosopher wrote a treatise entitled *On the Intellect and Character of Animals*, a work unfortunately lost, so that once again we are forced to rely on later testimonies on Theophrastus' teachings and on what are believed to be citations from his works embedded in the writings of others. Some have concluded that the ninth book of Aristotle's *History of Animals*, whose more generous interpretation of animal intellect appears to contradict Aristotle's pronouncements elsewhere, may be this lost treatise of Theophrastus or may at least be the work of Theophrastus. In *On Abstinence from Animal Flesh*, Porphyry reports (3.25) that Theophrastus, against Aristotle, stressed that all humans are akin to all animals because the principles (*archai*) of their bodies are alike: All have flesh and skin and bodily fluids.[24] Moreover, they are, in Theophrastus' estimation, alike in having appetites (*epithymiai*), angers (*orgai*), reason (*logismoi*), and perceptions (*aisthēseis*). He concludes his discussion of Theophrastus' teachings on human–animal kinship by stating (3.25) that "the race of all other animals would thus be akin (*oikeion*) to us and in all things related." If we may trust Porphyry's interpretation of Theophrastus' position, the successor of Aristotle went far beyond his master in attributing true reason (*logismos*) to animals, and in concluding that animals do share that *oikeiōsis* with humans that Stoicism would vigorously deny them.

From its inception, Stoicism was antiquity's most thoroughly anthropocentric school of philosophy, teaching that the goal of life was living in accord with nature, which was itself equivalent to living in accord with reason. Once the human attains to reason, it becomes his ethical project to direct his impulses toward those things that are *akin* to him, that is, to seek out the *oikeion*. In the case of human beings, this kinship is reflected in other humans, with whom each human has an affinity toward wisdom and ethical conduct. As Diogenes Laertius explains in his life of Zeno (335–263 BCE), the founder of Stoicism, all creatures at birth follow impulse (*hormē*), but "when reason has been added to those creatures that are rational, life for them lived in accord with reason becomes the natural life" (7.85). The problem that animals encounter vis-à-vis human beings is, according to Stoic teaching, inherent already in the makeup of the animal soul. The Stoic Chrysippus (ca. 280–207 BCE) taught that the soul, both of humans and of other animals, has at birth eight components: the five senses, the faculty of reproduction, the faculty of utterance, and a mysterious eighth part that the Stoics called the *hēgemonikon,* or "guiding principle."[25] In the human, the *hēgemonikon* develops into the faculty of reason, while in animals it remains forever irrational, a situation that precludes any moral relationship between the species since animals never develop a capacity for meaningful speech, which is a product of reason and which would allow ethical discourse between the species. Cicero explains the Stoic position on the consequences of a lack of reason in animals with stark clarity (*On Duties* 1.50): "In no respect are we further removed from the nature of beasts, in whom we often say that there is strength, as in the case of horses or lions, but we do not say that they have justice, fairness or goodness; for they are without reason and speech." Cicero correctly understood that in Stoic ethics, speech and moral standing are interrelated. Creatures that cannot express a desire to have their interests respected and their willingness to respect the interests of others fall outside the pale of morality. The language component of the Stoic case against animals arose as a byproduct of the school's conception of the makeup of the human and animal soul (*psychē*). The Stoics distinguished two forms of "reason" (*logos*): *logos endiathetos,* "inner reason, thought," controls and gives meaningful expression to the other type of reason, *logos prophorikos,* "uttered reason, meaningful speech." Since *logos endiathetos* was felt to arise in the *hēgemonikon,* which never attains rationality in animals, they have by their nature no capacity for articulate, meaningful speech, and their vocal utterances are without significance.[26]

In another of his philosophical dialogues, Cicero sets forth the consequences of lack of kinship with humans, now citing Chrysippus by name (*On the Ends of Good and Evil* 3.67): "But just as they think that there exist the bonds of right between human beings, so do they say that there are no bonds with the animals. Chrysippus has well observed that other things were born for the sake of mankind and the gods, but that humans were born for their own fellowship and society, so that humans can use them for their own purposes without wrongdoing." Cicero's allusion here to "fellowship and society" is surely a reference to the Stoic doctrine of *oikeiōsis*, that kinship that the Stoics declared to be impossible between humans and nonhuman animals. The Chrysippean position, as Cicero presents it here, had devastating consequences for animals. It becomes impossible to treat an animal unjustly or cruelly because they simply do not enter into the sphere of human moral concern. Aristotle's denial of reason to animals had been transformed by the Stoics into the basis for an exclusionist theory of human morality.

The sharp dichotomy between humans and other animal species based on intellectual criteria espoused by Stoic ethical philosophers proved enormously attractive to the early church fathers, which is perhaps not surprising in the case of two systems of thought that taught the primacy of the human being over other creatures and sought to point the way to salvation for that uniquely gifted and favored child of god, the human being. In *City of God* 1.20, Augustine explicates the biblical commandment against killing in such a way that plants and animals are excluded from the prohibition on the grounds that just as plants have no sensations, so animals have no reason (*ratio*). He specifically invokes the Stoic denial of "kinship" (*oikeiōsis*) between humans and animals when he calls animals creatures "that are not partners with us at all in the faculty of reason (*nulla nobis ratione sociantur*)." Sorabji observes of Augustine's understanding of Christ's attitude toward animals, "It is perfectly true that Christ did not spare them, and that is because Christ was a Stoic as regards animals. That is in effect what Augustine is saying. For he ascribes to Christ the Stoic theory that animals cannot be brought within the community of just dealings, because they lack reason."[27] Whether or not Christ was himself a Stoic in his views toward animals, it is likely that some of the less animal-friendly aspects of the Christian message have Stoic roots, most especially the belief that humans are fundamentally different from and superior to other animal species.[28]

The insistence of the Stoics on "kinship" (*oikeiōsis*) with human beings in the possession of intellectual faculties that include rationality manifesting itself in meaningful language as a prerequisite for moral considerability appears as well in the ethical teachings of their contemporaries and chief philosophical rivals, the Epicureans, a school not generally viewed as sharing many points of doctrine with the Stoics or indeed as demonstrating much interest in animals at all. Much of what survives of the works of Epicurus (341–270 BCE), the founder of the school, is preserved in the tenth book of Diogenes Laertius, including the text of three lengthy philosophical letters and a set of forty miscellaneous pronouncements of the master that summarize points of Epicurean doctrine, a collection that scholars variously designate as *Principal Doctrines* or *Sovereign Maxims*. In the thirty-second of these, Epicurus declares that animals and human tribes incapable of forming contracts or agreements (*synthēkai*) that require their participants to avoid harming each other or being harmed by each other, have no part in justice or injustice. The capacity for language as a prerequisite for justice is set forth in the thirty-third maxim, in which Epicurus states that absolute justice has never existed, but only a covenant arising from discourse between individuals who come together and agree on a policy of nonaggression. Epicurus' immediate successor as head of the school, Hermarchus, reaffirmed his master's teaching that animals were excluded from a relationship of justice with humans because of their inability to form contracts.[29] With Epicurus, we see the triumph of that anthropocentrism toward which Greek philosophical speculation on animals was tending in the fourth and third centuries BCE.

There is some evidence to suggest, however, that the rigorously anti-animal stance of earlier Stoic philosophy was softened somewhat in the refinements to the system introduced by at least one later representative of the school, although he ultimately did little to counteract the effects of his predecessors on subsequent treatment of animals at the hands of human beings. The "later Stoic" Posidonius (ca. 135–51 BCE), who wrote on subjects ranging from earthquakes to anthropology, is often credited with humanizing the sometimes harsh and forbidding teachings of Stoicism. Unfortunately, we are once again limited in our understanding of his doctrines by the poor state of preservation of his works, but even the scanty fragments that we do possess reveal that he was not averse to challenging the positions of earlier Stoics. He is reported to have questioned the statement of Chrysippus that animals are incapable of emotions because they are irrational and emotion arises from reason, charging that Chrysippus' assertion flies in the face of observable facts (fr. 159) and arguing that animals obviously feel desire and anger (fr. 33). Posidonius' most important contribution to animal psychology is his solution to the problem posed by Chrysippus' theory of emotions: He posited that animals' emotions arise from the nonrational parts of their souls, thus obviating the need for rationality in the production and expression of emotions (fr. 33).[30]

It would nevertheless be a mistake to conclude from evidence supplied by the fragments of Posidonius that later Stoicism adopted a uniformly milder stance in its position on humans' relationship with nonhuman species. Seneca (ca. 4 BCE–65 CE) (see Figure 6.3), Rome's most illustrious Stoic, set forth his views on animal psychology prominently in his collection of *Moral Letters*. He reports (*Moral Letters* 108) that he adopted a vegetarian regimen for the period of a year under the influence of his Neopythagorean teacher Sotion, but that he abandoned it on the urging of his father who hated philosophy, noting that his father had little trouble in convincing him to "eat better once again" (*Moral Letters* 108.22). In *Moral Letters* 121, Seneca seems to have reversed the trend in Stoic thinking on animals observable in Posidonius by reiterating the position of Chrysippus that while humans and animals may start life with apparently

FIGURE 6.3: *Herm of Seneca* (ca. 4 BCE–65 CE). Roman double herm (frontal view). First half of the 3rd century CE. Marble, h. 28 cm. Inv. Sk 391. Photo: Johannes Laurentius. Location: Antikensammlung, Staatliche Museen zu Berlin, Berlin, Germany. Photo Credit: Bildarchiv Preussischer Kulturbesitz/Art Resource, NY; ART186264.

similar mental capacities, the human intellect always has the *potential* to attain to rationality that the animal intellect does not, so that animals remain ultimately incapable of any kinship with humans, a reassertion of the doctrine of *oikeiōsis* central to the older Stoic position on animals.[31] Although Rome's greatest representative of the Stoic school did not evince any marked sympathy for animalkind, this cannot be said of Rome's greatest Epicurean, Lucretius (ca. 95–44 BCE). A fervent disciple of Epicurus, Lucretius left a detailed exposition of the school's atomistic view of the physical world in his didactic poem, *On the Nature of Things,* but in its extant form, it provides little insight into Epicurean ethics, so that we must form an appreciation for the poet-philosopher's views on animals from random comments spread throughout his text. He affectingly depicts the anguish of a mother cow deprived of her calf that has been led off to slaughter (*On the Nature of Things* 2.349–366), and his amusing portrait of a newborn calf at play in a pasture, frolicking on shaky legs while "drunk" on its mother's milk (*On the Nature of Things* 1. 259–261) is one of the most charming passages in his poem. While we will not find in Lucretius any organized and closely reasoned exposition on the nature of animal psychology in the manner of Aristotle, the Roman philosopher does present an idea almost unparalleled otherwise in ancient texts, that is, the belief that animals are capable of emotions like sadness and joy, and that they take simple pleasure in their own lives. Perhaps more important, he seems to have countenanced the idea that animals have mind. He observes, for example (*On the Nature of Things* 2.268), that a racehorse at the starting gate cannot burst forth as quickly as its mind (*mens*) would like to because the atomic substance of its body must be roused throughout its frame before it can follow the "urging of the mind" (*studium mentis*). In a later passage, in which Lucretius attempts to account for the disparate temperaments of animal species, he observes (*On the Nature of Things* 3.299) that stags are easily frightened because of their "chilly mind" (*frigida mens*). Although it might be an overstatement to see any real violation of Epicurean orthodoxy in Lucretius' touching portrayals of animals, or any intentional innovation in the teaching of a philosophical school notorious for discouraging variance from the master's own pronouncements, since, after all, animals are mentioned only incidentally in his poem, he was certainly more sympathetic to animal creation than were the vast majority of his fellow Romans.[32]

A philosophical document, also dating from the Roman period, that has much of interest for the study of ancient attitudes toward animals but that has received less attention than it merits, a circumstance attributable to the peculiar state of its preservation, is the dialogue *On Animals* by Philo of Alexandria (ca. 25 BCE–ca. 45 CE), the Jewish philosopher best known for his Stoic-influenced allegorizations of Scripture. Philo's treatise on animals, whose full title, *Alexander, or Whether Dumb Animals Possess Reason,* is all that survives of the Greek original beyond a few fragments, comes down to us solely in an Armenian translation dating from some period between the sixth and eighth century CE.[33] In this remarkable work, Philo is portrayed as bringing forth the transcript of a lecture that his nephew Alexander had delivered defending the position that animals are rational. The lecture is read aloud by Philo's grandnephew Lysimachus, after which Philo attempts to refute Alexander's case using Stoic arguments. Alexander's case occupies by far the greater portion of the text (*On Animals* 10–71), while Philo's brief refutation (77–100) comes off as surprisingly halfhearted and perfunctory. Alexander defends the position that animals are endowed with some degree of rationality by citing a number of arguments that were commonplaces in ancient accounts of animal wonders and had come to be considered by some classical authors to be evidence of the mental powers of animals, including the cleverness and elaborate workmanship observable in the construction of spiderwebs and beehives (*On Animals* 17–20). He argues as well that animals have an innate sense of justice and equality because they choose their leaders and follow them faithfully (*On Animals* 64). Alexander even alludes to the Stoic doctrine of the *hēgemonikon,* the governing principle of the soul that accords rationality to humans but remains irrational in other animal species, and directly contradicts the Stoic position by declaring (*On Animals* 29) that nature implanted a sovereign mind in every soul. Remarkably, Philo's refutation of Alexander's exposition relies more on ridicule than rational argument, and the Jewish philosopher prefaces his presentation with a warning that to argue as Alexander does that animals are rational is a sin against God (*On Animals* 77). The reader comes away from Philo's treatise with a much more favorable impression of animal intellect than Philo, as a proponent of the Stoic position, could have intended.[34]

Although we cannot look to the Roman age for a more animal-friendly brand of Stoicism, if we may judge from the examples of Seneca and Philo, the most elaborate and carefully argued case for rationality in animals and for the inclusion of animals in the sphere of human moral concern based on possession of that faculty, was developed by two Greek philosophers active in the Roman world, both of whom we have had occasion to mention earlier in this study. Ironically, their contribution to the debate on the moral status of animals remains largely unknown both to the general reader and to many modern animals rights philosophers. The prolific Plutarch is familiar to the modern reader as the author of moralizing biographies of Greek and Roman political and military figures, while his numerous treatises on ethical issues, known collectively as the *Moralia,* remain somewhat neglected. Three treatises included in the *Moralia* are devoted to animal issues. The longest of these, *On the Cleverness of Animals,* seeks to refute the Stoic denial of reason to animals and advances the position that humans have an obligation to treat other species with justice and compassion, while the two parts of his incomplete treatise *On the Eating of Flesh* offer the most detailed and impassioned argument for the necessity of abstinence from meat to survive from classical antiquity prior to the composition of Porphyry's *On Abstinence from Animal Flesh.* Far different in tone is his lighthearted dialogue *Gryllus,* a witty parody of the famous scene from the tenth book of Homer's *Odyssey* in which Odysseus petitions the witch Circe to reconvert his men into human beings from their animal state. In Plutarch's reimagining of the scene, the animals refuse the hero's offer and prefer their beastly state.[35] The Neoplatonist Porphyry, the second of our later advocates of animal rationality, drew heavily on Plutarch and devoted particular attention to the question of humans' potential debt of justice to nonhuman animals.

In the opening chapter of his dialogue *On the Cleverness of Animals,* one of the interlocutors reminds his companions that the previous day's discussion had been devoted to a demonstration that all animals are to some extent rational: "[We] said yesterday, as you know, that all animals partake in some manner of thought and reason" (*On the Cleverness of Animals* 960A). The listeners, who are a party of hunters, are reminded that it is after all this very quality of mental sharpness in their prey that renders hunting so challenging. Almost immediately after this, Plutarch takes up the attack on the Stoics when he has his speaker remark that one should not be surprised that all animals share in reason and understanding since every creature is born with a soul, and it is unreasonable to hold that the soul of any creature can contain both rational and irrational parts. Moreover, that very soul guarantees the possession of some intellectual faculties: "Every creature with a soul comes to birth capable of sensation and imagination" (960D). We recall that even the Stoics had admitted that all animals have a soul, albeit, in their view, a defective one. Now, Plutarch's speaker asks, would nature produce any animal with a soul merely to have it be sentient without at the same time intending that the animal employ that sentience toward the successful conduct of its life, through a knowledge of what it should flee and what it should pursue, that is, a recognition of its natural enemies and its natural food sources? (960E). Plutarch's interlocutor cites the Aristotelian philosopher Strato to reinforce his argument, "There is a treatise by Strato the natural philosopher, in fact, that demonstrates that it is impossible to have sensation without thought" (961A). Consequently, he continues, the Stoics are guilty of self-contradiction when they punish their dogs and horses with the intention of producing in them the sensation of repentance (*metanoia*), for it would be pointless to punish them if animals are incapable of reflecting on the purpose of punishment (961D).

Plutarch's speaker cites numerous examples of animal behaviors that indicate memories (*mnēmai*), emotions (*pathē*), and care for their offspring (*teknōn epimeleiai*), none of which would be possible without the possession of at least some degree of reason. He concludes from these observations, "Philosophers demonstrate by means of these things that animals have a share of reason" (966B). The notion that animals have a "share" of reason appears several times in the course of Plutarch's treatise *On the Cleverness of Animals* and is key to his understanding of animal intellect, for he criticizes the Stoics for mistakenly believing that creatures that were not designed by nature to display perfect reason have no reason at all. "True and perfect reason arises from care and education. Thus, all besouled creatures have a share of reason" (962C). The conclusion that Plutarch draws from this line of argument is far-reaching. It effectively challenges the Stoic denial of kinship (*oikeiōsis*) between humans and nonhuman species if this kinship rests, as the Stoics demanded, on the possession of reason, and it calls into question the Stoic assertion that the *hēgemonikon,* the "guiding principle" of the soul, fails in the case of animals to advance beyond a prerational stage. Finally, it rejects the Stoic belief that humans can owe nothing to other animals because they are fundamentally unlike humans. Animals, in Plutarch's view, are creatures that fall within the scope of human moral concern and merit just treatment from humans.

Plutarch develops an argument for the necessity of justice toward animals that is virtually unparalleled in extant ancient sources, claiming that animals themselves have an understanding of the concept of justice and actively seek it from human beings.[36] In his treatise *On the Eating of Flesh,* Plutarch imagines a heartrending scene of a food animal at the point of slaughter whose cries and shrieks humans mistakenly assume are inarticulate when they are in fact "cries for justice" (*dikaiologias*) (*On the Eating of Flesh* 994E). Plutarch here seems to question the Stoic idea that animals are incapable of that meaningful language (*logos prophorikos*) that arises from reason. The fault, he suggests, lies in the humans who cannot understand the language of animals.[37] It was self-evident to Plutarch that, if animals are to some extent rational and are therefore akin to humans, and can likewise express themselves in a language, albeit one incomprehensible to humans, a vegetarian regimen was incumbent on all individuals who sought to live an ethical life. To this argument for abstention that depends on rationality as a criterion for inclusion in the sphere of human moral concern Plutarch adds yet another argument that is seldom encountered in writers before his time: that animals deserve compassion from humans simply because they are capable of suffering. Unfortunately, he notes, they do not receive it. "Nothing shames us," he charges (*On the Eating of Flesh* 994E), "not the flowery tint of their flesh, not their persuasive utterances, not their clean demeanor and extraordinary intelligence, but for the sake of a bit of meat we deprive them of the light of the sun, of the brightness of day, of that lifetime to which they are entitled by birth."

Relations between humans and animals are treated in a more humorous fashion in Plutarch's brief dialogue *Gryllus,* in which the pig Gryllus, whose name means "oinker" or "squeaker," and who is one of Circe's pig-converts from among Odysseus' crew, declines Odysseus' offer of reconversion into the human state on the grounds that animals are in fact superior to human beings (they modestly mate only once a year, he notes, in contrast to lustful humans) and do not misapply their intelligence toward the acquisition of useless pleasures and luxuries.[38] Animals, he argues, live more in accord with nature than do humans who pervert their natural gifts. Gryllus declares himself quite satisfied with his new status as an animal: "Since I have entered my new body, I wonder at those arguments by which I was once persuaded that all creatures excepting humans are irrational and senseless" (*Gryllus* 992C).

Although he was not a systematic philosopher in the manner of Aristotle and was willing to appropriate any argument that would support his positions, Plutarch nevertheless considered Plato to be his philosophical mentor and can be considered an adherent of the so-called New Academy, whose most important leader was Carneades (ca. 189–ca. 129 BCE). Central to the New Academy's stance was its opposition to doctrinaire Stoicism with its emphasis on the primacy of the human being. It is not surprising, then, that Plutarch came out so strongly against the Stoic denial of reason to animals and of any obligation on the part of humans to treat animals with even a modicum of compassion, and it was natural that the Neoplatonist Porphyry, in the third century CE, looked to Plutarch for inspiration in the composition of his lengthy treatise *On Abstinence from Animal Flesh*. Reflecting Platonism's concern for the welfare of the human soul and its suspicion of the detrimental effects of bodily desires, Neoplatonism sought to draw the human being closer to the divine through an avoidance of corporal contamination. The consumption of animal flesh was considered by the Neoplatonists to contribute to that contamination. Porphyry's treatise marshals an impressive array of arguments for abstention and offers, in its first book, the fullest exposition of the *anti*vegetarian position to survive from antiquity, which Porphyry then undertook to refute in the subsequent books of his treatise.[39] We have encountered some of the arguments of the carnivore in earlier writers. Porphyry relates, for example, that the common person who knows nothing of philosophy believes that humans wage a just war against creatures that seek to harm us and that would overrun the world if their numbers were not kept in check by humans. Porphyry replies that it is ridiculous to hold that animals must be controlled in number by humans because animal species, both those that humans consume and those that they do not, have natural predators that keep their numbers in check (*On Abstinence from Animal Flesh* 1.53).

It is the third book of Porphyry's treatise that exercises the greatest fascination for the student of ancient philosophical attitudes toward animals, for here he sets forth his case for rationality in animals and for the consequent debt of justice toward them. In the opening chapters of this book, Porphyry cites the Stoic doctrine of two types of reason (*logos*), the internal (*endiathetos*) and the external (*prophorikos*) that is manifested in speech, to argue that there is no reason to suppose, with the Stoics, that an animal has not "thought what it has experienced" (*On Abstinence from Animal Flesh* 3.3) before saying what it proceeds to say. That is, it is foolish to assert that the utterances of an animal do not represent the externalization of some internal thought processes. The fact that animal utterances are meaningless to humans is without significance, since a Greek may not understand an Indian or a Syrian but does not conclude from that fact that the utterances of such persons are without meaning (3.3). We are justified only in concluding that animals may be *less* rational than humans, not that they are irrational (3.7). Animals, like humans, are born with certain capacities, like the ability to pursue appropriate nourishment and to avoid enemies, but, as Plutarch had observed, time and education, supplied by conspecifics, heighten this innate knowledge.

Porphyry's demonstration of rationality in animals leads him naturally to his plea for just treatment for animals, a plea based on the belief that animals are after all *akin* (*oikeion*) to humans. If it is true of animals that they have perceptions, as they must in order to secure food and to escape enemies, and if they feel pain, fear, and distress and can therefore be injured, as is clearly the case, then they must fall within the sphere of human moral concern. "The followers of Zeno," Porphyry reminds the reader (3.19), "make this kinship (*oikeiōsin*) the origin of justice." He goes on to conclude, "Is it not irrational, when we see many humans living by perception alone, without intelligence and reason, to think that there is some bond of justice with such persons, and not with our plow animals and with the dog that shares our house and with those beasts that provide us milk?" (3.19). This justice, Porphyry asserts (3.26–27), consists of doing no harm to animals that do us no harm, even if we are justified in eliminating those species that seek to do us harm. "Justice," Porphyry maintains (3.26), "lies in being restrained and harmless toward those beings that do not harm us." Obviously, human beings concerned with living an ethical life would not feel themselves justified in consuming creatures that are akin to them in having sentience and reason and in being harmless as well. To this point in his argument, Porphyry's defense of abstention closely mirrors the sort of argumentation on which Plutarch's case is built, but as a Neoplatonist, Porphyry adds a type of argument that does not figure at all prominently in Plutarch. He argues as well that a meat diet arouses negative passions and mental troubles that hinder the human soul's ascent to true Being (*On Abstinence from Animal Flesh* 1.33). Here Porphyry seems to take a page from Pythagoras, although his case for abstention contains a much more highly developed concern for animals as intelligent and sensitive beings than is detectable in testimonies relating to Pythagoras' case for abstention.

A millennium of Greco-Roman philosophical thought separates the age of Pythagoras and his fellow pre-Socratics from that of Porphyry, in the course of which many of the intellectual presuppositions of the subsequent debate on animals' moral status found their earliest expression. In the pronouncements of Aristotle and the Stoics, we see the full flowering of the idea that the exclusive possession of reason by the human species precludes any real kinship between humans and nonhuman animals and leads to the natural inferiority of other animal species, a notion that is still central to philosophical opposition to the concept of "animal rights" and forms the cornerstone of the anthropocentrism on which that opposition rests.[40] Although extant texts and testimonies do not justify any claim that classical antiquity could boast an infant animal rights movement or that any ancient thinker was an "animal rightist" in any real sense, not least because we cannot always determine what motivated apparently animal-friendly utterances by ancient thinkers, we are justified in concluding that Greek and Roman philosophy at least articulated many of the questions that are still asked today and formulated carefully reasoned, if sometimes contradictory, positions on many of the issues that still inform the debate on what constitutes humans' proper ethical stance toward those creatures that share their world.

CHAPTER SEVEN

Animals into Art in the Ancient World

CHRISTINE MORRIS

Vultures with great, fringed wings at Çatal Hüyük, cow-eared Hathor gazing forth from the capitals of Egyptian temples, dappled bulls charging in the bull-games in Minoan Crete, majestically rearing horses on the Parthenon frieze, the fierce she-wolf that nurtures the founder of Rome: animals in ancient art are memorable, full of artistic grace and power, and resonant with the multiple interactions between humans and animals.

Animals have been a major theme in ancient art since humans first put pigment on the walls of dark caves in the Paleolithic period to create stunning animal images such as bison, mammoths, horses, and deer. Such images can be examined from many angles: from an aesthetic perspective; as windows on the practical roles of animals as providers of food and other resources; as depictions of companions; or as potential dangers and predators in the landscape. Beyond this, animals, and images of them, also operate in almost all human societies as symbols, referents, and metaphors, a role that has been elegantly expressed by Stanley Tambiah though the phrase "animals are good to think and good to prohibit."[1] Exploration of this expressive role of animals in the arts of the various cultures of the Mediterranean will provide a central theme for this chapter.

A key element in the human encounter with animals is domestication; through this process particular animals such as cattle, sheep, and dogs were drawn into closer relationships with human individuals and societies. Domestication led to both a physical and cognitive separation of domesticated and wild animals, which is played out in many ways. The ancient Greeks, for example, deemed only domesticated animals suitable for sacrifice to the gods. The Neolithic site of Çatal Hüyük rises from the Konya plain of modern Turkey. Its people lived in a settlement of closely packed, small, mud-brick houses, many of which have remarkable wall paintings (both painted and in relief) of powerful animals, most notably bulls, wild boar, stags, bears, vultures, and large felines. A pair of confronted felines sculpted in relief plaster dominates a wall; their large spots suggest that leopards are intended, and similar spotted creatures are also to be found in small-scale sculptures where humans appear to be riding on them. Felines also appear on the most famous image from the site, a clay figurine of a generously proportioned, seated female, who rests her hands on the heads of two felines that appear to form the arms of her seat.[2] Her identity is hotly contested—many would interpret her as a "Mother Goddess," though archaeologists are now skeptical about interpreting each and every female image in early art as a "goddess." Whoever she is, the association with dangerous felines in combination with the seated posture evokes power and perhaps control over the natural world. The original excavator of the site, James Mellaart, interpreted much of the iconography as relating to "the cult of the Mother Goddess." The large (but often headless) figures with splayed limbs on the walls were interpreted as goddesses in a birthing posture.[3] A more recent find of a sealing with a figure in this posture, but with an animal head (possibly that of a bear), opens up the possibility that the large images are also animals or even composite figures, neither fully human nor animal, thus emphasizing further the significance of animal imagery in the rich artistic repertoire of the site.

Another powerful creature in the Çatal artistic repertoire is the vulture. The vultures have great, fringed wings, and they swoop down and appear to attack tiny human figures, who are headless. Mellaart argued that the vultures were associated with the highly distinctive burial practice of excarnation known from other cultures (for example, the "sky burials" of Tibet,[4] or the Parsee "Towers of Silence" in India), in which the human body is not buried but placed outside and picked clean by birds of prey.[5] Recent evidence, however, indicates that the people of Çatal were buried intact rather than having their bodies first exposed to vultures, and this demands from us a less literal reading of the imagery. In addition, it has been noted that the paintings are closely associated with concentrations of burials within the houses, and using ethnographic analogy, the current excavators speculate that the powerful animal imagery could be related to communication with or protection from the spirits of the dead and the ancestors.

The most commonly repeated animal imagery on the site is bovine, ranging from painted images to sculpted and relief heads in association with actual skulls and horns of bovines. One painted image shows a silhouette scene of a massive, heavy-bodied wild bull or aurochs facing right, its tongue lolling from an open mouth. Male hunters with weapons surround it, yet the humans seem small and puny alongside the animal. Animal skulls and horns are embedded within plastered forms and are sometimes placed within a plaster projection with only the tip visible. Mellaart interpreted the plaster projections as female breasts (again referring back to a fertility goddess), but this argument is undermined by the placement of the "breasts" in vertical rows on the wall. The integration of animal bones into the art is also intriguing, and the blurring of the boundaries between animal remains and animal representations could perhaps be thought of as a way of harnessing the power of the animal enclosed within for the benefit of the human community.

The prevalence of wild and powerful animals in the art of Çatal Hüyük has long seemed striking in the context of a community thought to be largely dependent on agriculture and domesticated animals. Recent analysis of the animal remains suggests a more complicated picture in which sheep and goat were domesticated but cattle were still wild.[6] Ian Hodder, the current excavator, has argued that the animal imagery at Çatal could represent the "domestication of the wild" by bringing it symbolically into the household, and that there is a specific link between the wild cattle imagery and the burial of the ancestors within the houses.[7]

Mesopotamia, the land between the rivers, is home to some of the earliest cities in the world and to art and imagery produced for the ruling elite who lived in palaces and were buried with every sign of conspicuous display, such as the mid-third millennium Royal Tombs of Ur. The lavish finds from these Royal Tombs made headline news worldwide when their excavator, Sir Leonard Woolley, discovered them within a larger burial area in 1928, and they include many stunning representations of animals. One of the most famous objects from the royal burials is the so-called "Standard of Ur";[8] the scenes were inlaid into a now decayed wooden frame in shell and red limestone on a deep-blue lapis lazuli background. The two main sides are conventionally known as "war" and "peace," and they include an array of animals. The "war" side shows a very early image of the Sumerian army, and we see chariots driving into battle drawn by donkeys. On the "peace" side, the main theme seems to be the bountiful nature of the land, expressed through a banquet and formal processions of people bringing animals: One man carries pairs of fish, others lead cattle and goats, and perhaps most striking is the group of sheep with curling horns and undulating, zebra-like lines indicating their long shaggy coats.

Another stunning work of art from Ur is a gold and lapis lazuli bull's head which was attached to the front of a lyre.[9] The bull sports a long beard made from pieces of lapis set into a silver backing. The front of the sound box is decorated with a series of inlaid shell plaques. These show animals, some with human features, engaged in preparations for a banquet—a dog carries an offering table piled with animal parts, a lion brings a large jar and bowl, and a seated equid plays a bull lyre. A bear helps to support the lyre, while a smaller animal perched on the bear's leg plays a *sistrum* (rattle). In a separate panel a hero is flanked by human-headed bulls. This melding of human and bull features (bulls with beards, bulls with human heads) seems to be closely linked to kingship in Mesopotamia.

The fluidity of human–animal boundaries is perhaps best known from Egyptian art and religion, where gods and goddesses were represented in the form of animals or with hybrid human–animal features. The gap between ancient Egyptian perceptions and later Christian thought is well illustrated by Clement of Alexandria, who writes disparagingly of entering a beautiful Egyptian temple only to find "not the god for whom we have been looking inside, the god toward whom we have hastened, but a cat, or a crocodile, or a native snake, or similar animals, which should not be in a temple, but in a cleft or a den, or on a dung heap."[10] Clement, like many commentators on the use of animal imagery in Egyptian religion, made the mistake of thinking that the Egyptians practiced zoolatry or that they worshipped animals in a literal way. Rather, the animals chosen seem to embody particular attributes or manifestations of divine power, and the multifaceted nature of the gods could be expressively communicated through multiple, shifting bodily combinations and indeed by the commonly used epithet "rich in manifestations."[11]

The relationship between deity and animal forms was complex. Several different goddesses—Hathor, Isis, Nut, and Neith—could be represented as cows, and there are strong links between these cow goddesses and Egyptian kingship.[12] In addition to taking a fully bovine form or sporting a cow-head, Hathor is unique in that her face gazes out at the viewer in human form but with the large soft ears of a cow. Certain deities could take several different animals forms. For example, the god Thoth (deity of learning and patron of scribes) could be manifested in the form of the sacred ibis (*Theskiornis aethiopicus*). Sadly, this elegant bird with its slender down-turned bill can no longer be found on the Egyptian Nile, though it was a common sight up until the nineteenth century.[13] Thoth also appeared in a quite different animal form, that of the baboon. One fine Eighteenth-Dynasty example is a quartzite statue of a squatting baboon in the British Museum (see Figure 7.1). This large male baboon displays a well-developed shaggy mane and a long muzzle, and the image is imbued both with physical strength and an air of dignified mystery. The baboon also had more general religious connotations since it was associated in Egyptian thought with the daily rebirth of the sun in the form of Re (or Ra). In hymns we are told that it is the baboons who "announce Re when this great god is to be born again … they dance for him, they jump gaily for him, they sing for him, they sing praises for him, they shout out for him."[14] This extravagant description is in fact an embellishment of real baboon behavior since upon waking baboons do sometimes jump around in the warmth of the rising sun and make loud noises.

FIGURE 7.1: Quartzite figure of a baboon, British Museum. Photo Credit: Dr. Cybelle Greenlaw.

For this reason baboons are often shown standing on their hind legs and raising their arms in adoration toward the sun rising on the eastern horizon.

Among the stranger creatures in the divine bestiary are composite or hybrid animals. The goddess Taweret, protector of women in childbirth, brings together several distinctive creatures of the Nile. She takes the form of a pregnant hippo-potamus with large, sagging breasts and lionlike paws and wears a crocodile on her back. The combined powers of these animals were surely seen as efficacious in protecting vulnerable women in childbirth, while the monstrous visual effect may be a way of "externalizing their internal power to protect."[15] It can surely be no coincidence that the hippopotamus is particularly ferocious in guarding her young and that the crocodile mother is unusual among reptiles in guarding the eggs and then carrying the young down to the water once hatched.

Unsurprisingly, the teeming life of the river Nile, the very lifeblood of Egypt, is vibrantly depicted in the arts of ancient Egypt. One of the most stunning ex-amples of the genre of hunting in the marshes comes from a group of paintings from the New Kingdom tomb of a Theban official, Nebamun[16] (see Figure 7.2). He stands on a delicate papyrus boat and is accompanied by his young son and his wife, though her elaborate dress, the cone of scented perfume on her head, and the sistrum in her left hand seem more appropriate to a feast or party than a hunting expedition. The presence of a large duck at the front of the boat may

FIGURE 7.2: Fowling in the marshes: fragment of wall painting from the tomb of Nebamun (no. 10), Thebes, Egypt, 18th Dynasty, ca. 1350 BCE. (EA, 37977). Location: British Museum, London, Great Britain. Photo Credit: Heritage Image Partnership/ Art Resource, NY; ART177442.

suggest a subtle sexual dimension to the scene since ducks are considered to have erotic connotations in Egyptian art and literature. These observations serve to remind us that Egyptian tomb paintings are not simple images of everyday reality, but rather represent the ideal life as well as symbolize rebirth and new life. Below the boat the Nile waters teem with plump fish and water plants, while in front of Nebamun the papyrus thicket and the air are thronged with a rich variety of waterbirds. Nebamun holds a throw-stick and in his other hand grasps three live decoy herons firmly by the legs. Some of the birds still perch on the heads of the papyrus protecting a nest of eggs, some panic and take flight, while others struggle to escape from the teeth and claws of Nebamun's pet cat. The scene is exceptional in its use of delicate color, especially the blues and grays, and the fine-textured effects in the rendering of the animals: the softness of the birds' wings, the rougher fur of the cat, the iridescent scales of the fish below, and the delicately painted, fluttering butterflies that fill the smaller spaces and add to the overall sense of the abundant life of the papyrus swampland.

The busy movement in the scene, as Nebamun and his feline hunting companion spread panic amongst the roosting birds, contrasts with the space behind, filled with orderly rows of hieroglyphs. The text immediately behind Nebamun aptly describes him as "taking recreation and seeing what is good in the place of eternity" (in other words, the afterlife). The hieroglyphs in the upper area also provide a good example of the importance of animals, and especially birds, in the Egyptian writing system. There are two examples of the sign for the letter *m*, which takes the form of the barn owl. This bird of prey is instantly recognizable through its distinctive coloring and also the large moon-shaped face. Egyptian art in general favors profile views of both humans and animals; the frontal face of the barn-owl glyph is a notable exception, making it unique among the bird hieroglyphs. Among the numerous other birds of prey that appear in Egyptian art and as hieroglyphs, the falcon is of special importance as the emblem of Horus, son of Osiris, and symbol of Egyptian rulership. Horus himself could be shown as falcon-headed or in falcon form, and the meaning of his name, "lofty or distant one," is reflected in the flight of the falcon high in the sky. Each pharaoh was considered a living embodiment of Horus, and his "Horus name" is introduced by the falcon hieroglyph.[17] Houlihan describes the Horus falcon "as the nearest thing the Egyptians had to a national bird," while noting that the image cannot be tied down to any one species.[18] Parts of animals could also serve as hieroglyphs—a good avian example is the elegant plume of the ostrich, which was both a hieroglyph and the symbol of Maat, goddess of truth and justice, who wears the ostrich plume on her head.

The beautiful paintings of the tomb of Nebamun are notable not only for the hunting scene discussed earlier, but also for a whole range of animal depictions that display the wealth and status of the tomb owner. In a series of scenes, animals are brought before Nebamun for inspection, and the scribes are shown conducting a census.[19] Herdsmen bring groups of cattle, both short-horned and long-horned types, forward. As is typical in Egyptian art, the overlapping animals are differentiated by the use of contrasting colors, but the artist has gone further in individualizing the animals by creating a stunning array of dappled, piebald, and spotted hides. In another scene a closely packed group of geese, again differentiated through delicate use of color and body markings, are being counted. Some have already been placed in baskets, and the group in general is given a sense of movement and life by the varied poses of the geese, some pecking at the ground, others flapping their wings.

The animal world could also be a source of danger, and poisonous snakes and scorpions were a very real threat to the ancient Egyptians, so it is not surprising that numerous spells and medicinal treatments against these dangerous creatures are preserved in Egyptian texts, nor that Apophis, the archenemy of the sun god Ra, was envisioned in the form of a serpent. However, that which is dangerous can also be harnessed as a protector, so snake imagery is also intimately associated with royal power in the form of the snake "uraeus." The term "uraeus" refers to the distinctive attack posture of an enraged cobra, its head rearing up and its hood expanded, ready to spit venom. The rearing cobra or uraeus appears together with the lappet-faced vulture on the pharaoh's crown, a fearsome duo that symbolized the union of the Upper and Lower kingdoms in the persons of the "Two Ladies," the goddesses Nekhbet and Wadjet.

Egyptian art reveals a lively curiosity about animals from foreign lands, and as in many societies the elite expressed their power and knowledge through displays of exotic goods including animals. A major artistic source for the depiction of exotic animals is the mortuary temple of the female pharaoh Hatshepsut at Deir el-Bahri. The painted relief carvings show scenes of the famous expedition to the land of Punt (perhaps located in southern Sudan or Ethiopia) from which the Egyptians obtained highly valued myrrh and frankincense. These images show life in Punt in considerable detail, including its animals (giraffe, rhinoceros, baboons, tropical fish) as well as exotic animals and animal products being brought back to Egypt. Some of these animals may have been kept in royal game parks or menageries, while a pair of cheetahs seems to have joined the royal household, since these sleek felines are shown with collars and leashes in a scene depicting the queen's personal retinue. A painting from the New Kingdom tomb of Sobkhotepe shows vividly rendered scenes of foreigners presenting tribute to Tuthmosis IV.[20] Among them are a group of black men from tropical Africa, and animals are prominent among their exotic offerings. So, alongside gold rings from the mines of Nubia and logs of precious ebony wood, they bring giraffe tails (perhaps to be made into fly whisks) and a leopard skin. A vervet monkey is perched on the shoulder of one of the men, while a leash holds a stately baboon marching beside him.

Imported, exotic creatures such as monkeys could be treasured—if rather showy—pets, but Egyptian art amply testifies to the close relations between humans and a wide range of animal companions. Dogs, then as now, were loyal companions, guards, and hunting partners. Human affection for pet dogs can be seen in tomb imagery where dogs sit under their owners' seats, by the fact that they are given personal names (and unusually among animals these are sometimes names used for humans), and by the excavation of burials of treasured canine companions.[21] The cat, too, finds a place in the favored spot under its owner's chair from the Middle Kingdom onward, and one charming scene shows a group of pets frolicking under the throne of Queen Tiye in an otherwise formal ceremonial scene; rather improbably, a cat hooks its leg around a duck in a companionable manner, while a green monkey leaps playfully over them!

More overt humor is found in satirical scenes from later Egyptian art where animals play out human roles. Such scenes appear on satirical papyri and on ostraka (limestone or pottery fragments used as cheaper media for drawing). Often, animal relationships are inverted in a quirky way, as on an ostrakon where a mouse occupies the role of the lady, drinking wine and sniffing her lotus flower, while being served by two attentive cat-servants. Elsewhere, on the Turin papyrus, the familiar theme of the pharaoh and his army attacking a city is turned into a mouse-king in his chariot drawn by dogs and a walled city defended by cats.[22] The theme of the mouse lording it over the cat is reminiscent of a Tom and Jerry cartoon and suggests that some aspects of humor can transcend cultural differences of time and space. Other humorous animal scenes show hyenas herding goats, a lion and an antelope playing a board-game of *senet*, and even an entire animal orchestra with lion and donkey harpists, a banjo-strumming crocodile, and a flute-playing monkey.

The Bronze Age cultures of the Aegean developed into palace-based societies during the second millennium BCE, later than their eastern neighbors, contact with whom may have provided one of the catalysts toward state formation. The civilizations of the Aegean are often characterized in terms of the perceived contrasts between the "peaceful" Minoans of the island of Crete and the "warlike" Mycenaeans in mainland Greece. Such evaluations, of course, oversimplify and caricature both groups, yet the fluid, graceful style of Minoan art and its focus on the natural world strongly suggest that plant and animal imagery was of particular importance to the Minoan worldview. In comparison with Egyptian art, the flora and fauna in Aegean art can appear more lively and naturalistic. Yet the reality is that Egyptian animals are far more accurately observed and represented (so that particular species can be identified), whereas plants and animals in Aegean art can be remarkably hard to pin down and are more impressionistic than they first seem.

Perhaps most striking is the strong focus on imagery of the inhabitants of the sea, such as dolphins, octopus, fish, and triton shells. A defining feature of the painted pottery of the neopalatial period is the Marine Style.[23] The octopus is a favorite image; its tentacles twist and turn across the surface of the vase as if into every nook and cranny, creating an extraordinary sense of unity between the design and the vase form (see Figure 7.3). Large eyes confront the viewer, and the suckers are turned into a continuous frill of dotted circles along the

FIGURE 7.3: Minoan vase decorated with an octopus, from Palaikastro, Crete, ca. 1500 BCE. Location: Archaeological Museum, Heraklion, Crete, Greece. Photo Credit: Scala/Art Resource, NY; ART101664.

inner edges of the tentacles. An appropriate marine environment is created for the octopus by the swirls of seaweed and anemones that artists painted between the tentacles. A far more unusual creature in the Marine Style repertoire is a relative of the octopus, the paper nautilus or argonaut (*Argonauta argo*). The scientific name derives from Greek mythology and means "traveler on the Argo," referring to Jason and the Argonauts. This association arose from the mistaken idea that the nautilus used its arms to propel itself.[24] The earliest known representations of the creature are found in Minoan art, where it is shown with several tentacles curling upward from the shell.[25] The representations must show a female nautilus since only the female has a shell, specifically built as an egg case to protect the eggs. It is unclear whether the Minoans were aware of this, though it is somewhat tempting to infer a symbolic significance associated with fecundity and new life for the argonaut motif. Since the nautilus lives only in the deep open sea and is rarely seen, Minoan knowledge of its form must surely have come from seeing it on the water's surface while on long-distance sailing expeditions. The Marine Style is associated with a relatively narrow range of vase shapes relating primarily to the manipulation of liquids, and it has been suggested that these vases were used primarily in ritual contexts. Sea creatures continue to appear on pottery and in other media, though over time the images became ever more stylized so that the once swirling tentacles are regimented into neat sinuous rows.

A well-known fresco from the palace of Knossos depicts graceful dolphins swimming in a watery environment with smaller fish and seaweed. Although visitors to the palace today see the dolphin fresco on the wall of the so-called "Queen's megaron," it is more likely that the fresco in fact belongs on the floor of a room above, thus creating the unusual experience of walking on the world of the sea. The degree and range of interest in marine imagery in Minoan art is remarkable and cannot be explained simply as a product of an island society, since other Mediterranean islands did not generate such distinctive and pervasive marine imagery. While the significance of marine iconography was surely complex and polyvalent, it is likely that the importance of marine images and objects (such as shells) in ritual contexts was a significant factor in the popularity of these motifs.

Fresco paintings are a rich source of animal imagery in the Aegean, and those from the island of Thera are exceptionally well preserved as a result of a volcanic eruption that buried the town of Akrotiri during the early part of the late Bronze Age. The fresco of the Boxing Boys and the Antelopes from building B1 offers a good example of animal symbolism in the Aegean.[26] The whole room is "wallpapered" with fresco; in one tall narrow panel, two young boys, perhaps seven to eight years of age, are engaged in a bout of boxing. Their high status is indicated by their jewelry, their age by their distinctive hair-locks on an otherwise shaved head and by their bodily form—the relatively large heads and rounded bellies characteristic of children. The rest of the room is covered by antelopes, including a pair located directly adjacent to the boys. The animals are painted directly onto a plain white background (typical of Theran frescoes) using simple, calligraphic outline. One single flowing line draws the eye all the way along the backs of the animals and through the arched tails, while the softness of the underbelly and of the mouth area is rendered by shading. An intriguing feature of the antelopes is that they were certainly not indigenous to the Aegean and that the depictions seem to combine visual features of an African antelope with the Cretan *agrimi* (wild goat). This "hybridity" could be due to unfamiliarity with the African animal, yet the same apparent disregard for accuracy is found in other Aegean depictions of animals and plants, suggesting that reproducing reality was not a priority.

When the fresco was first discovered, it was suggested that the pair of antelopes was engaged in a courting ritual, and there seemed therefore to be no thematic connection with the boxing boys. However, more careful attention to the postures of the antelopes has shown without doubt that these are two male antelopes engaged in ritualized aggressive display.[27] The artist has communicated this through the raised tails and the way that the antelopes sidestep each other and lock glances. Thus, the behavior of the antelopes parallels that of the boxers: They are a pair, they are young males, and they engage in combat. In other words, the parallels between animal and human behavior are clearly recognized, and the animal world is drawn on to mirror and emphasize the ritualized combat of the humans.

Although exotic animals play a much smaller role in Aegean art than in Egyptian art, an exotic and interesting animal visitor in Aegean imagery is the monkey, which very likely came (whether in physical reality or only in iconography) from North Africa. An early example (ca. 2500 BCE or later) of the monkey is a knob-shaped seal from the Trapeza cave.[28] Here the simian sits upright supported by its own curving tail. In later imagery from frescoes, the monkeys appear in more complex scenes that suggest the significance of this exotic creature within an Aegean frame of reference. A fragmentary fresco from Knossos shows monkeys wearing harnesses amid a setting of saffron crocuses growing in containers. The link between the monkeys and the crocus is more fully expressed in a much more elaborate fresco from building Xeste 3 on Thera.[29] Extending over the walls of two separate stories, the fresco shows young women gathering crocuses for their saffron, most likely in relation to a female rite of passage to womanhood. On the upper story, the saffron stamens have been collected and are brought to a seated female who is flanked by two creatures, a griffin with raised wings standing behind her, and in front of her a monkey who offers her the saffron stamens. The presence of the griffin, as well as other iconographic markers (such as the tripartite platform on which she sits), indicate that she is a goddess. Of particular interest is the way that the monkey functions as intermediary between the goddess and the humans who offer the saffron. The two animals, the monkey and griffin, together act as liminal markers, defining and separating the goddess from the human world of the saffron gatherers. The important symbolic link between the goddess and the world of both plants and animals is also more subtly expressed through aquatic imagery.[30] She wears several splendid necklaces, one of ducks and one of dragonflies.[31] Both these creatures are depicted in their natural environment on the adjacent wall where ducks nest amidst reeds, and one even brings a dragonfly to feed the young ducklings, perhaps evoking ideas of nurturing and new life.

Ever present in Minoan art is the image of the bull. Like the lion the bull is a widespread symbol of strength across the Mediterranean, often in relation to royal or divine power. In art, bulls and lions attack and defeat their animal prey, but they in turn are defeated in combat by human beings whether in lion hunts or more ritualized contests such as bull-leaping. Bulls appear throughout Aegean art but they do seem to have especially strong symbolic associations with the palace of Knossos.[32] A series of fresco panels show bull-leaping (discussed in other chapters in this volume), while a charging bull (perhaps also part of a bull-leaping contest), rendered in the rarer technique of relief fresco, met the Bronze Age visitor to Knossos at the impressive north entrance passage[33] (see Figure 7.4). The excavator, Sir Arthur Evans, describes this relief bull as "one of the noblest revelations of Minoan art" and notes the way the artist has expressed the power and vitality of the creature, "the upstanding ear marks intense excitement; the tongue protrudes, the hot breath seems to blow through the nostrils. The folds of the dewlap show that the head was in a lowered position—it is that of a bull coursing wildly."[34] The Minoans were highly skilled in carving vessels from various types of stone, among them vases in the form of animal heads. A very fine example is a bull's head vase from Knossos; it is carved from a relatively soft greenish-black stone called steatite, with inlays in other semiprecious materials: rock crystal and red jasper for the eyes and shell for the area around the nostrils. The horns (now reconstructed) were probably made from gilded wood.

FIGURE 7.4: Charging bull from the north entrance passage at Knossos. Photo Credit: Dr. Alan Peatfield.

The Minoans, like many societies, practiced animal sacrifice, and the artistic evidence draws our attention again to the bull as a prime gift for the gods. This appears most clearly on a late Bronze Age limestone sarcophagus from Ayia Triadha in south-central Crete. The sarcophagus is painted in polychrome fresco technique, and it shows scenes of offering and animal sacrifice.[35] On one of the long sides, the bull takes center stage, tightly trussed up on a low table under which lie two goats (perhaps also awaiting sacrifice). The bull's head is turned outward to face the viewer. In an artistic tradition that favors the profile view for both people and animals, this is striking, and is probably intended to signal the death of the animal in the same way as the frontal bull's head or bucranium in scenes on seal-stones. Indeed, the bucranium, as both head and skull, has remained a familiar image through Greek and Roman times and into Neoclassical art where it often appears with garlands as part of a decorative relief frieze, its original link with death and sacrifice largely forgotten.

But bulls are pervasive not only in Minoan art; they are also a strong presence in Greek myths connected with the island of Crete. Or, as Roberto Calasso so succinctly puts it, "In any Cretan story, there's a bull at the beginning and a bull at the end."[36] Europa, a Phoenician princess, is carried off to Crete on the back of a white bull (Zeus in disguise), and the most famous Cretan bull, the bull-man Minotaur, is born as a result of the unnatural passion of Pasiphae, wife of King Minos, for a bull. The monstrous man-eating Minotaur, imprisoned in the labyrinth at Knossos, is finally slain by the Athenian hero Theseus. A visual bridge between the later myth and Bronze Age art appears in an Aegean-style fresco found at the site of Avaris (modern Tel el-Dab'a) in the Nile Delta. A scene of bull-leaping (strongly associated with Knossos, as noted earlier) shows a leaper vaulting over the bull. The background of the scene is a maze pattern, and it is hard to resist linking the maze with Knossos and the later story of the labyrinth.

The Mycenaean culture of the Greek mainland adopted many themes and techniques from the arts of their Minoan neighbors, but their imagery shows a distinctive interest in warfare and hunting. Thus, in the Shaft Graves of Mycenae, a number of different objects, such as an inlaid dagger and gold rings, depict humans fighting lions. Confronted lions also appear on the famous "Lion Gate" at Mycenae.[37] The lions are carved in relief from limestone, though their separately attached heads (now missing) were most likely made from another material, and they mask the relieving triangle above the massive lintel stone of the entrance to the citadel. Unique to Mycenae, the Lion Gate may depict the special symbolic protectors of the citadel.

Mycenaean palaces were also adorned with frescoes, and again war and hunting are constant themes. From Tiryns in the Argolid comes a fine scene of a boar hunt. Ladies riding in chariots drawn by horses with their manes tied up in proud plumes accompany the hunters, who have trapped their quarry in a stand of marshy reeds, and then attack with nets and spears. Assisting the hunters are the lean hunting dogs, dappled unrealistically in shades of pink and blue. Alongside the lion and the bull, the boar was a formidable and dangerous opponent; once angered a boar will attack relentlessly with its sharp tusks. The Mycenaeans made these white tusks into boars' tusk helmets. Given that it took some thirty to forty tusks to construct a single helmet, this represented a very visible display of hunting prowess, and perhaps also indicated that the hunter had appropriated the power of the defeated animals.[38]

With the collapse of the Bronze Age civilizations of the Mediterranean came a hiatus in artistic production in many areas. The Greek world, in particular, entered a dark age in which imagery of any kind was rare. The development of Greek art after this time is synonymous with the birth of Western art in which the human figure takes center stage, as a glance through any book on Greek art will attest. Yet animals continue to play important and richly symbolic roles in the imagery of the classical world. A particularly rich source of animal imagery is the poetry of Homer, based on older oral traditions but taking a written form by the late eighth century BCE. In the *Iliad* the poet uses animal similes repeatedly to evoke the physical and emotional world of the battling Greeks and Trojans. Much of the imagery takes predatory animals such as the lion or boar as parallels for the power of the heroes on the battlefield. Hector and Ajax, for example, fight with the ferocity of lions against boars. Elsewhere, the imagery is of predator and prey, victor and victim: Greek heroes are likened to the lion while the Trojans become a helpless flock of sheep or young deer. The lone hero is like the fierce but unyielding boar trapped in the thicket, reminding us of the boar-hunting scene from the Mycenaean palace of Tiryns discussed earlier:

> As when closing about a wild boar the hounds and the lusty young men rush him, and he comes out of his lair in the deep of a thicket grinding to an edge the white fangs in the crook of the jawbones, and these sweep in all about him, and the vaunt of his teeth uprises as they await him, terrible though he is, without wavering; so closing on Odysseus beloved of Zeus the Trojans rushed him. (*Iliad* 9, 413–420)

The protective and nurturing instincts of animals are also called on, as when heroes stand over the dead bodies of their comrades in the same fiercely protective way as a lion guards her cubs or a mother cow her young calf. Finally, a complex and evocative set of animal metaphors is brought into play when Achilles refuses Hector's request for a truce over their dead bodies (*Iliad* 22, 260–267). He argues that men do not swear oaths to lions (Hector being the wounded lion), and that wolves do not make treaties with lambs.

A key area for the emergence of pictorial art is Athens in the eighth century BCE, and of the animal world, horses are the first to appear in the geometric style of the time. Painted in angular silhouette and sometimes with trumpet-shaped noses, they pull chariots in funeral processions and bring warriors to battle. Horses are frequent, too, as bronze offerings at the major sanctuaries, both as stand-alone figurines and as attachments on the handles of impressive bronze tripod cauldrons. Horses, then as now, signaled status and wealth, because of the resources needed to graze these beasts in a marginal Mediterranean climate.

New and exotic animals begin to appear in numbers with the influx of Near Eastern ideas in the succeeding seventh century. Artists in Corinth warmed quickly to these "orientalizing" ideas, and animals of all kinds, some exotic, others not, are the main decoration on Protocorinthian pottery. Lion, boars, and bulls pace, while deer and goats lower their heads to graze, but predator and prey have all become decorative elements separated by dotted rosettes. Over time the rosettes get bigger and more intrusive, and the animal bodies become strangely elongated as the painters seek to fill the friezes with less effort and fewer animals. The Macmillan *aryballos* (perfumed oil container) in the British Museum both depicts animals and "is" an animal. The painted friezes, with details picked out through incision and added color, show hoplite warfare and scenes of the hunt with horse-riders, dogs, and hares, but it is the upper part of the vase, modeled in the shape of a lion's head, that really catches the eye. The lion's jaws are open showing his sharp teeth, and the lion imagery resonates with the themes of war and hunting below. However, this is male warrior ideology in a tiny, perfumed package, since the entire vase stands only 7 centimeters high, and the perfumed oil would have emerged spectacularly over the lion's red lolling tongue!

Fantastic creatures such as sphinxes and griffins are newly discovered through contacts with the East. Knowledge of them seems to be lost (at least in the visual arts) by the end of the Bronze Age. But early Greek art is also replete with all manner of other monsters, either hybrid animals or hybrid human-animals, whose primary task is to confront and be defeated by the heroes of Greek myth. Whereas in Egyptian thought and art, hybridity was a mark of the power of the divine, hybridity in the Greek world is largely presented as negative or ambivalent. The addition of animal features to a primarily anthropomorphic figure served to express its inherent monstrosity. Thus, Medusa, the Gorgon with the ability to turn men to stone, can appear as a female figure, but with wings, huge fangs, and the famous snake-infested hair. It is easy from a modern perspective to see the snake as a purely negative feature, and snake characteristics are indeed a feature of numerous monsters in Greek mythology, the Hydra, Echidna, and Pytho, to name but a few. But in different company, snakes could also carry other connotations. The goddess Athena wears a protective aegis (breastplate) fringed with snakes, and a snake lived on the Acropolis as part of her cult. In art the gold and ivory (chryselephantine) statue of Athena that dominated the interior of the fifth-century BCE Parthenon included a huge snake, coiled comfortably in the interior of Athena's domed hoplite shield. While the Greeks, on the whole, envisaged their gods and goddesses in anthropomorphic form, many of their deities were strongly linked to specific animals, so the snake is also closely associated with the healing cult of Asclepius. Statues of the god often show the snake wrapped around his staff (an image used in modern medicine, for example, in the logo of the World Health Organization), and relief sculptures dedicated by grateful worshippers sometimes showed the snake visiting the patient sleeping in the god's sanctuary in the hope of a cure.

Birds, too, had particular divine associations. Athenian coinage showed the owl of their patron deity Athena, the gentle dove was associated with Aphrodite, the peacock with Hera, and the fierce eagle with Zeus, king of the gods. Special relationships between deities and animals extend also into sacrificial practices. Demeter was held to favor pigs on her altars, and this is reflected in the offerings of pig figurines in her sanctuaries. A deity with intense links to animals is Artemis, so it is appropriate to look at her animal world in a little more detail. A very old title associated with Artemis is "*Potnia Theron*," or Mistress of the Animals, and in this guise she is depicted either flanked by wild animals or grasping them. She appears as *Potnia Theron* on the handles of an early sixth-century BCE crater known as the François Vase; here the goddess is winged, and in one hand she grasps a great-antlered stag, while in the other a panther is lifted by its neck and seems to swing helplessly above the ground-line at her side (see Figure 7.5). Artemis is a huntress, and her delight in the hunt is vividly expressed in the opening lines of the Homeric Hymn to Artemis: "I sing of Artemis of the golden arrows, chaste virgin of the noisy hunt, who delights in her shafts and strikes down the stag." But Artemis was also a protector of wild animals, and the dual role is neatly captured in an artistic image, a Roman marble statue (a copy of classical Greek bronze work) where she protectively grasps a leaping stag by the head, but with the other hand has reached up to take an arrow from her quiver.[39] Her protective role also extended to young people, since boys and girls were thought of by the Greeks as belonging to the wild and needing to be "tamed" or brought into a civilized adult state through reaching adulthood and taking on adult roles. As protector of the young she appears embracing children and animals, and thus takes on the role of a *kourotrophos* (nurturer) despite her own virginal state. The goddess who protects can also destroy, and the myth of Aktaeon is a good example of animal metamorphosis. In the story, Aktaeon, a hunter, comes upon the goddess bathing, and as a punishment she turns him into a stag (so that the hunter becomes the hunted) and his own hunting dogs turn upon him.[40]

The bear is especially associated with Artemis, and this may relate in part to her nurturing role since bears are highly protective toward their young, and the Greeks even thought that the bear cub was born unformed and licked into shape by the mother. This is, of course, not true, but bears are exceptionally helpless when born and parallels with human babies and their care can be

FIGURE 7.5: Detail from *François Vase: Diana and Ajax with the corpse of Achilles*. Ergotimos (6th century BCE, potter) and Kleitias (575–560 BCE, vase painter). Location: Museo Archeologico, Florence, Italy. Photo Credit: Scala/Art Resource, NY; ART41340.

readily made. In the cult of Artemis at Brauron in eastern Attica, young girls took part in rituals in which they are said to be "little bears" (*arktoi*); ancient sources offer various explanations for the rituals, but they all revolve around a story in which the goddess is propitiated through these rituals after a bear is treated badly or killed by humans.[41]

The bear is a central character in another myth involving Artemis. A young woman, Callisto, is a follower of Artemis, but is pursued by Zeus and becomes pregnant. The poor girl is first expelled from Artemis' followers and then, after the birth of her child Arkas, is transformed into a bear by a furious Hera (in one of her many acts of revenge for Zeus' endless infidelities). Like the Aktaeon story, metamorphosis into an animal is the punishment. In this case we have a moving description of Callisto's transformation and subsequent state of mind from Ovid:

> Callisto spread her arms in suppliant prayer; her arms began to bristle with black hair, her hands to be bent with fingers turning to curved claws; she use her hands as feet, and the face that once delighted Jupiter grew ugly with grinning jaws. Her power of speech was lost, with no prayer or entreaties could she win pity, and a hoarse and frightening growl was her only utterance. Yet Callisto's human mind remained even when she had become a bear; with never-ceasing moans she made known her suffering; ... How often was she pursued over the rocky hill by the baying hounds; how often did the huntress run in fear from the hunters! Often she hid herself (forgetting what she was—and though a bear, shrank from the sight of bears. (*Metamorphoses* 2, 477–500)

Like the earlier myth of Aktaeon, Callisto's sad story (though she is eventually released from her suffering and turned into a constellation by Zeus) reveals divine punishment as one important aspect of animal metamorphosis. But while such bodily changes (together with hybridity) are expressive of how the breaking down of boundaries between human and animal can threaten identity and the very idea of what it is to be human, metamorphosis in other myths can act as a reprieve or release, and in the case of the gods is a power they can call on at will. Thus Zeus becomes a bull to transport Europa to Crete, or as an eagle he brings the Trojan prince Ganymede up to Olympus as his cupbearer.

Mutability of the animal–human boundary is also expressed by the melding of the two into composite creatures that share a horsey nature, centaurs and satyrs. The satyr takes mainly human form but with the important additions of the ears and tail of a horse (though in later Hellenistic and Roman times the satyr can be more goatlike); he belongs to the convivial world of Dionysus and is thus highly visible on painted pottery destined for use in the symposium (aristocratic drinking party). The animal elements serve to underline the satyr's lack of self-control and moderation, as does his partaking of undiluted wine and his constant state of sexual readiness, and this overall package served as a "cautionary model of antisocial irresponsibility."[42] The man-horse mixture of the centaur is more complex. In the earliest examples a fully human body is conjoined at the buttocks with the body and rear legs of a horse, though later all four legs become equine. The first clear example of a centaur in Greece comes from Lefkandi in Euboia, and is a tenth-century BCE terracotta figurine standing some 36 centimeters tall.[43] An intentional gash on the left foreleg suggests that it represents a particular centaur, Chiron, who was wounded by an arrow of Herakles. Chiron is the "wise centaur" who behaves against the centaur norm; he schools heroes such as Achilles and Jason and trains Asclepius in the healing arts. In keeping with his special status, he is distinguished iconographically from other centaurs in classical art by his human forelegs and by the added dignity of a tunic or cloak.[44] The generality of centaurs, though, are troublesome creatures, and the battle of the Greek Lapiths against the centaurs is a stock theme in Greek temple art, being one of a number of ways of expressing the idea of Greek civilized, socially ordered behavior in contrast to the barbaric and disorderly world of the "other."

As stressed earlier, the human form is the central preoccupation of Greek art, but this in no way means that animals were not sensitively observed and depicted. This is well illustrated by the sculptures of the Parthenon, built in the mid-fifth century BCE while the Athenians were at the height of their powers. Ancient viewers would have looked up through the colonnade and glimpsed sections of a continuous frieze carved in low relief high on the exterior wall of the temple chamber. The frieze shows the procession of the Panathenaic festival, and almost half of it is taken up with a cavalcade of mounted horsemen. The procession is full of movement and excitement as the horsemen rein in their eager mounts; these rear up, creating in places a veritable forest of overlapping legs as the cavalcade moves, sometimes four deep, along the north and south sides of the frieze.[45] Quieter moments occur near the less crowded beginning of the procession where the horses wait (some patiently) to be mounted, but others rear up majestically revealing the delicately carved veining and musculature of their bellies.[46] Other animals, woolly sheep and sleek cattle, are nearer the front of the procession; they await sacrifice in honor of the goddess Athena. Most are quite docile, but one or two of the cattle buck quite violently, and one raises its head as if to protest.[47] This memorable image is believed to have been the inspiration for the imagery in Keats's poem "Ode on a Grecian Urn": "Who are these coming to the sacrifice? To what green altar, O mysterious priest, Lead'st thou that heifer lowing at the skies, And all her silken flanks with garlands drest?" Horses also appear on both pediments of the Parthenon. Confronted chariot groups frame the contest of Athena and Poseidon for possession of Athens on the west side. The horses in the corners of the east pediment belong to the chariots of Helios (Sun) and Selene (Moon), and they cleverly represent the cosmic passage of the particular day made unique by the birth of Athena at the center of the image. Selene's horses have completed their nightly journey, and one preserved head with its bulging eyes, pressed-back ears, and open mouth instantly conveys the noble animal's utter exhaustion.

Some of the most stunning depictions of animals in Roman art are in scenes from the games and spectacles held in the Roman amphitheaters, where wild and exotic animals were either displayed or died in combat, animal pitted against either human or animal. Since this topic is treated in detail in chapter 4, the focus here is on other contexts. Quintessentially Roman is the image of the she-wolf suckling the twins Romulus and Remus, since this image takes us to the story of the very foundation of Rome. The image was well known from coins (see Figure 7.6), and it continued to be so iconic of Rome that it appeared on the poster for the 1960 Olympic games held there. A larger than life-size bronze wolf of Etruscan manufacture (ca. 500 BCE), known as the Capitoline Wolf, is usually associated with this myth, although the chubby babes about to suckle at the wolf's teats are, in fact, a later Renaissance addition to the statue group. The wolf's milk-filled teats contrast with the lean body with its protruding ribs, and the fur at the neck and shoulders is presented as a pleasing, though unrealistic, pattern of regular curls. The bared teeth and the tense posture both suggest the fierce nature of the wolf.

The affection in which many Romans held their pets is well documented in art, literature, and inscriptions, and Toynbee notes that "love for canine pets in particular was one of the most attractive features of the ancient Roman character."[48] Dogs had practical uses in hunting and as guards, the latter function delightfully recorded through the chained dog in the "cave canem" (beware of the dog) mosaic from Pompeii (see Figure 7.7). In addition, many pet dogs were clearly cosseted by doting owners, so that we find epitaphs and tombstones for these much-missed companions. Dogs also appear with their reclining owners in funerary art. On a funerary relief from Rome, Ulpia Epigone, a stylish Flavian lady, half-nude in the style of a Venus statue, has a lapdog peeping out from under her left armpit.[49] Dogs also appear, sometimes playful, sometimes curled up quietly, beside children on funerary couches and sarcophagi.[50] The imagery may operate at several levels. There is no reason to doubt that some images

FIGURE 7.6: Coin showing she-wolf suckling Romulus and Remus. Credit: Department of Classics, Trinity College Dublin.

FIGURE 7.7: *Cave canem*. Pompeiian mosaic. Location: House of the Tragic Poet, Pompeii, Italy. Photo Credit: Scala/Art Resource, NY; ART180958.

portray treasured pets, but these canine companions may also be more general symbols of fidelity (a concept that is found also in later Western art) or perhaps even, through connections with deities of the underworld and of healing, evoke ideas of death and rebirth.[51]

Birds and fish were also popular pets. Fish were displayed in ponds and aquaria, and eels (*murena*) were a special favorite. While the literary sources may sometimes exaggerate and satirize, they do give us vivid vignettes of fish-loving Romans. Thus, they regale us with stories of eels that responded to their owners' voices, their fins adorned with earrings, and owners grieving over deceased fish as if they had lost a family member.[52] In art the numerous mosaics depicting the rich harvest of the sea may reflect both the contents of the fishponds of the wealthy, and the gourmet consumption of marine life at the tables of the Roman elite. A mosaic panel from Pompeii shows a vivid scene of marine life with fine detail and subtle gradations of color (made possible by the use of tiny mosaic tiles that create an effect closer to painting). Form and coloring are so acutely observed that it is possible to distinguish more than twenty edible species, including bass, mullet, dogfish, and squid. The dramatic focus of the piece is a deadly fight between an octopus and a lobster that are intertwined in combat while an eel swims toward them. Marine imagery was suitable for a range of contexts. The edible species in the panel discussed above would have made a delightful centerpiece in a Roman dining room, but fishy scenes were also highly appropriate around ornamental fountains, pools, and bathhouses. Floor decorations in bath complexes might include a "marine thiasos," an underwater parade of Neptune, god of the sea, together with the other denizens of the sea. An example in the black-and-white style from Ostia shows the typical swirling movement of these scenes. Neptune rides across the center, pulled by his sea-horses (with horsey foreparts and long serpentine tails), while around him swim other sea creatures, including cupids riding dolphins.

Birds, like fish, were kept both as a source of food and as valued pets. For example, Pliny extols the musical skills of the nightingale and relates that such birds could fetch extremely high prices, sometimes costing as much as a slave. A more exotic bird, the peacock, also fetched exorbitant prices. It was, of course, much admired for its jewel-colored tail. According to myth Juno created the tail of her favorite bird by placing the hundred eyes of Argus on it. In one of Aesop's fables the peacock complains that the song of the nightingale pleases the ear but that he has an ugly voice, and Juno cheers him up by saying, "But you far excel in beauty and in size. The splendor of the emerald shines in your neck and you unfold a tail gorgeous with painted plumage" (*Fables*, 211). A painted peacock perches in the foreground on a fresco from a villa at Oplontis in the bay of Naples, dating to the first century CE. Its gorgeous tail trails down over a ledge, contributing to the illusion of an image that looks onto distant space. Peacocks appear frequently in Roman funerary art as a symbol of immortality, and a similar meaning was carried into early Christian art where the peacock symbolized everlasting life.[53]

By virtue of their special link to Juno, peacocks are shown on a variety of Roman imperial coins. The iconography on coins was an important vehicle for communicating Roman power and ideology since coins were widely distributed throughout the Roman world, and animals are a highly visible part of these images of power. The peacock, the eagle, and the owl together represent the Capitoline triad of gods (Jupiter, Juno, and Minerva) on coins from Hadrian's reign. A succession of imperial wives and daughters associated themselves with Juno (queen of heaven) through peacock imagery, and on yet other coins the peacock symbolized the deification of imperial ladies such as Faustina, Julia Domna, and Paulina through the association of the spread tail with the vault of the starry heavens. The parallel elevation of the emperor to the heavens was associated with the ultimate imperial image, the eagle. On coinage, an iconic

Egyptian creature, the crocodile, was chosen to mark Augustus' defeat of Antony and Cleopatra and the conquest of Egypt. On some coins the crocodile is shown alone with the words "Aegypto capta" (Egypt captured); on others it is chained to a palm tree. Another foreign animal, the elephant, appears on coins in a military context. Members of a particular noble Roman family, the gens Caecilia, adopted the elephant as their family emblem after Lucius Caecilius Metellus won a battle against the Carthaginians using elephants in 250 BCE. An elephant trampling a serpent appears on a coin issued by Julius Caesar, and the imagery is thought to represent good triumphing over evil in reference to Caesar's defeat of Pompey at Pharsalus.[54]

The mythological figure of Orpheus brings the world of animals together in a harmonious composition. Images of this magical singer charming the animals and birds through his music are particularly well represented on mosaic floors, though the theme is also to be found in sculpture, gems, and pottery (see Figure 4.7 in chapter 4). Only the depiction of the Roman games (quite different in tone) offered the artist comparable scope for bringing together such a rich and varied collection of animals, giving the theme an obvious decorative appeal. Moreover, the main theme of the creation of an idyllic and harmonious world expressed through Orpheus' pacification of wild creatures would have brought an appropriate sense of calm to contexts where the imagery accompanied a pond or fountain,[55] as well as evoking from the viewer a sense of bodily enchantment through sight and sound. On a mosaic from Paphos in Cyprus a seated Orpheus is surrounded by animals; some sit quietly at his feet, others stop in midstep to gaze back at him, their turned heads and raised paws indicating their rapt attention.[56] The mosaic is made mainly from local stones, but more expensive glass is used to pick out the eyes of the animals, the birds' wings, and Orpheus' tunic. Other, more formal arrangements show Orpheus in a central panel with the animals arranged in panels around him, while two examples from Roman Britain show the musician and animals within a series of concentric circles.[57] The theme of Orpheus and the animals continues to be popular in the later Roman and early Byzantine period, and debate continues over whether specific images should be read as largely decorative or whether they carry Christian connotations.[58] Clear examples of Orpheus morphing into the Christian "Good Shepherd" come from Ostia and Rome in catacomb paintings and sarcophagi, that is, from explicitly funerary contexts. The significant change in some of these early examples is that fewer animals are shown, and there is a focus on sheep, thus emphasizing the shift in meaning. Elsewhere, Orpheus retains his wilder range of beasts, and it is rather harder to be sure whether the imagery was intended to have specifically Christian connotations. But in both cases the gentle imagery of Orpheus and the beasts represents a world of animals in ancient art in which humans are very much in control, and the animals are idyllically at peace with one another.

NOTES

Introduction

1. Linda Kalof, *Looking at Animals in Human History* (London: Reaktion Books, 2007). This essay is an expanded and revised version of selected material from chapters 1, 2, and 3 of *Looking at Animals*.
2. Jean Clottes, *Chauvet Cave: The Art of Earliest Times*, trans. Paul G. Bahn (Salt Lake City: University of Utah Press, 2003).
3. James Serpell, *In the Company of Animals: A Study of Human-Animal Relationships* (Oxford: Basil Blackwell, 1986).
4. Juliet Clutton-Brock, *A Natural History of Domesticated Mammals* (New York: Cambridge University Press, 1999).
5. Calvin W. Schwabe, "Animals in the Ancient World," in *Animals and Human Society: Changing Perspectives*, ed. Aubrey Manning and James Serpell (London: Routledge, 1994), pp. 36–58.
6. Paul Collins, "A Goat Fit for a King," *ART News* 102, no. 7 (2003): 106, 108.
7. Schwabe, "Ancient World," pp. 37–38.
8. Schwabe, "Ancient World," pp. 40–41.
9. Schwabe, "Ancient World," p. 53.
10. Schwabe, "Ancient World," p. 53.
11. Patrick F. Houlihan, *The Animal World of the Pharaohs* (London: Thames and Hudson, 1996).
12. Francis Klingender, *Animals in Art and Thought to the End of the Middle Ages*, ed. Evelyn Antal and John Harthan (Cambridge: MIT Press, 1971).
13. Donald P. Hansen, "Art of the Royal Tombs of Ur: A Brief Interpretation," in *Treasures from the Royal Tombs of Ur*, ed. Richard L. Zettler and Lee Horne (Philadelphia: University of Pennsylvania Museum, 1998), pp. 43–59.
14. Hansen, "Art of the Royal Tombs," pp. 45–46.
15. Collins, "Goat," p. 108; Hansen, "Art of the Royal Tombs," p. 62.
16. Hansen, "Art of the Royal Tombs," pp. 49, 62. On the tree-climbing behavior of goats, see J. Donald Hughes, *Pan's Travail: Environmental Problems of the Ancient Greeks and Romans* (Baltimore: Johns Hopkins University Press, 1994), p. 31.

17. Clutton-Brock, *Domesticated Mammals*, p. 126.

18. Schwabe, "Ancient World," p. 40.

19. Hughes, *Pan's Travail*, p. 135.

20. Clutton-Brock, *Domesticated Mammals*, pp. 108–113.

21. Plinio Prioreschi, *Roman Medicine* (Omaha, NE: Horatius Press, 2003).

22. L. T. Yablonsky, "Burial Place of a Massagetan Warrior," *Antiquity* 64 (1990): 288–296.

23. Clutton-Brock, *Domesticated Mammals*, p. 40.

24. Clutton-Brock, *Domesticated Mammals*, p. 60.

25. Dorothy Phillips, *Ancient Egyptian Animals* (New York: Metropolitan Museum of Art Picture Books, 1948).

26. Katharine M. Rogers, *The Cat and the Human Imagination: Feline Images from Bast to Garfield* (Ann Arbor: University of Michigan Press, 1998).

27. Clutton-Brock, *Domesticated Mammals*, p. 138.

28. Bob Brier, "Case of the Dummy Mummy," *Archaeology* 54 (2001): 28–29.

29. Howard Hayes Scullard, *The Elephant in the Greek and Roman World* (Ithaca: Cornell University Press, 1974).

30. Clutton-Brock, *Domesticated Mammals*, 149.

31. J.M.C. Toynbee, *Animals in Roman Life and Art* (London: Camelot Press, 1973).

32. David Matz, *Daily Life of the Ancient Romans* (Westport, CT: Greenwood Press, 2002).

33. Houlihan, *Animal World*, pp. 42–43.

34. John Kinloch Anderson, *Hunting in the Ancient World* (Berkeley: University of California Press, 1985).

35. Christine E. Morris, "In Pursuit of the White Tusked Boar: Aspects of Hunting in Mycenaean Society," in *Celebrations of Death and Divinity in the Bronze Age Argolid*, ed. Robin Hagg and Gullog C. Nordquist (Stockholm: Paul Astroms Forlag, 1990), pp. 151–156.

36. Ephraim David, "Hunting in Spartan Society and Consciousness," *Echos du Monde Classique/Classical Views* 37 (1993): 393–413.

37. Judith M. Barringer, *The Hunt in Ancient Greece* (Baltimore: Johns Hopkins University Press, 2001).

38. Xenophon, "On Hunting," trans. H. G. Dakyns, http://www.gutenberg.org/dirs/etext98/sport10.txt (accessed April 2005).

39. Thomas Veltre, "Menageries, Metaphors, and Meanings," in *New Worlds, New Animals: From Menagerie to Zoological Park in the Nineteenth Century*, ed. R. J. Hoage and William A. Deiss (Baltimore: Johns Hopkins University Press, 1996), pp. 19–29.

40. Varro, cited in Anderson, *Hunting*, p. 86.

41. Toynbee, *Animals in Roman Life*, p. 20.

42. Keith Hopkins, *Death and Renewal: Sociological Studies in Roman History* (New York: Cambridge University Press, 1983).

43. Hopkins, *Death and Renewal*, pp. 15–16.

44. Paul Veyne, *Bread and Circuses: Historical Sociology and Political Pluralism*, trans. Brian Pearce (London: Penguin Press, 1990).

45. Veyne, *Bread and Circuses*, pp. 400–401.

46. K. M. Coleman, "Fatal Charades: Roman Executions Staged as Mythological Enactments," *Journal of Roman Studies* 80 (1990): 44–73.

47. Alison Futrell, *Blood in the Arena: The Spectacle of Roman Power* (Austin: University of Texas Press, 1997).

48. Shelby Brown, "Death as Decoration: Scenes from the Arena on Roman Domestic Mosaics," in *Pornography and Representation in Greece and Rome*, ed. Amy Richlin (New York: Oxford University Press, 1992), pp. 180–211.

49. Thomas Wiedemann, *Emperors and Gladiators* (London and New York: Routledge, 1992).

50. George Jennison, *Animals for Show and Pleasure in Ancient Rome* (Manchester: Manchester University Press, 1937).

51. David L. Bomgardner, "The Trade in Wild Beasts for Roman Spectacles: A Green Perspective," *Anthropozoologica* 16 (1992): 161–166.

52. Futrell, *Blood in the Arena*, pp. 24–26.

53. Futrell, *Blood in the Arena*, pp. 24–26.

54. Jo-Ann Shelton, "Dancing and Dying: The Display of Elephants in Ancient Roman Arenas," in *Daimonopylai: Essays in Classics and the Classical Tradition*, ed. Mark Joyal and Rory B. Egan (Winnipeg: University of Manitoba, Centre for Hellenic Civilization, 2004), p. 367.

55. Donald G. Kyle, *Spectacles of Death in Ancient Rome* (New York: Routledge, 1998).

56. J.M.C. Toynbee is the authority on the Latin and Greek works that reference animals in Roman life. The major literary sources are Varro, Columella, Pliny the Elder, Martial, Plutarch, Arrian, Oppian, and Aelian (see Toynbee, *Animals in Roman Life*, p. 23).

57. William M. Johnson, *The Rose-Tinted Menagerie: A History of Animals in Entertainment, from Ancient Rome to the Twentieth Century* (London: Heretic Books, 1990).

58. Kyle, *Spectacles of Death*, p. 19.

59. Claudian, "De consulate stilichonis," book Iii, http://penelope.uchicago.edu/Thayer/E/Roman/Texts/Claudian/De_Consulatu_Stilichonis/3*.html.

60. Jennison, *Animals for Show*, pp. 141–149.

61. Jennison, *Animals for Show*, p. 149.

62. Toynbee, *Animals in Roman Life*, p. 19.

63. Jennison, *Animals for Show*, pp. 159–162.

64. Claudian, quoted in Jennison, *Animals for Show*, p. 160. Christian writers often used the unwillingness of animals to attack martyrs in the arena as a sign of the martyr's innocence (see Wiedemann, *Emperors and Gladiators*, p. 89).

65. Roland Auguet, *Cruelty and Civilization: The Roman Games* (New York: Routledge, 1972).

66. Dio Cassius, "Roman History," book Xxxix (39), http://penelope.uchicago.edu/Thayer/E/Roman/Texts/Cassius_Dio/39*.html.

67. Hopkins, *Death and Renewal*, p. 28.

68. Hopkins, *Death and Renewal*, p. 29. On the use of public punishment as a strategy of social control, see Michel Foucault, *Discipline and Punish* (New York: Vintage, 1977/1995).

69. Brown, "Death as Decoration," p. 181; Coleman, "Fatal Charades," p. 58.

70. Coleman, "Fatal Charades," p. 59.

71. Brown, "Death as Decoration," p. 208.

72. Coleman, "Fatal Charades," p. 54.

73. Wiedemann, *Emperors and Gladiators*, p. 56.

74. Futrell, *Blood in the Arena*, p. 15.

75. Nigel Spivey, *Etruscan Art* (London: Thames and Hudson, 1997).

76. Jose M. Galan, "Bullfight Scenes in Ancient Egyptian Tombs," *Journal of Egyptian Archeology* 80 (1994): 81–96.

77. Pliny the Elder, *Natural History: A Selection*, trans. John F. Healy (London: Penguin, 2004).

78. Veltre, "Menageries," p. 19.

79. Veltre, "Menageries," p. 20.

80. Houlihan, *Animal World*, p. 195.

81. Houlihan, *Animal World*, p. 196.

82. Pliny the Elder, *Natural History*, p. 108.

83. Plutarch, "Pyrrhus," http://penelope.uchicago.edu/Thayer/E/Roman/Texts/Plutarch/Lives/Pyrrhus*.html (accessed April 22, 2005).

84. Houlihan, *Animal World*, p. 199.

85. Houlihan, *Animal World*, p. 200.

86. Hughes, *Pan's Travail*, p. 108.

87. Hughes, *Pan's Travail*, p. 108. On Aristotle and dissections, see also Scullard, *Elephant*.

88. R. J. Hoage, Anne Roskell, and Jane Mansour, "Menageries and Zoos to 1900," in *New Worlds, New Animals: From Menagerie to Zoological Park in the Nineteenth Century,* ed. R. J. Hoage and William A. Deiss (Baltimore: Johns Hopkins University Press, 1996), p. 10.

89. Hoage, Roskell, and Mansour, "Menageries and Zoos," p. 10.

90. Paul Plass, *The Game of Death in Ancient Rome* (Madison: University of Wisconsin Press, 1995).

91. Hughes, *Pan's Travail*, p. 109.

92. Michael Lahanas, "Galen," www.mlahanas.de/Greeks/Galen.htm (accessed November 18, 2004).

93. Pliny the Elder, *The Natural History*, Book VIII, *The Nature of the Terrestrial Animal*, ed. John Bostock and H. T. Riley, http://www.perseus.tufts.edu/cgi-bin/ptext?doc=Perseus%3Atext%3A1999.02.0137&query=toc:head%3D%23333 (accessed November 14, 2005).

94. Pliny the Elder, *The Natural History*, Book Ix, *The Natural History of Fishes*, ed. John Bostock and H. T. Riley, http://www.perseus.tufts.edu/cgi-bin/ptext?doc=Perseus%3Atext%3A1999.02.0137&query=toc:head%3D%23418 (accessed November 14, 2005).

95. Pliny the Elder, *Natural History*, p. 129.

96. Johnson, *Rose-Tinted Menagerie*, p. 31.

97. Vernon N. Kisling, Jr., "Ancient Collections and Menageries," in *Zoo and Aquarium History: Ancient Animal Collections to Zoological Gardens*, ed. Vernon N. Kisling, Jr. (Boca Raton: CRC, 2001), pp. 1–47.

98. Joseph Strutt, *The Sports and Pastimes of the People of England*, ed. J. C. Cox (London: Augustus M. Kelley, 1903), pp. 195–197.

99. John F. Healy, "The Life and Character of Pliny the Elder," in Pliny the Elder, *Natural History*, pp. ix–xxxx.

Chapter 1

1. Paul Shepard, *Thinking Animals: Animals and the Development of Human Intelligence* (New York: Viking Press, 1978), p. 2.

2. Shepard, *Thinking Animals*.

3. Shepard, *Thinking Animals*, p. 50.

4. Shepard, *Thinking Animals*.

5. Shepard, *Thinking Animals*, p. 51.

6. Shepard, *Thinking Animals*.

7. Shepard, *Thinking Animals*, pp. 26, 27.

8. Kenneth Clark, *Animals and Men: Their Relationship as Reflected in Western Art from Prehistory to the Present Day* (New York: William Morrow & Co., 1977), p. 14.

9. Clark, *Animals and Men*. See also Shepard, *Thinking Animals*.

10. Francis Klingender, *Animals in Art and Thought to the End of the Middle Ages* (London: Routledge & Kegan Paul, 1971), p. 383.

11. Shepard, *Thinking Animals*, p. 57.

12. Shepard, *Thinking Animals*, p. 59.

13. Shepard, *Thinking Animals*.

14. Joseph D. Clark, *Beastly Folklore* (Metuchen, NJ: Scarecrow Press, 1968), cited in Shepard, *Thinking Animals*, p. 28.

15. Klingender, *Animals in Art and Thought*, p. 84.

16. Klingender, *Animals in Art and Thought*.

17. Margaret Blount, *Animal Land: The Creatures of Children's Fiction* (New York: Willliam Morrow & Co., 1975), p. 15.

18. Joseph Campbell, *Historical Atlas of World Mythology*, vol. 1, *The Way of the Animal Powers*, pt. 1, *Mythologies of the Primitive Hunters and Gatherers* (New York: Harper & Row, 1988), p. 8.

19. Jeremy Poynting, "From Ancestral to Creole: Humans and Animals in a West Indian Scale of Values," in *Monsters, Tricksters, and Sacred Cows: Animal Tales and American Identities*, ed. A. James Arnold (Charlottesville: University of Virginia Press, 1996), p. 206.

20. Poynting, "From Ancestral to Creole," p. 212.

21. Campbell, *Historical Atlas*, vol. 1, pt. 2, *Mythologies of the Great Hunt*, p. xiii.

22. Knud Rasmussen, "Intellectual Life of the Iglulik Eskimos," *Report of the Fifth Thule Expedition 1921–24*, The Danish Expedition to Arctic North America, vol. 7, no. 1 (1929): p. 56, cited in Yi-Fu Tuan, *Dominance and Affection: The Making of Pets* (New Haven: Yale University Press, 1984), p. 91.

23. Campbell, *Historical Atlas*, vol. 2, *The Way of the Seeded Earth*, pt. 1, *The Sacrifice*, p. 10.

24. Barry Holstun Lopez, *Of Wolves and Men* (New York: Charles Scribner's Sons, 1978), p. 90.

25. Campbell, *Historical Atlas*, vol. 1, pt. 2, p. 148.

26. James Serpell, *In the Company of Animals: A Study of Human-Animal Relationships* (Oxford: Basil Blackwell, 1986), p. 145.

27. Robert Ardrey, *The Hunting Hypothesis* (New York: Atheneum, 1976), p. 10.

28. Ardrey, *Hunting Hypothesis*, p. 161. Ardrey, a successful writer of plays and screenplays (e.g., *Four Horsemen of the Apocalypse*, *Khartoum*), claimed "hard evidence …, from the field and the laboratory" that hunting and carnivory shaped humanity (p. 11). Similar views of humans as predators appear in his earlier works, *African Genesis* (1961), *The Territorial Imperative* (1966), and *The Social Contract* (1970). The same views have been popularized by other writers, including Desmond Morris, Robin Fox, Lionel Tiger, Konrad Lorenz, and Joseph Campbell. Paul Shepard, while his works are not as popular, established the same views in

Deep Ecology circles. For more discussion on the exaggeration of hunting in human evolution, see Jim Mason, *An Unnatural Order: The Roots of Our Destruction of Nature* (New York: Lantern Books, 2005), pp. 70–83.

29. Tuan, *Dominance and Affection*, p. 71.

30. Henry S. Sharp, "The Null Case: The Chipewyan," in *Woman the Gatherer*, ed. Frances Dahlberg (New Haven: Yale University Press, 1981), p. 227.

31. Campbell, *Historical Atlas*, vol. 2, pt. 1, p. 9.

32. Richard E. Leakey and Roger Lewin, *Origins: What New Discoveries Reveal about the Emergence of Our Species and Its Possible Future* (New York: E. P. Dutton, 1977), p. 174.

33. German sociologist and zoologist Richard Lewinsohn believed that the concepts of money and property arose from the early herders' obsession with their herds. See Richard Lewinsohn, *Animals, Men, and Myths* (New York: Harper and Bros., 1954), p. 69.

34. Klingender, *Animals in Art and Thought*, p. 30.

35. Alfred W. Crosby, *Ecological Imperialism: The Biological Expansion of Europe, 900–1900* (Cambridge: Cambridge University Press, 1986), p. 23.

36. Lewinsohn, *Animals, Men, and Myths*, p. 68.

37. Lewinsohn, *Animals, Men, and Myths*, p. 69.

38. Shepard, *Thinking Animals*, p. 154.

39. B.A.L. Cranstone, "Animal Husbandry: The Evidence from Ethnography," in *The Domestication and Exploitation of Plants and Animals*, ed. Peter J. Ucko and B. W. Dimbleby (Chicago: Aldine, 1969), p. 261.

40. Marvin Harris, *Cannibals and Kings: The Origins of Cultures* (New York: Random House, 1977), p. 62. See also Anthony Leeds and Andrew P. Vayda, eds., *Man, Culture, and Animals: The Role of Animals in Human Ecological Adjustments* (Washington, DC: American Association for the Advancement of Science, 1965); Keith Thomas, *Man and the Natural World: A History of the Modern Sensibility* (New York: Pantheon Books, 1983).

41. Campbell, *Historical Atlas*, vol. 2, pt. 1, p. 74.

42. Thomas, *Man and the Natural World*, p. 46.

43. Gerhard Lenski and Jean Lenski, *Human Societies: An Introduction to Macrosociology*, 4th ed. (New York: McGraw-Hill, 1982), p. 224.

44. Lenski and Lenski, *Human Societies*, p. 224.

45. Gerhard Lenski, Patrick Nolan, and Jean Lenski, *Human Societies: An Introduction to Macrosociology*, 7th ed. (New York: McGraw-Hill, 1995), p. 227.

46. Mason, *Unnatural Order*.

47. Clark, *Animals and Men*, p. 18.

48. Serpell, *Company of Animals*, p. 168.

49. Walter Burkert, *Homo Necans: The Anthropology of Ancient Greek Sacrificial Ritual and Myth*, trans. Peter Bing (Berkeley: University of California Press, 1983), pp. 3–12, cited in Serpell, *Company of Animals*, p. 168.

50. Clark, *Animals and Men*, p. 53.

51. John Rodman, "The Dolphin Papers," *North American Review* 2 (spring 1974): 20.

52. Klingender, *Animals in Art and Thought*, p. 41.

53. Klingender, *Animals in Art and Thought*, p. 40.

54. Klingender, *Animals in Art and Thought*, p. 45.

55. Klingender, *Animals in Art and Thought*.

56. Klingender, *Animals in Art and Thought*, p. 46.

57. Clark, *Animals and Men*, p. 17.

58. Klingender, *Animals in Art and Thought*, p. 47.

59. Klingender, *Animals in Art and Thought*, p. 48.

60. Kate Millet, *Sexual Politics* (Garden City, NY: Doubleday, 1970), p. 28.

61. Millet, *Sexual Politics*, p. 51.

62. Hesiod, *Theogony*, trans. Norman O. Brown (Indianapolis: Liberal Arts Press, 1953), p. 70, cited in Millet, *Sexual Politics*, p. 51.

63. Millet, *Sexual Politics*, p. 52.

64. *Millet, Sexual Politics*, p. 54.

65. Gerda Lerner, *The Creation of Patriarchy* (New York: Oxford University Press, 1986).

66. Paul Shepard, *Nature and Madness* (San Francisco: Sierra Club Books, 1982).

67. With due respect to Juliet Clutton-Brock, a contributor to this volume. See her book *The Walking Larder: Patterns of Domestication, Pastoralism, and Predation* (London: Unwin Hyman, 1989).

68. Shepard, *Thinking Animals*, p. 154.

69. Clark, *Animals and Men*, p. 54.

Chapter 2

1. Richard E. Leakey and Roger Lewin, *Origins: What New Discoveries Reveal about the Emergence of Our Species and Its Possible Future* (New York: E. P. Dutton, 1977), p. 117; Donald C. Johansen and James Shreeve, *Lucy's Child: The Search for Our Beginnings* (New York: Morrow, 1989), p. 209.

2. 1 Samuel 17:34–36.

3. Patrick F. Houlihan, "Animals in Egyptian Art and Hieroglyphs," in *A History of the Animal World in the Ancient Near East*, ed. Billie Jean Collins (Leiden: Brill, 2002), pp. 110–114.

4. Herrmann Kees, *Ancient Egypt: A Cultural Topography* (Chicago: University of Chicago Press, 1951), p. 20.

5. Karl W. Butzer, *Early Hydraulic Civilization in Egypt* (Chicago: University of Chicago Press, 1976), pp. 26–27.

6. Butzer, *Early Hydraulic Civilization*, pp. 86–87.

7. Isaiah 18:1.

8. Kees, *Ancient Egypt*, pp. 93–94.

9. Kees, *Ancient Egypt*, p. 95. The lion was sacred to Bastet as cat-goddess.

10. JoAnn Scurlock, "Animals in Ancient Mesopotamian Religion," in Collins, *History of the Animal World*, pp. 370–371.

11. Benjamin R. Foster, "Animals in Mesopotamian Literature," in Collins, *History of the Animal World*, p. 285.

12. N. K. Sandars, trans., *The Epic of Gilgamesh* (Harmondsworth: Penguin Books, 1960), p. 94.

13. John Kinloch Anderson, *Hunting in the Ancient World* (Berkeley: University of California Press, 1985), p. 14.

14. J. Donald Hughes, *Pan's Travail: Environmental Problems of the Ancient Greeks and Romans* (Baltimore: Johns Hopkins University Press, 1994).

15. Katherine M. D. Dunbabin, *The Mosaics of Roman North Africa* (Oxford: Oxford University Press, 1978), no. 32.

16. Aristophanes *Birds* 529–530.

17. Athenaeus *Deipnosophists* 5.198D–201C.

18. William Radcliffe, *Fishing from the Earliest Times* (Chicago: Ares Publishers, 1974), p. 256.

19. Horace *Satires* 2.4.73; Martial 3.77. 5, 5.11.94.

20. Pliny *Natural History* 9.79.

21. Radcliffe, *Fishing*, pp. 159–160.

22. Pliny *Natural History* 9.79.

23. Pliny *Natural History* 9.79.

24. Aristotle *De generatione animalium* 3.11; Ludwig Friedländer, *Roman Life and Manners under the Early Empire* (London: George Routledge and Sons, 1909–1913), vol. 2, p. 165.

25. Xenophon *Cynegeticus* 12.1; Anderson, *Hunting*, p. 17.

26. Xenophon *Constitution of Sparta* 2.7–8; Plutarch *Lycurgus* 12.1–2, 17–18; Athenaeus *Deipnosophists* 4.141C.

27. Polybius 5.84; Pliny *Natural History* 8.9.

28. Howard Hayes Scullard, *The Elephant in the Greek and Roman World* (Ithaca: Cornell University Press, 1974), p. 24.

29. Homer *Iliad* 11.129, 544–556; 18.573–586.

30. Anderson, *Hunting*, pp. 15, 25.

31. Anderson, *Hunting*, pp. 70–73.

32. Plato *Laws* 7.822D–824B.

33. Anderson, *Hunting*, pp. 76–80.

34. Elizabeth Carney, "Hunting and the Macedonian Elite: Sharing the Rivalry of the Chase," in *The Hellenistic World: New Perspectives*, ed. Daniel Ogden, (London: Gerald Duckworth, 2002), pp. 59–80.

35. Judith M. Barringer, *The Hunt in Ancient Greece* (Baltimore: Johns Hopkins University Press, 2001, p. 186.

36. Scriptores Historiae Augustae *Hadrian* 20.13; Anderson, *Hunting*, p. 169, n. 12.

37. Dio Cassius 69.10.3.

38. *Codex of Theodosius* 15.11.1.

39. Homer *Odyssey* 19.418–458.

40. Plutarch *Anthony* 29.2.

41. Plutarch *On the Cleverness of Animals* 9.

42. Xenophon *Anabasis* 1.2.7; *Cyropaedia* 1.4.4–15.

43. Varro *De re rustica* 3.13.1–3.

44. Ausonius *Moselle*.

45. Pindar *Nemean Ode* 3.51–52.

46. Anderson, *Hunting*, p. 14.

47. Xenophon *Horsemanship* 8.1–10; Perses *Anthologia Palatina* 6.112.

48. Ctesias 4.26; Aristotle *Historia animalium* 9.620A32; Aristotle, *De mirabilibus auscultationibus* 118.841B15; Anderson, *Hunting*, p. xii.

49. Xenophon *Cynegeticus* 11.1–4.

50. Xenophon *Cynegeticus* 9.1–7.

51. Anderson, *Hunting*, pp. 5, 10.

52. Anderson, *Hunting*, p. 14 n. 50, and pp. 38–39, 158.

53. Xenophon *Cynegeticus* 2.9; 9, 11–20.

54. John Richard Thornhill Pollard, *Birds in Greek Life and Myth* (London: Thames and Hudson, 1977), p. 104.

55. Xenophon *Anabasis* 1.5.2; Aelian *De natura animalium* 14.7.

56. Homer *Odyssey* 10.124.

57. Radcliffe, *Fishing*, p. 242.

58. Martial *Epigrams* 5.18.7–8; Aelian *De natura animalium* 14.22; 15.1; Radcliffe, *Fishing*, p. 158.

59. Plato *Laws* 7.824C.

60. Oppian *Halieutica* 3.29–31.

61. Radcliffe, *Fishing*, p. 242.

62. Radcliffe, *Fishing*, pp. 231–233; Mikhail Rostovtzeff, *The Social and Economic History of the Roman Empire*, 2nd ed. (Oxford: Clarendon Press, 1957), vol. 1, p. 287.

63. Justinian *Corpus iuris, Digest* 44.3.7.

64. Dio Chrysostom *Oratio* 7 ("The Euboean Discourse").

65. Matt Cartmill, *A View to Death in the Morning: Hunting and Nature through History* (Cambridge: Harvard University Press, 1993), pp. 32–33.

66. Homer *Odyssey* 10.156–177; 12.297–396.

67. James George Frazer, *The Golden Bough: A Study of Magic and Religion* (New York: Macmillan, 1935), vol. 8, p. 221.

68. Diodorus Siculus 22.5.

69. Arrian *Cynegetica* 34.1.–36.4.

70. Xenophon *Cynegeticus* 5.14; cf. Arrian *Cynegetica* 16.1–7.

71. Xenophon *Anabasis* 5.3.7–10.

72. Homer *Odyssey* 2.181–182.

73. Pollard, *Birds in Greek Life*, p. 15.

74. Ovid *Fasti* 5.539–541; Charles Bergman, *Orion's Legacy: A Cultural History of Man as Hunter* (New York: Dutton, 1996), p. 77.

75. *Anthologia Graeca* 4.202.

76. Anderson, *Hunting*, p. 4 n. 7, and p. 157.

77. Herodotus 7.125–126.

78. Aristotle *Historia animalium* 6.31.579b7; 8.28.606b15.

79. Pausanias 3.20.5; 8.23.6.

80. Jacques Blondel and James Aronson, *Biology and Wildlife of the Mediterranean Region* (Oxford: Oxford University Press, 1999), pp. 234–238; David Attenborough, *The First Eden: The Mediterranean World and Man* (Boston: Little, Brown and Co., 1987), pp. 28–31.

81. Ammianus Marcellinus 18.7; 22.15.24; Themistius *Orations* 10. p. 140a; William Charles Brice, ed., *Environmental History of the Near and Middle East since the Last Ice Age* (New York: Academic Press, 1978), p. 141; Friedländer, *Roman Life and Manners*, vol. 2, p. 67.

82. Vergil *Eclogues* 5.29.

83. Aristophanes *Birds* 504–575.

84. Radcliffe, *Fishing*, p. 230.

85. Suetonius *Tiberius* 34; Pliny *Natural History* 930.

86. Ellen Churchill Semple, *The Geography of the Mediterranean Region: Its Relation to Ancient History* (New York: Henry Holt and Co., 1931), pp. 446–454.

87. Xenophon *Cynegeticus* 5. 22.

88. Pausanias 8.38.5.

89. Apollodorus *Bibliotheca* 3.9.2.

90. The Romans killed countless wild animals in the mock hunts (*venationes*) in the arena.

91. Apollodorus *Bibliotheca* 3.30.

92. Hugh Lloyd-Jones, "Artemis and Iphigeneia," *Journal of Hellenic Studies* 103 (1983): 87–102.

93. Euripides *Bacchae* 337–340.

94. Sophocles *Electra* 563–572.

95. Sophocles *Electra* 563–572.

96. Pausanias 8.54.5.

97. Herodotus 8.41.2.

98. Plutarch *On the Cleverness of Animals* 35.11.

99. Aelian *De natura animalium* 8.4; Plutarch *Moralia* 976A; Pausanias 7.22.4.

100. Pausanias 1.32.1.

101. Apollodorus *Bibliotheca* 3.104–105.

102. Lilly Kahil, "The Mythological Repertoire of Brauron," in *Ancient Greek Art and Iconography*, ed. Warren G. Moon, (Madison: University of Wisconsin Press, 1983), pp. 231–244.

103. J. Donald Hughes, "Artemis: Goddess of Conservation," *Forest and Conservation History* 34 (1990): 191–197.

104. Aristophanes *Birds* 70; Pollard, *Birds in Greek Life*, p. 108; George Jennison, *Animals for Show and Pleasure in Ancient Rome* (Manchester: Manchester University Press, 1937), p. 18.

105. Livy 39.22; Friedländer, *Roman Life and Manners*, vol. 2, p. 62.

106. Scullard, *Elephant*, p. 250.

107. *Res gestae* 22.3.

108. Aurelius Victor *Caesares* 1.25.

109. Friedländer, *Roman Life and Manners*, vol. 2, p. 66.

110. Friedländer, *Roman Life and Manners*, vol. 2, p. 63; Jennison, *Animals for Show*, p. 174.

111. Symmachus *Epistles* 5.60, 62.

112. Edicts of Honorius and Theodosius, *Codex Theodosianus* 15.11.1, 2.

113. Pliny *Natural History* 36.40; Jennison, *Animals for Show*, p. 174.

114. Hermann Dembeck, *Animals and Men* (Garden City, NY: Natural History Press, 1961), p. 53.

115. Cicero *Ad familiares* 7.1.3; Dio Cassius 39.38.2–4; Pliny *Natural History* 8.7. (20–21); Anderson, *Hunting*, p. 87.

116. Cicero *Letters to Atticus* 6.1.21; *Letters to Friends* 2.11.2.

117. Dio Cassius 39.38.2–4; Pliny *Natural History* 8.7 (20–21).

118. Varro, *Saturae Menippeae* 161, 293–296, 361; J. Aymard, *Essai sur les chasses romaines des origines à la fin du siècle des Antonins* (Paris: Bibliothèque des Ecoles Francaises d'Athenes et de Rome, fasc. 171, 1951), pp. 60–63; Anderson, *Hunting*, p. 87.

119. Anderson, *Hunting*, p. 86.

120. Arrian *Cynegetica* 16.6–8.

121. Ovid *Metamorphoses* 15.60–143.

122. Plutarch *Moralia* 962C–D.

123. Plutarch *Moralia* 996F.

124. According to commentators, Sisyphus seduced Odysseus' mother, Anticlea, daughter of Autolycus, shortly before her marriage to Laertes, Odysseus' ostensible father.

125. Plutarch *Moralia* 999A, referring to Hesiod *Works and Days* 277–279.

Chapter 3

1. Juliet Clutton-Brock, *A Natural History of Domesticated Mammals*, 2nd ed. (Cambridge: Cambridge University Press/The Natural History Museum, 1999), p. 32.

2. A. Gentry, J. Clutton-Brock, and C. P. Groves, "The Naming of Wild Animal Species and Their Domestic Derivatives," *Journal of Archaeological Science* 31 (2004): 645–651.

3. Clutton-Brock, *Domesticated Mammals*, p. 40.

4. Clutton-Brock, *Domesticated Mammals*, p. 32.

5. K. Dobney and G. Larson, "Genetics and Animal Domestication: New Windows on an Elusive Process," *Journal of Zoology* 269 (2006): 261–271.

6. Patrick F. Houlihan, *The Animal World of the Pharaohs* (London: Thames and Hudson, 1996), p. 204, fig. 141.

7. A. Beja-Pereira, P. England, N. Ferrand, S. Jordan, A. Bakhiet, M. Abdalla, M. Mashkour, J. Jordana, P. Taberlet, and G. Luikart, "African Origins of the Domestic Donkey," *Science* 304 (2004): 1781.

8. J. Marshall, ed., *Mohenjo-Daro and the Indus Civilization*, vol. 1 (London: Arthur Probsthaim, 1931).

9. A. M. Khazanov, *Nomads from the Outside World*, trans. J. Crookenden (Cambridge: Cambridge University Press, 1984).

10. A. Sherratt and G. Clark, eds., *The Cambridge Encyclopedia of Archaeology* (Cambridge: Cambridge University Press, 1980), pp. 361–364.

11. T. Ingold, *Hunters, Pastoralists, and Ranchers* (Cambridge: Cambridge University Press, 1980), pp. 82–133.

12. Juliet Clutton-Brock, "Cattle, Sheep, and Goats South of the Sahara: An Archaeozoological Perspective," in *Origins and Development of African Livestock: Archaeology, Genetics, Linguistics, and Ethnography*, ed. R. M. Blench and K. C. MacDonald (New York: Routledge, 2000), pp. 30–37.

13. D. W. Phillipson, *African Archaeology*, 2nd ed. (Cambridge: Cambridge University Press, 1993).

14. A. B. Smith, *Pastoralism in Africa: Origins and Development Ecology* (London: Hurst & Co, 1992), pp. 72–100.

15. M. Kadwell, M. Fernandez, H. Stanley, R. Baldi, J. Wheeler, R. Rosadio, and M. Bruford, "Genetic Analysis Reveals the Wild Ancestors of the Llama and the Alpaca," *Proceedings of the Royal Society of London* B 268 (2001): 2575–2584.

16. Juliet Clutton-Brock, "Origins of the Dog: Domestication and Early History," in *The Domestic Dog*, ed. James Serpell (Cambridge: Cambridge University Press, 1995), pp. 14–15.

17. J. Koler-Matznick, I. Brisbin, M. Feinstein, and S. Bulmer, "An Updated Description of the New Guinea Singing Dog (*Canis hallstromi* Troughton, 1957)," *Journal of Zoology* 261 (2003): 109–118.

18. C. Groves, *Ancestors for the Pigs: Taxonomy and Phylogeny of the Genus Sus*, Department of Prehistory, Research School of Pacific Studies, Australian National University, Technical Bulletin No. 3 (1981).

19. R. D. Barnett, *Assyrian Palace Reliefs in the British Museum* (London: British Museum, 1970).

20. Juliet Clutton-Brock, *Horse Power: A History of the Horse and Donkey in Human Societies* (Cambridge: Natural History Museum Publication and Harvard University Press, 1992).

21. N. Postgate, *The First Empires* (Oxford: Elsevier Phaidon, 1977).

22. G. Rawlinson, trans., *The Histories of Herodotus* (London: J. M. Dent and Sons, 1970), bk. 2, pp. 110–182.

23. Clutton-Brock, *Horse Power*, p. 83.

24. E. V. Rieu, trans., *Homer: The Odyssey* (Baltimore: Penguin Books, 1946), bk. 17, p. 266.

25. M. Hammond, trans., *Homer: The Iliad* (New York: Penguin Books, 1987), bk. 23, p. 379.

26. P. A. Brunt, trans., *Arrian: History of Alexander and Indica* (Cambridge: Harvard University Press, Loeb Classical Library, 1983), bk. 5, 19, 4, vol. 2, p. 61.

27. J. S. Watson, trans., *On Hunting*, in *Xenophon's Minor Works* (London: George Bell & Sons, Bohn's Classical Library, 1884), chap. 6, 1, p. 348.

28. J. S. Watson, trans., *On Horsemanship*, in *Xenophon's Minor Works*, chap. 2, 5, p. 273.

29. S. A. Handford, *Caesar: The Conquest of Gaul* (New York: Penguin Books, 1951), V, I, p. 126, fn.

30. Rawlinson, *Histories of Herodotus*, bk. 4, 72, p. 315.

31. Clutton-Brock, *Horse Power*, pp. 96–102.

32. H. L. Jones, trans., *The Geography of Strabo* (Cambridge: Harvard University Press, Loeb Classical Library, 1983), bk. 7, 3,7, vol. 3, p. 199.

33. E. S. Forster and E. Heffner, trans., *Lucius Junius Moderatus Columella on Agriculture, Books V–IX* (Cambridge: Harvard University Press, Loeb Classical Library, 1968), vol. 2.

34. C. Pharr, trans., *The Theodosian Code and Novels and the Sirmondian Constitutions* (Princeton: Princeton University Press, 1952).

35. J. Bostock and H. T. Riley, trans., *The Natural History of Pliny* (London: Bohn's Classical Library, 1856), vol. 1V, bk. XVIII, 48.

36. B. Radice, trans., *Pliny Letters, Books I–VII* (Cambridge: Harvard University Press, Loeb Classical Library, 1969), bk. V, vi, 9–11, p. 341.

37. H. B. Ash, trans., *Lucius Junius Moderatus Columella on Agriculture, Books I–IV* (Cambridge: Harvard University Press, Loeb Classical Library, 1993), vol. 1, bk. II, ii, 22–24, p. 123.

38. Lynn White, Jr., *Medieval Technology and Social Change* (Oxford: Oxford University Press, 1962), pp. 41–45.

39. W. Probert, trans., *The Ancient Laws of Cambria* (London: E. Williams, 1823), pp. 222–253.

40. Probert, *Ancient Laws of Cambria*, pp. 223–229.

41. Probert, *Ancient Laws of Cambria*, p. 237.

42. Clutton-Brock, *Horse Power*, p. 76.

43. Juliet Clutton-Brock, "The Spread of Domestic Animals in Africa," in *The Archaeology of Africa: Food, Metals and Towns*, ed. T. Shaw, P. Sinclair, B. Andah, and A. Okpoko (Cambridge: Cambridge University Press, 1993), pp. 61–70.

44. Smith, *Pastoralism in Africa*.

45. Clutton-Brock, "Cattle, Sheep, and Goats," pp. 30–37.

46. A. B. Smith, "The Origins of the Domesticated Animals of Southern Africa," in *Origins and Development of African Livestock: Archaeology, Genetics, Linguistics, and Ethnography*, ed. R. M. Blench and K. C. MacDonald (New York: Routledge, 2000), pp. 222–238.

47. K. Ramsay, L. Harris, and A. Kotzé, *Landrace Breeds: South Africa's Indigenous and Locally Developed Farm Animals* (Pretoria: Farm Animal Conservation Trust, Pretoria, 1999).

48. J. Clutton-Brock and N. Hammond, "Hot Dogs: Comestible Canids in Preclassic Maya Culture at Cuello, Belize," *Journal of Archaeological Science* 21 (1994): 819–826.

49. M. A. Schwartz, *A History of Dogs in the Early Americas* (New Haven and London: Yale University Press, 1997).

50. H. Epstein, *Domestic Animals of China* (Farnham Royal, Bucks: Commonwealth Agricultural Bureaux, 1969), p. 136.

51. Z. Zhang, "Goldfish," in *Evolution of Domesticated Animals*, ed. I. L. Mason (New York: Longman, 1984), p. 382.

52. S. Piggott, *The Earliest Wheeled Transport: From the Atlantic Coast to the Caspian Sea* (London: Thames and Hudson, 1983), p. 14.

53. Piggott, *Earliest Wheeled Transport*, p. 15

54. White, *Medieval Technology*, p. 56.

55. White, *Medieval Technology*, p. 2.

56. And, incidentally, by Native Americans after horses had been introduced to North and South America.

57. Watson, *On Horsemanship*, chap. 12, 13, p. 301.

Chapter 4

1. N. Marinatos, "The 'Export' Significance of Minoan Bull Hunting and Bull-Leaping Scenes," *Egypt and the Levant: International Journal of Egyptian Archaeology* 40 (1994): 89–93; J. Pinsent, "Bull-Leaping," in *Minoan Society*, ed. O. Krzysz-kowska and L. Nixon (Bristol: Bristol Classical Press, 1983), pp. 259–271; A. Ward, "The Cretan Bull Sports," *Antiquity* 42 (1968): 117–122; J. G. Younger, "Bronze Age Representations of Aegean Bull-Leaping," *American Journal of Archaeology* 80 (1976): 125–137; J. G. Younger, "Bronze Age Representations of Aegean Bull-Games III," *Aegaeum* 12 (1995): 507–545.

2. Marinatos, "Export," pp. 90–92, argues that none of the leapers were women.

3. Younger, "Bull-Games," p. 523.

4. Younger, "Bull-Games," p. 521.

5. Ward, "Cretan Bull Sports," pp. 117–122, maintains that the events occurred near an altar where the bull would later be sacrificed.

6. Younger, "Bull-Leaping," pp. 125–136. Pinsent, "Bull-Leaping," p. 260, cautions that we are viewing not photographs, but conventionalized renderings of actions and people.

7. A stone *rhyton* (drinking cup) seems to portray a leaper impaled by the bull's horns. However Younger, "Bull-Games," p. 524, suggests the artist has simply produced an awkward juxtaposition of the bull's horns and the (uninjured) leaper's body. See also S. Marinatos and M. Hirmer, *Crete and Mycenae* (London: Thames and Hudson, 1960), pls. 182–185. An agate seal from perhaps Priene depicts a leaper falling head first above the bull's head. See Younger, "Bull-Leaping," p. 130; Pinsent, "Bull-Leaping," p. 261; and Ward, "Cretan Bull Sports," p. 120.

8. F. Zeunon, *A History of Domesticated Animals* (London: Hutchinson & Co., 1963), p. 229.

9. Younger, "Bull-Games," plates LX, and Zeunon, *History*, p. 232. Drinking cups found at Sparta in mainland Greece, but originating from Crete, depict the netting of bulls. See E. Davis, *The Vapheio Cups and Aegean Gold and Silver Ware* (New York: Garland, 1977), pp. 256–257.

10. Zeunon, *History*, p. 235.

11. Zeunon, *History*, pp. 208–210.

12. D. Collon, "Bull-Leaping in Syria," *Egypt and the Levant: International Journal of Egyptian Archaeology* 40 (1994): 80–88, argues that the bull had become a cult object in Asia Minor in the sixth millennium BCE.

13. R. F. Willetts, *The Civilizations of Ancient Crete* (Berkeley and Los Angeles: University of California Press, 1977), p. 31, discusses the head and horn motif and the bull as an object of worship.

14. Willetts, *Civilizations*, pp. 104–114, analyzes the possible historical reality behind these myths.

15. Zeunon, *History*, p. 234, suggests that when Crete was the dominant power in the Aegean, the Athenians (and perhaps others) sent to Cnossus a tribute of humans who faced death in confrontations with bulls in a type of human sacrifice.

16. The word labyrinth may be connected to a Lydian (Asia Minor) word, *labrys*, which designates the two-headed ax used to kill bulls at sacrifices. These axes appear frequently in Minoan art, usually in connection with images of bulls' heads or horns. Thus, the word labyrinth may signify not a maze, but rather a place for sacrificing either bulls or humans (see note 15).

17. Younger, "Bull-Games," pp. 518–521, and Ward, "Cretan Bull Sports," pp. 117–122, discuss bull-leaping as a prelude to sacrifice.

18. Suetonius *Claudius* 21.3; Pliny the Elder *Naturalis historia* 8.70.182; Dio Cassius 61.9.1.

19. P. Vigneron, *Le cheval dans l'antiquite greco-romaine* (Nancy: Annales de L'est, 1968), pl. 78b.

20. H. Dessau, *Inscriptiones latinae selectae (= ILS)* (1916; repr., Berlin: Weidman, 1954), # 5053.

21. Judith M. Barringer, *The Hunt in Ancient Greece* (Baltimore and London: Johns Hopkins University Press, 2001), pp. 89–95; E. Csapo, "Deep Ambivalence: Notes on a Greek Cockfight," *Phoenix* 47 (1993): 1–28 (part 1) and 115–124 (parts 2–4); J. Dumont, "Les combats du coq furent-ils un sport?," *Pallas* 34 (1988): 33–47; H. Hoffmann, "Hahnenkampf in Athen: Zur Ikonologie einer attischen Bildformel," *Revue Archeologique* (1974): 195–220.

22. C. Geertz, "Deep Play: Notes on the Balinese Cockfight," in *Myth, Symbol, and Culture*, ed. C. Geertz (New York: W. W. Norton and Company, 1971), p. 24.

23. Geertz, "Deep Play," p. 10.

24. Geertz, "Deep Play," p. 5: "the deep psychological identification of Balinese men with their cocks is unmistakable. The double entendre here is deliberate."

25. A cockfight is depicted on the chair of the high priest at the Theater of Dionysus; see Hoffmann, "Hahnenkampf," p. 196, fig. 1.

26. Plutarch *Moralia* 1049a.

27. Csapo, "Deep Ambivalence," p. 10.

28. Lucian *Gallus* 3.

29. M. Bentz, *Panathenaische Preisamphoren* Antike Kunst, Beiheft 18 (Basel, 1998), pp. 51–53.

30. Hoffmann, "Hahnenkampf," p. 203.

31. Hoffmann, "Hahnenkampf," p. 201, fig. 3, and p. 202, fig. 6. For literary associations of cocks with Herakles, see Aelian *Natura animalium* 17.46, and Plutarch *Moralia* 696e.

32. Aristotle *Historia animalium* 488 b 4.

33. Hoffmann, "Hahnenkampf," p. 206, fig. 11, and Barringer, *Hunt*, p. 94, fig. 54.

34. Pliny *NH* 10.24.27; Cicero *De divinatione* 1.34.74, 2.26.56.

35. Csapo, "Deep Ambivalence," p. 22.

36. Aristophanes *Birds* 70 and 71; Pliny *NH* 10.24.47.

37. Barringer, *Hunt*, pp. 89–95.

38. Barringer, *Hunt*, p. 74, fig. 32; p. 76, fig. 35; p. 81, fig. 44.

39. Hoffmann, "Hahnenkampf," p. 211, fig. 15.

40. Csapo, "Deep Ambivalence," p. 27, suggests that the cock may be a warning to the young object of affection that, as soldiers watching cockfights learned, submission meant enslavement.

41. M. Gwyn Morgan, "Three Non-Roman Blood Sports," *Classical Quarterly* 25 (1975): 117–122.

42. Aristotle, *Politics* 1256a: "The art of war is duly employed against wild animals."

43. F. van Straten, "Greek Sacrificial Representations: Livestock Prices and Religious Mentality," in *Gifts to the Gods*, ed. T. Linders and G. Norquist (Uppsala: Boreas, 1987), pp. 164–165.

44. Pliny *NH* 8.70.180; Varro *De re rustica* 2.5.3; Columella *DRR* 6. Praef. 7. Aelian *VH* 5.14 also lauds the ox as an ally of humans.

45. *Hecatomb*: the Greek word *hecaton* means "one hundred," but the word *hecatomb* was sometimes used loosely to mean "a very large number of cattle."

46. In the days following the procession and sacrifice, there were athletic and artistic contests and horse races. The prize for the athletic contests was a large, beautifully decorated vase filled with olive oil (the olive tree was sacred to Athena). On one side was an image of Athena, on the other, a depiction of the event for which the vase was awarded. See note 29 above.

47. K. J. Rosivach, *The System of Public Sacrifice in Fourth-Century Athens* (Atlanta: Scholars Press, 1994), p. 159.

48. Rosivach, *System*, p. 161, and M. H. Jameson, "Sacrifice and Animal Husbandry in Classical Greece," in *Pastoral Economies in Classical Antiquity*, ed. C. R. Whitaker (Cambridge: Cambridge University Press, 1988), pp. 87–88.

49. I. Jenkins, *The Parthenon Frieze* (London: British Museum Press, 1994), pp. 24–26, outlines the controversy about interpreting the activities on the frieze as an actual or generalized or idealized rendering of the Panathenaic procession.

50. F. van Straten, *Hiera Kala: Images of Animal Sacrifice in Archaic and Classical Greece* (Leiden: Brill, 1995), pp. 100–102. The same author, in "Sacrificial Representations," pp. 159–160, provides images of a bull restrained by ropes (figure 1) and a bull tethered at the altar (figure 5).

51. See Jenkins, *Parthenon Frieze*, pp. 72–73.

52. The examination of entrails for signals from the gods (a procedure known as *extispicium*) was an important element of Roman religion.

53. A lengthy account of an animal sacrifice appears in Homer's *Odyssey* 3.430–463.

54. R. Gordon, "The Moment of Death: Art and the Ritual of Greek Sacrifice," in *World Art: Themes of Unity in Diversity*, ed. I. Lavin (University Park: Pennsylvania State University Press, 1989), pp. 570–571.

55. Hesiod *Theogony* 535–557.

56. In the Roman world, meat acquired from sacrificed animals was sometimes sold at markets. Pliny the Younger *Letter* 10.96, mentions that Christians refused to buy such meat. Cf. 1 Corinthians 10:18–21.

57. H. Foley, *Ritual Irony* (Ithaca and London: Cornell University Press, 1985), pp. 26–52, provides a summary of the complex and contentious issue of the origins and meanings of animal sacrifices.

58. J. Heath, *The Talking Greeks: Speech, Animals, and the Other in Homer, Aeschylus, and Plato* (Cambridge: Cambridge University Press, 2005), p. 3.

59. Rosivach, *System*, p. 3. On p. 66, he estimates that an Athenian man would participate and receive meat in forty to forty-five sacrifices a year. See also Jameson, "Sacrifice," p. 105. Heath, *Talking Greeks*, p. 2, remarks that the "average American eats 197 pounds of meat each year … Athens, on the other hand, which may have provided its citizens with twice as much meat as most other cities, probably distributed less than five pounds of beef yearly to individuals in public sacrifices."

60. See George Jennison, *Animals for Show and Pleasure in Ancient Rome* (Manchester: University of Manchester Press, 1937; repr., Philadelphia: University of Pennsylvania Press, 2005), pp. 30–35; E. E. Rice, *The Grand Procession of Ptolemy Philadelphus* (Oxford: Oxford University Press, 1983); K. M. Coleman, "Ptolemy Philadelphus and the Roman Amphitheater," in *Roman Theater and Society*, ed. W. J. Slater (Ann Arbor: University of Michigan Press, 1996), pp. 49–68.

61. Plutarch *Antonius* 27.

62. V. Foertmeyer, "The Dating of the *Pompe* of Ptolemy II Philadelphus," *Historia* 37 (1988): 90–104. Also Rice, *Grand Procession*, pp. 4 and 5, 38–42.

63. Athenaeus *Deipnosophistai* (Catalog of Wondrous Events) 197 C–203 B. Rice, *Grand Procession*, provides both the Greek text and an English translation. Athenaeus' account is based on an earlier account, written by Callixeinus (Kallixeinos). See Rice, *Grand Procession*, pp. 164–171, and Coleman, "Ptolemy Philadelphus," p. 50.

64. Rice, *Grand Procession*, pp. 35 and 36.

65. Dionysus' journey from India to the Mediterranean world was not portrayed as a triumph until the Hellenistic period, when historians claimed that it provided a parallel to the Indian triumph of Alexander, who was said to be a descendant of Dionysus; Rice, *Grand Procession*, pp. 83–86.

66. W. W. Tarn, "Two Notes on Ptolemaic History," *JHS* 53 (1933): 58–59. The Ptolemies claimed relationship to Alexander through common descent from Dionysus. Asserting relationship with Alexander was a means to legitimize the Ptolemies as Alexander's heirs in Egypt.

67. Coleman, "Ptolemy Philadelphus," p. 50.

68. I have followed the identifications of these species made by Jennison, *Animals*, pp. 30–35, and Rice, *Grand Procession*, pp. 88–99.

69. W. W. Tarn, *Hellenistic Civilization* (London: Arnold, 1952), p. 183.

70. Jennison, *Animals*, p. 34.

71. Diodorus 3.36.3. Strabo 17.1.5 writes that the Ptolemies were patrons of science.

72. Ptolemy II may have displayed elephants in his procession to warn his Seleucid rivals, who possessed some of the war elephants captured by Alexander in India, that he, Ptolemy, also had access to these formidable beasts.

73. Roland Auguet, *Cruelty and Civilization: The Roman Games* (1972; repr., London and New York: Routledge, 1994); Thomas Wiedemann, *Emperors and Gladiators* (London and New York: Routledge, 1992); Donald G. Kyle, *Spectacles of Death*

in Ancient Rome (London and New York: Routledge, 1998); Alison Futrell, *Blood in the Arena: The Spectacle of Roman Power* (Austin: University of Texas Press, 1997).

74. Dio *Epitome* 66.25; Suetonius *Titus* 7.3. Suetonius reports that five thousand animals were killed in just one day.

75. Dio *Epitome* 68.15.

76. Shelby Brown, "Death as Decoration: Scenes from the Arena on Roman Domestic Mosaics," in *Pornography and Representation in Greece and Rome*, ed. Amy Richlin (New York and Oxford: Oxford University Press, 1992), p. 184.

77. *ILS* 5062.

78. Libanius *Epistle* 1399. 2 and 3.

79. Also *Ad familiares* 8.2.2, 8.4.5, 8.6.5, 8.8.10, 8.9.3; *Ad Atticum* 5.21.5, 6.1.21; and Plutarch *Cicero* 36.5.

80. Pliny *NH* 8.20.53; Seneca *De brevitate vitae* 13.6.

81. Cicero *Ad fam.* 7.1.3; Pliny *NH* 8.7 (20 and 21), 20 (53), 24 (64), 29 (71); Seneca *Brev. vit.* 13.6; Dio Cassius 39.38.2–4.

82. Pliny *NH* 8.7 (22), 20 (53), 27 (69); Dio 43.22 and 23.

83. Ovid *Fasti* 4.681–682, and 5.371–372; Martial 8.67.3 and 4.

84. Brown, "Death as Decoration," p. 207.

85. Polybius 31.29.1–12; Cicero *Natura deorum* 2.64 (161) and *Tusculanae disputationes* 2.17 (40).

86. Consider the hunting party described by Pliny the Younger *Epistle* 1.6 (also: 5.6.46, 5.18.2, 9.10, 9.36.6).

87. Paul Plass, *The Game of Death in Ancient Rome* (Madison: University of Wisconsin Press, 1995), p. 18, comments on the "conspicuous consumption of public resources measured by both blood and money and carrying the symbolic meaning which frequently accompanies consumption."

88. Jo-Ann Shelton, "Dancing and Dying: The Display of Elephants in Ancient Roman Arenas," in *Daimonopylai: Essays in Classics and the Classical Tradition*, ed. Mark Joyal and Rory B. Egan (Winnipeg: University of Manitoba, Centre for Hellenic Civilization, 2004), pp. 363–382.

89. Also at Probus' spectacles, thousands of ostriches, deer, boars, and wild sheep were turned loose in the arena, and audience members were allowed to seize as many as they wanted, presumably to slaughter and eat.

90. K. M. Coleman, "Fatal Charades: Roman Executions Staged as Mythological Enactments," *JRS* 80 (1990): 44–73.

91. Katherine Dunbabin, *The Mosaics of Roman North Africa* (Oxford and New York: Clarendon Press, 1978), pp. 67–70; Wiedemann, *Emperors*, pp. 16 and 17.

Chapter 5

1. The information in this chapter is the result of a more than twenty-year collaboration between veterinarian and epidemiologist Calvin Schwabe and myself, an Egyptologist with a background in paleobiology. The reader is referred to Andrew Gordon and Calvin Schwabe, *The Quick and the Dead: Biomedical Theory in Ancient Egypt* (Leiden: Brill.Styx, 2004), for a fuller development of themes discussed here and for fuller notes and bibliography. With a few exceptions, only references not in *Quick and the Dead* and/or direct quotations will be cited here.

2. Andrew Gordon, "Origins of Ancient Egyptian Medicine, Part 1: Some Egypto-logical Evidence," *KMT* 1 (1990): 26–29; Gordon and Schwabe, *Quick and the Dead*, pp. 1–13.

3. H. E. Sigerist, *A History of Medicine*, vol. 1, *Primitive and Archaic Medicine* (New York: Oxford University Press, 1967), p. 352.

4. James Allen, *The Art of Medicine in Ancient Egypt* (New York: Metropolitan Museum of Art, 2005), p. 70.

5. Warren Dawson, *Magician and Leech: A Study in the Beginnings of Medicine with Special Reference to Ancient Egypt* (London: Methuen & Co., 1929), p. 74.

6. Dawson, *Magician and Leech*, p. 74.

7. Dawson, *Magician and Leech*, p. 74.

8. G. Elliot Smith and Warren Dawson, *Egyptian Mummies* (New York: Dial Press, 1924), p. 8.

9. J. R. Harris, "Medicine," in *The Legacy of Egypt*, ed. J. R. Harris, 2nd ed. (Oxford: Clarendon Press, 1971), p. 125.

10. Bruno Halioua and Bernard Ziskind, *Medicine in the Days of the Pharaohs* (Cambridge: Belknap Press, 2005), p. 44.

11. Halioua and Ziskind, *Medicine*, p. 179. Calvin Schwabe and I hypothesize that the maintaining in health and sacrifice of animals led directly to the start of the development of a scientifically based medicine.

12. James Breasted, *Development of Religion and Thought in Ancient Egypt: Lectures Delivered on the Morse Foundation at Union Theological Seminary* (New York: Charles Scribner's Sons, 1912), p. ix.

13. Breasted, *Development*, pp. ix–x.

14. John Nunn, *Ancient Egyptian Medicine* (Norman: University of Oklahoma Press, 1996), p. 34. In the section devoted to the Kahun Gynecological Papyrus, Nunn claims the veterinary papyrus is a subsection of it, even though the two are written in different hands and styles.

15. Halioua and Ziskind, *Medicine*, p. 192. They also claim it is part of the Kahun Gynecological Papyrus. Perhaps both books get their information from Ghalioun-gui, who claims that the veterinary papyrus is an older section of the papyrus. See Paul Ghalioungui, *The House of Life: Magic and Medical Science in Ancient Egypt* (Amsterdam: B. M. Israël, 1973), p. 36.

16. F. Ll. Griffith, *Hieratic Papyri from Kahun and Gurob (Principally of the Middle Kingdom)* (London: Bernard Quaritch, 1898), table of contents and pp. 5, 12.

17. Hermann Grapow, *Grundriss der Medizin der alten Ägypter*, vol. 2 (Berlin: Akademie Verlag, 1954), p. 88.

18. Alan Gardiner, *Ancient Egyptian Onomastica* (Oxford: Oxford University Press, 1947), vol. 1, p. 6.

19. Gardiner, *Ancient Egyptian Onomastica*, vol. 1, p. 15.

20. Gardiner, *Ancient Egyptian Onomastica*, vol. 1, p. 15.

21. In one instance, an epithet of a priest of Sekhmet, Ahanakht, is "he who knows bulls" (Ghalioungui, *House of Life*, p. 137).

22. This is why the Egyptians were comfortable putting an animal head on a human body in representations of selected gods. With respect to the Greeks, for example, there is Aristotle's dictum that man is an animal meant to live in a polis.

23. Because of the lack of human dissection, the assumption that the human female's uterus was bicornuate continued in the work of Galen and lasted until the Renaissance.

24. W. G. Waddell, trans., *Manetho* (Cambridge: Harvard University Press, 1940), p. ix. Manetho's own name may come from the Egyptian "Truth of Thoth." Another idea is his name may mean "groom" or more literally "horse herdsman." If the latter, then his family may have dealt with animals and their health.

25. C. J. Bleeker, *Hathor and Thoth: Two Key Figures of the Ancient Egyptian Religion* (Leiden: E. J. Brill, 1973), pp. 142, 156.

26. R. E. Walker, "The Veterinary Papyrus of Kahun," *Veterinary Record* 76 (1964): 198.

27. Walker, *Veterinary Papyrus*, p. 198.

28. For a fuller version of the ideas expressed herein, see Gordon and Schwabe, *Quick and the Dead*, pp. 31–55.

29. E. E. Evans-Pritchard, *The Nuer: A Description of the Modes of Livelihood and Political Institutions of a Nilotic People* (Oxford: Clarendon Press, 1940), p. 16.

30. Evans-Pritchard, *Nuer*, p. 19.

31. The genetic estimate of about 7000 BCE for African cattle domestication has been disputed by anthropological researchers. Diane Gifford-Gonzalez, "Animal Disease Challenges to the Emergence of Pastoralism in Sub-Saharan Africa," *African Archaeological Review* 17 (2000): 98.

32. Toby Wilkinson, *Genesis of the Pharaohs: Dramatic New Discoveries Rewrite the Origins of Ancient Egypt* (New York: Thames and Hudson, 2003), p. 101.

33. Wilkinson, *Genesis*, pp. 98–99.

34. Wilkinson, *Genesis*, pp. 98, 104.

35. Wilkinson, *Genesis*, p. 101.

36. Gardiner, *Ancient Egyptian Onomastica*, vol. 1, pp. 4–5.

37. J. E. Quibell, *The Ramesseum* (London: Bernard Quaritch [Egyptian Research Account, 1896], 1898), p. 3 and pl. III.

38. Allen, *Art of Medicine*, pp. 28–30.

39. Quibell, *Ramesseum*, pl. III; Allen, *Art of Medicine*, p. 29.

40. Gardiner, *Ancient Egyptian Onomastica*, vol. 1, pp. 15–19.

41. For a fuller development of this theme with additional citations, see Gordon and Schwabe, *Quick and the Dead*, pp. 95–148; Calvin Schwabe and Andrew Gordon, "The Egyptian *w3s*-Scepter: A Possible Biological Origin as a Dried Bull's Penis in Relation to an Ancient Theory on Bones as the Source of Semen," Working Paper Series No. 53 (Davis: Agricultural History Center, University of California, 1989), fn. 19 and 129; Calvin Schwabe, Joyce Adams, and Carleton Hodge, "Egyptian Beliefs about the Bull's Spine; An Anatomical Origin for Ankh," *Anthropological Linguistics* 24 (1982): 447–450.

42. James Breasted, *The Edwin Smith Surgical Papyrus* (Chicago: University of Chicago Press, 1930), vol. 1, pp. 323–332, argues that the case reads that a dislocation of the lower cervical vertebrae would cause an erection with the dribbling of urine, while the dislocation of the middle cervical vertebra would cause erection with spontaneous seminal emission (*mns3*), while Allen, *Art of Medicine*, p. 91, translates the disputed word *mns3* as "erection" rather than "seminal emission." The modern consensus on the Egyptian word does tend toward "erection," but Breasted's transliteration of the hieratic into hieroglyphs does show the word *Hr(y)-ib* for "middle." Also, Breasted noted (p. 323) that, in modern times, a criminal whose neck is broken from hanging may experience a spontaneous seminal emission.

43. Allen, *Art of Medicine*, p. 70.

44. The translations are those of Faulkner; I have occasionally tweaked them. R. O. Faulkner, *The Ancient Egyptian Pyramid Texts* (Oxford: Clarendon Press, 1969), p. 149.

45. Faulkner, *Pyramid Texts*, pp. 206–207.

46. Faulkner, *Pyramid Texts*, p. 36.

47. R. O. Faulkner, *The Ancient Egyptian Coffin Texts* (Warminster: Aris & Phillips, 1977), vol. 2, p. 153.

48. Faulkner, *Pyramid Texts*, p. 98.

49. Serge Sauneron, "Le germe dans les os," *Bulletin de l'Institut français d'Archéologie orientale* 60 (1960): 21.

50. Sauneron, "Le germe," p. 21.

51. Sauneron, "Le germe," p. 21.

52. The six books dealt with anatomy and physiology, general diseases, healer's instruments, remedies, eye diseases, and gynecology. Only healer's instruments are not represented in the remaining ancient Egyptian medical papyri.

53. Halioua and Ziskind, *Medicine*, p. 183. Translation from the French by DeBevoise.

54. Louis Ginzberg, *The Legends of the Jews* (Philadelphia: Jewish Publication Society of America, 1925), vol. 5, p. 81.

55. Ginzberg, *Legends of the Jews*, vol. 1, p. 336.

56. B. Lincoln, *Priests, Warriors, and Cattle: A Study in the Ecology of Religions* (Berkeley: University of California Press, 1981), p. 72.

57. N. H. Keswani, "The Concepts of Generation, Reproduction, Evolution and Human Development As Found in the Writings of Indian (Hindu) Scholars during the Early Period (up to 1299 A.D.) of Indian History," *Bulletin of the National Institute of Science, India* 21 (1963): 218.

58. Keswani, *Concepts*, p. 211.

59. R. Huffman, *Nuer-English Dictionary* (Berlin: Dietrich Reimer, 1929), p. 21.

60. Schwabe, Adams, and Hodge, "Egyptian Beliefs," p. 454.

61. For a fuller development of this theme with additional citations, see Gordon and Schwabe, *Quick and the Dead*, pp. 15–30, 73–93, 168–171; Andrew Gordon, "The K3 as an Animating Force," *Journal of the American Research Center in Egypt* 33 (1996): 31–35; Andrew Gordon and Calvin Schwabe, "'Live Flesh' and 'Opening-of-the-Mouth': Biomedical, Ethnological, and Egyptological Aspects," in *Proceedings of the Seventh International Congress of Egyptologists, Cambridge, 3–9 September 1995*, ed. C. J. Eyre, (Leuven: Peeters, 1998), pp. 461–469.

62. Zaki Saad, *The Excavations at Helwan: Art and Civilization in the First and Second Egyptian Dynasties* (Norman: University of Oklahoma Press, 1969), pp. 43–45, 61–63, figs. 11–13, and pls. 45 and 55; Zaki Saad, *Ceiling Stelae in Second Dynasty Tombs from the Excavations at Helwan* (Le Caire: l'Institut français d'Archéologie orientale, 1957), p. 6.

63. Gordon and Schwabe, "'Live Flesh,'" p. 466.

64. Faulkner, *Pyramid Texts*, p. 3.

65. Liselotte Buchheim, "Die Verordnung von 'lebendem' Fleisch in altägyptischen Papyri," *Sudhoffs Archiv für Geschichte der Medizin und der Naturwissenschaften* 44 (1960): 109. Translated from the German.

66. Guido Majno, *The Healing Hand: Man and Wound in the Ancient World* (Cambridge: Harvard University Press, 1975), p. 107.

Chapter 6

1. J. Donald Hughes, *Pan's Travail: Environmental Problems of the Ancient Greeks and Romans* (Baltimore: Johns Hopkins University Press, 1994), p. 110.

2. Hughes, *Pan's Travail*, p. 111.

3. Liliane Bodson, "Attitudes towards Animals in Greco-Roman Antiquity," *International Journal for the Study of Animal Problems* 4 (1983): 314.

4. Richard Sorabji, *Animal Minds and Human Morals: The Origins of the Western Debate* (Ithaca: Cornell University Press, 1993), p. 156.

5. Peter Singer, *Animal Liberation: A New Ethics for Our Treatment of Animals* (New York: Avon, 1975), p. 196.

6. Richard D. Ryder, *Animal Revolution: Changing Attitudes towards Speciesism* (Oxford: Blackwell, 1989), p. 22.

7. Sorabji, *Animal Minds*, pp. 7–28.

8. Rod Preece and Lorna Cunningham, *Animal Welfare and Human Values* (Waterloo: Wilfrid Laurier University Press, 1993), p. 14.

9. A readable general introduction to the thought of the pre-Socratics, with individual chapters devoted to each prominent thinker and philosophical school, is found in Edward Hussey, *The Presocratics* (New York: Scribners, 1972).

10. Although it is often held that Pythagoras left no writings, Diogenes Laertius (third century CE) claims, in the course of his life of Pythagoras, that this notion is absurd, and he then proceeds to list the pre-Socratic's works (*Lives and Opinions of Eminent Philosophers* 8. 6–7).

11. This passage from Porphyry is cited as Empedocles fr. 139DK in Hermann Diels and Walther Kranz, eds., *Die Fragmente der Vorsokratiker* (Berlin: Weidmann, 1951). The fragments of the pre-Socratics included in the collection of Diels and Kranz are available in English translation in Kathleen Freeman, *Ancilla to the Pre-Socratic Philosophers* (Cambridge: Harvard University Press, 1978). The poetic fragments of Empedocles are now available, with extensive commentary, in Brad Inwood, *The Poem of Empedocles: A Text and Translation with Introduction* (Toronto: University of Toronto, 1992), where fr. 139DK=fr. 124 Inwood.

12. Damianos Tsekourakis, "Pythagoreanism or Platonism in Ancient Medicine? The Reasons for Vegetarianism in Plutarch's 'Moralia'," *Aufstieg und Niedergang der römischen Welt* 2, 36. 1 (1987): 370.

13. Tsekourakis, "Pythagoreanism or Platonism," p. 379.

14. All translations from Greek and Latin texts in this study are my own.

15. Daniel A. Dombrowski, *The Philosophy of Vegetarianism* (Amherst: University of Massachusetts Press, 1984), p. 56.

16. In "The Greek Anthropocentric View of Man," *Harvard Studies in Classical Philology* 85 (1981): 239–259, Robert Renehan demonstrates that Greek thought is full of expressions like those of Xenophon in which human attainments are declared to be unique in the realm of animals, and he names this sort of assertion the "man alone of animals" commonplace, which he traces in Greek writers as early as Hesiod.

17. Sorabji, *Animal Minds*, p. 10. Plato's ultimate inability to resolve the issue of animal rationality was commented on more recently by Urs Dierauer, "Das Verhältnis von Mensch und Tier im griechisch-römischen Denken," in *Tiere und Menschen: Geschichte und Aktualität eines prekären Verhältnisses*, ed. Paul Münch and

Rainer Walz (Paderborn: Schöningh, 1998), p. 51: "Platon hat sich also nie ganz eindeutig zur Frage der Tiervernunft geäußert."

18. On the "man alone of animals" motif in Greek philosophical thought, see note 16 above.

19. For a discussion of this peculiar idea in ancient thought, see Stephen T. Newmyer, "Paws to Reflect: Ancients and Moderns on the Religious Sensibilities of Animals," *Quaderni Urbinati di Cultura Classica*, n.s., 75, no. 3 (2003): 111–129.

20. The use that Greek philosophers made of such examples of animal behaviors to argue that animals are or are not rational is treated in Sherwood Owen Dickerman, "Some Stock Examples of Animal Intelligence in Greek Psychology," *Transactions of the American Philological Association* 42 (1911): 123–130.

21. The contribution that Aristotle's doctrine of "continuity" or "biological gradualism" made to the later idea of the *scala naturae*, or Great Chain of Being, is discussed in A. O. Lovejoy, *The Great Chain of Being* (Cambridge: Harvard University Press, 1948), pp. 55–59.

22. Sorabji, *Animal Minds*, p. 2.

23. The bibliography on the complex doctrine of *oikeiōsis* is remarkably rich. Particularly helpful are S. J. Pembroke, "Oikeiôsis," in *Problems in Stoicism*, ed. A. A. Long, (London: Athlone, 1971), pp. 114–149; and Gisela Striker, "The Role of *Oikeiosis* in Stoic Ethics," *Oxford Studies in Ancient Philosophy* 1 (1983): 145–167.

24. It is not clear whether the Theophrastean arguments mentioned here by Porphyry were derived from his lost work, *On the Intellect and Character of Animals*, or from his more famous work, *On Piety*, also lost, which is known to have contained arguments against the sacrifice of animals on the grounds that they are sentient and intelligent creatures. For Theophrastus' arguments against animal sacrifice, see Dirk Obbink, "The Origin of Greek Sacrifice: Theophrastus on Religion and Cultural History," in *Theophrastean Studies on Natural Science, Physics and Metaphysics, Ethics, Religion, and Rhetoric*, ed. William W. Fortenbaugh and Robert W. Sharples (New Brunswick: Transaction Books, 1988), pp. 272–295.

25. The fragments of the earlier Stoics, including Chrysippus, are collected in the four volumes of Johannes von Arnim, ed., *Stoicorum Veterum Fragmenta* (Stuttgart: Teubner, 1903–1924). The fragment of Chrysippus alluded to in our study is designated as *SVF* 2. 827.

26. A detailed discussion of the Stoic theory of speech and language in animals is offered in Stephen T. Newmyer, "Speaking of Beasts: The Stoics and Plutarch on Animal Reason and the Modern Case against Animals," *Quaderni Urbinati di Cultura Classica*, n.s., 63, no. 3 (1999): 99–110.

27. Sorabji, *Animal Minds*, pp. 195–196.

28. The overall influence of Christianity on the treatment of animals throughout history has been variously assessed. Animal rights philosophers have tended to see that influence as largely pernicious. On the willingness of early civilizations to cause suffering to animals while valuing humans more highly, Richard D. Ryder, *Animal Revolution*, p. 27, charges, "The religion which could have changed this emphasis through its principle of Love, Christianity, did not do so ... because it magnified the gulf between human and nonhuman. ..." Peter Singer, *Animal Liberation*, p. 200, writes similarly, "Christianity left nonhumans as decidedly outside the pale of human sympathy as ever they were in Roman times." Theologian Andrew Linzey, *Animal Theology* (Urbana: University of Illinois Press, 1995), attempts to show that Christian theol-

ogy has through the ages been in fact more animal-friendly than some critics have charged.

29. Epicurean contract theory is discussed in Phillip Mitsis, *Epicurus' Ethical Theory: The Pleasures of Invulnerability* (Ithaca: Cornell University Press, 1988), pp. 79–92, without any reference, however, to the place of animals in such contracts.

30. The numbering of the fragments of Posidonius followed in this study is that found in Ludwig Edelstein and I. G. Kidd, eds., *Posidonius I: The Fragments* (Cambridge: Cambridge University Press, 1972).

31. The Roman contribution to *oikeiōsis* theory, with particular reference to its appearance in the works of Cicero and Seneca, is investigated in Gretchen Reydams-Schils, "Human Bonding and *Oikeiōsis* in Roman Stoicism," *Oxford Studies in Ancient Philosophy* 22 (2002): 221–251.

32. Jo-Ann Shelton, "Contracts with Animals: Lucretius, *De rerum natura*," *Between the Species* 11 (1995): 115–121, argues that Lucretius held that humans were capable of forming contracts with some animal species while excluding other species from such contracts. This was done, Lucretius maintains, for the purpose of securing that "pleasure" (*voluptas*) that constituted the highest good in Epicurean philosophy. If Shelton's reading of Lucretius is correct, he could unquestionably be credited with doctrinal innovation in the matter of Epicurean contract theory.

33. Philo's work can now be studied in the superb edition of Abraham Terian, *Philonis Alexandrini de Animalibus: The Armenian Text with an Introduction, Translation, and Commentary* (Chico: Scholars Press, 1981).

34. For a detailed examination of Philo's debt to Stoicism in *On Animals*, see Stephen T. Newmyer, "Philo on Animal Psychology: Sources and Moral Implications," in *From Athens to Jerusalem: Medicine in Hellenized Jewish Lore and in Early Christian Literature*, ed. Samuel Kottek and Manfred Horstmanshoff (Rotterdam: Erasmus, 2000), pp. 143–155.

35. Plutarch's three treatises are analyzed in their relation to the ancient tradition of philosophical speculation on the nature of animalkind and are shown to anticipate a number of arguments prominently advanced by modern animal rights philosophers in Stephen T. Newmyer, *Animals, Rights, and Reason in Plutarch and Modern Ethics* (Oxford: Routledge, 2006).

36. The views of Plutarch and of modern animal psychologists on the possibility of a sense of justice at work in animal behavior are discussed in Stephen T. Newmyer, "Just Beasts? Plutarch and Modern Science on the Sense of Fair Play in Animals," *Classical Outlook* 74, no. 3 (1997): 85–88.

37. On the language of animals, see note 26.

38. The idea, infrequently encountered in ancient literature, that animals are actually superior to human beings has been dubbed "theriophily" by George Boas and is discussed in his article "Theriophily," in *Dictionary of the History of Ideas*, ed. Philip P. Wiener (New York: Scribners, 1973), vol. 4, pp. 384–389.

39. A useful discussion of Porphyry's treatise is given in Dombrowski, *Philosophy of Vegetarianism*, pp. 107–119. His ideas are developed further in Daniel A. Dombrowski, "Porphyry and Vegetarianism: A Contemporary Philosophical Approach," *Aufstieg und Niedergang der römischen Welt* 2, 36. 1 (1987): 774–791.

40. An extremely informative survey of the influence of classical philosophical thought on subsequent philosophical speculation on animals is offered in Gary Steiner,

Anthropocentrism and Its Discontents: The Moral Status of Animals in the History of Western Philosophy (Pittsburgh: University of Pittsburgh Press, 2005).

Chapter 7

1. Stanley J. Tambiah, "Animals Are Good to Think and Good to Prohibit," in *Culture, Thought, and Social Action* (Cambridge: Harvard University Press, 1985), pp. 169–211; see also D. Sperber, "Why Are Perfect Animals, Hybrids and Monsters Food for Symbolic Thought?" *Method and Theory in the Study of Religion 8*, no. 2 (1996): 143–169.

2. James Mellaart, *Çatal Hüyük: A Neolithic Town in Anatolia* (London: Thames and Hudson, 1967), pl. 67; fig. 52.

3. Mellaart, *Çatal Hüyük*, e.g., rooms VII.1 and VII.23.

4. For a dramatic recounting of such practices in Tibet, see Xue Xinran, *Sky Burial: An Epic Love Story of Tibet* (New York: Random House, 2005).

5. Mellaart, *Çatal Hüyük*, p. 204.

6. M. Balter, *The Goddess and the Bull: Çatalhöyük: An Archaeological Journey to the Dawn of Civilization* (New York: Free Press, 2005), pp. 292–308.

7. Balter, *Goddess and Bull*, pp. 323–324; I. Hodder, "The Lady and the Seed," in *Archaeology beyond Dialogue*, ed. I. Hodder (Salt Lake City: University of Utah Press, 2003), pp. 155–163.

8. J. Reade, *Mesopotamia* (London: British Museum Press, 1991), fig. 5, pp. 49–51.

9. Richard L. Zettler and Lee Horne, eds., *Treasures from the Royal Tombs of Ur* (Philadelphia: University of Pennsylvania Museum of Archaeology and Anthropology, 1998), p. 55, no. 3.

10. Clement of Alexandra, *Paedagogos*, ch. 2.

11. Lynn M. Meskell and Rosemary A. Joyce, *Embodied Lives: Figuring Ancient Maya and Egyptian Experience* (London: Routledge, 2003), p. 84.

12. Patrick F. Houlihan, *The Animal World of the Pharaohs* (London: Thames and Hudson, 1996), p. 105 (plate xix shows the young Amenhotep II suckling from Hathor in the form of a cow).

13. Houlihan, *Animal World*, pp. 158, 161.

14. Cited in Houlihan, *Animal World*, p. 96.

15. Meskell and Joyce, *Embodied Lives*, p. 82.

16. The Nebamun paintings are in the British Museum; they were acquired ca. 1821 by Henry Salt in Thebes. (See T.G.H. James, *Egyptian Painting and Drawing in the British Museum* [London: British Museum Press, 1985], pp. 26–28 and fig. 25.)

17. M. Collier and B. Manley, *How to Read Egyptian Hieroglyphs* (London: British Museum Press, 1998), p. 20.

18. Houlihan, *Animal World*, p. 160.

19. James, *Egyptian Painting*, p. 31 with fig. 30.

20. James, *Egyptian Painting*, p. 24 with fig. 25.

21. Houlihan, *Animal World*, p. 78.

22. Houlihan, *Animal World*, p. 211, fig. 146.

23. S. Marinatos and M. Hirmer, *Crete and Mycenae* (London: Thames and Hudson, 1960), pls. 85–87.

24. Aristotle, *History of Animals*, 622b.

25. Marinatos and Hirmer, *Crete and Mycenae*, pl. 85.

26. C. Doumas, *The Wall-Paintings of Thera* (Athens: The Thera Foundation, 1992), pp. 112–119.

27. L. Morgan, "Of Animals and Men," in *Klados: Essays in Honour of J. N. Coldstream*, ed. C. Morris (London: Institute of Classical Studies, 1995), pp. 171–184.

28. S. Hood, *The Arts in Prehistoric Greece* (Harmondsworth: Penguin, 1978), p. 212, fig. 210c.

29. Doumas, *Wall-Paintings of Thera*, pp. 158–159.

30. M. Zeimbeki, "Nurturing the Natural: A Cognitive Approach in the Study of the Xeste 3 Aquatic Imagery," in *Authochthon: Papers Presented to O.T.P.K. Dickinson on the Occasion of His Retirement*, ed. A. Dakouri-Hild and S. Sherratt (Oxford: British Archaeological Reports, 2005), pp. 242–251.

31. Doumas, *Wall-Paintings of Thera*, pp. 162–163.

32. B. Hallager and E. Hallager, "The Knossian Bull—Political Propaganda in Neopalatial Crete," in *Politeia: Society and State in the Aegean Bronze Age*, Aegaeum 12, ed. R. Laffineur and W. D. Niemeier (Liège: Université de Liège, 1995), pp. 547–556.

33. Marinatos and Hirmer, *Crete and Mycenae*, pl. XIV.

34. A. J. Evans, *The Palace of Minos at Knossos*, vol. 3 (London: Macmillan, 1930), p. 172.

35. Marinatos and Hirmer, *Crete and Mycenae*, pl. XXVIII.

36. R. Calasso, *The Marriage of Cadmus and Harmony* (London: Vintage, 1994), p. 21.

37. Marinatos and Hirmer, *Crete and Mycenae*, pl. 141.

38. Christine E. Morris, "In Pursuit of the White Tusked Boar: Aspects of Hunting in Mycenaean Society," in *Celebrations of Death and Divinity in the Bronze Age Argolid*, ed. Robin Hagg and Gullog C. Nordquist (Stockholm: Paul Astroms Forlag, 1990), pp. 149–156.

39. A. Pasquier, *The Louvre: Greek, Roman, and Etruscan Antiquities* (Paris: Scala, 1991), p. 42; For similar images see E. D. Reeder, *Pandora: Women in Ancient Greece* (New Haven: Princeton University Press, 1995), p. 310 (vase), 311 (terracotta figurine).

40. Ovid *Metamorphoses* 3.138–255.

41. Reeder, *Pandora*, p. 321.

42. J. M. Padgett, *The Centaur's Smile: The Human Animal in Early Greek Art* (New Haven: Princeton University Press, 2003), p. 28.

43. Padgett, *Centaur's Smile*, p. 8, fig. 3.

44. Padgett, *Centaur's Smile*, pp. 17–20 with fig. 15.

45. I. Jenkins, *The Parthenon Frieze* (London: British Museum, 1994).

46. Jenkins, *Parthenon Frieze*, pp. 104–109 (west frieze).

47. Jenkins, *Parthenon Frieze*, p. 72 (south frieze).

48. J.M.C. Toynbee, *Animals in Roman Life and Art* (1973; repr., Baltimore and London: Johns Hopkins University Press, 1996), p. 109.

49. Eve D'Ambra, "The Cult of Virtues and the Funerary Relief of Ulpia Epigone," in *Roman Art in Context: An Anthology*, ed. Eve D'Ambra (Englewood Cliffs, NJ: Prentice-Hall, 1993), pp. 104–114.

50. Toynbee, *Animals in Roman Life*, p. 111.

51. Toynbee, *Animals in Roman Life*, p. 123.

52. Toynbee, *Animals in Roman Life*, pp. 210–211.

53. Toynbee, *Animals in Roman Life*, pp. 252–253.

54. Toynbee, *Animals in Roman Life*, pp. 34–38.

55. Toynbee, *Animals in Roman Life*, pp. 288–289; J. Huskinson, "Routes to Reception: The Case of Orpheus in Early Christian Art," *The Reception of Classical Texts and Images, Open University Conference January 1996*, http://www2.open.ac.uk/ClassicalStudies/GreekPlays/conf96/huskinson.htm.
56. D. Michaelides, *Cypriot Mosaics*, Picture Book 7 (Nicosia: Department of Antiquities, 1987; 2nd ed., 1992), p. 6.
57. Toynbee, *Animals in Roman Life*, p. 292 (mosaics from Circencester and Woodchester; it is suggested that the latter may have had a water feature at the center).
58. Huskinson, "Routes to Reception," offers a useful review of the debate.

BIBLIOGRAPHY

Aldred, Cyril. *Egypt to the End of the Old Kingdom*. New York: McGraw-Hill, 1965.

Allen, James. *The Art of Medicine in Ancient Egypt*. New York: Metropolitan Museum of Art, 2005.

Anderson, John Kinloch. *Hunting in the Ancient World*. Berkeley: University of California Press, 1985.

Ardrey, Robert. *African Genesis: A Personal Investigation into the Animal Origins and Nature of Man*. New York: Atheneum, 1961.

Ardrey, Robert. *The Territorial Imperative: A Personal Inquiry into the Animal Origins of Property and Nations*. New York: Atheneum, 1966.

Ardrey, Robert. *The Social Contract: A Personal Inquiry into Evolutionary Sources of Order and Disorder*. New York: Atheneum, 1970.

Ardrey, Robert. *The Hunting Hypothesis*. New York: Atheneum, 1976.

Arnim, Johannes von, ed. *Stoicorum Veterum Fragmenta*. Stuttgart: Teubner, 1903–1924.

Attenborough, David. *The First Eden: The Mediterranean World and Man*. Boston: Little, Brown and Co., 1987.

Auguet, Roland. *Cruelty and Civilization: The Roman Games*. New York: Routledge, 1972. Reprint, London and New York: Routledge, 1994.

Aymard, J. *Essai sur les chasses romaines des origines à la fin du siècle des Antonins*. Paris: Bibliothèque des Ecoles Francaises d'Athenes et de Rome, fasc. 171, 1951.

Balter, M. *The Goddess and the Bull: Catalhöyük: An Archaeological Journey to the Dawn of Civilization*. New York: Free Press, 2005.

Barnett, R.D. *Assyrian Palace Reliefs in the British Museum*. London: British Museum, 1970.

Barringer, Judith M. *The Hunt in Ancient Greece*. Baltimore: Johns Hopkins University Press, 2001.

Beja-Pereira, A., P. England, N. Ferrand, S. Jordan, A. Bakhiet, M. Abdalla, M. Mashkour, J. Jordana, P. Taberlet, and G. Luikart. "African Origins of the Domestic Donkey." *Science* 304 (2004): 1781.

Bell, Lanny. "Luxor Temple and the Cult of the Royal Ka." *Journal of Near Eastern Studies* 44 (1985), 251–294.

Bentz, M. *Panathenaische Preisamphoren*. Antike Kunst, Beiheft 18. Basel, 1998.

Bergman, Charles. *Orion's Legacy: A Cultural History of Man as Hunter.* New York: Dutton, 1996.

Bleeker, C.J. *Hathor and Thoth: Two Key Figures of the Ancient Egyptian Religion.* Leiden: E.J. Brill, 1973.

Blondel, James, and James Aronson. *Biology and Wildlife of the Mediterranean Region.* Oxford: Oxford University Press, 1999.

Blount, Margaret. *Animal Land: The Creatures of Children's Fiction.* New York: William Morrow & Co., 1975.

Boas, G. "Theriophily." In *Dictionary of the History of Ideas,* edited by Philip P. Wiener, vol. 4, pp. 384–389. New York: Scribners, 1973.

Bodson, Liliane. "Attitudes towards Animals in Greco-Roman Antiquity." *International Journal for the Study of Animal Problems* 4 (1983): 312–320.

Bomgardner, David L. "The Trade in Wild Beasts for Roman Spectacles: A Green Perspective." *Anthropozoologica* 16 (1992): 161–166.

Bostock, J., and H.T. Riley, trans. *The Natural History of Pliny.* London: Bohn's Classical Library, 1856.

Breasted, James. *Development of Religion and Thought in Ancient Egypt: Lectures Delivered on the Morse Foundation at Union Theological Seminary.* New York: Charles Scribner's Sons, 1912.

Breasted, James. *The Edwin Smith Surgical Papyrus.* Vols. 1–2. Chicago: University of Chicago Press, 1930.

Brice, William Charles, ed. *Environmental History of the Near and Middle East since the Last Ice Age.* New York: Academic Press, 1978.

Brier, Bob. "Case of the Dummy Mummy." *Archaeology* 54 (2001): 28–29.

Brown, Shelby. "Death as Decoration: Scenes from the Arena on Roman Domestic Mosaics." In *Pornography and Representation in Greece and Rome,* edited by Amy Richlin, pp. 180–211. New York: Oxford University Press, 1992.

Brunt, P.A., trans. *Arrian: History of Alexander and Indica.* 2 vols. Cambridge: Harvard University Press, Loeb Classical Library, 1983.

Buchheim, Liselotte. "Die Verordnung von 'lebendem' Fleisch in altägyptischen Papyri." *Sudhoffs Archiv für Geschichte der Medizin und der Naturwissenschaften* 44 (1960): 97–116.

Burkert, Walter. *Homo Necans: The Anthropology of Ancient Greek Sacrificial Ritual and Myth.* Translated by Peter Bing. Berkeley: University of California Press, 1983.

Butzer, Karl W. *Early Hydraulic Civilization in Egypt.* Chicago: University of Chicago Press, 1976.

Calasso, R. *The Marriage of Cadmus and Harmony.* London: Vintage, 1994.

Campbell, Joseph. *Historical Atlas of World Mythology.* Vol. 1, *The Way of the Animal Powers.* New York: Harper & Row, 1988.

Campbell, Joseph. *Historical Atlas of World Mythology.* Vol. 2, *The Way of the Seeded Earth.* New York: Harper & Row, 1988.

Carney, Elizabeth. "Hunting and the Macedonian Elite: Sharing the Rivalry of the Chase." In *The Hellenistic World: New Perspectives,* edited by Daniel Ogden, pp. 59–80. London: Gerald Duckworth, 2002.

Cartmill, Matt. *A View to Death in the Morning: Hunting and Nature through History.* Cambridge: Harvard University Press, 1993.

Cassius, Dio. *Roman History,* book XXXIX (39). http://penelope.uchicago.edu/Thayer/E/Roman/Texts/Cassius_Dio/39*.html (accessed April 2006).

Childe, V. G. *New Light on the Most Ancient Near East.* New York: Norton, 1969.

Clark, Joseph D. *Beastly Folklore*. Metuchen, NJ: Scarecrow Press, 1968.

Clark, Kenneth. *Animals and Men: Their Relationship as Reflected in Western Art from Prehistory to the Present Day*. New York: William Morrow & Co., 1977.

Claudian. "De consulate stilichonis," book III. http://penelope.uchicago.edu/Thayer/E/Roman/Texts/Claudian/De_Consulatu_Stilichonis/3*.html (accessed April 2006).

Clottes, Jean. *Chauvet Cave: The Art of Earliest Times*. Translated by Paul G. Bahn. Salt Lake City: University of Utah Press, 2003.

Clutton-Brock, Juliet. *The Walking Larder: Patterns of Domestication, Pastoralism, and Predation*. London: Unwin Hyman, 1989.

Clutton-Brock, Juliet. *Horse Power: A History of the Horse and Donkey in Human Societies*. Cambridge: Natural History Museum Publication and Harvard University Press, 1992.

Clutton-Brock, Juliet. "The Spread of Domestic Animals in Africa." In *The Archaeology of Africa: Food, Metals and Towns*, edited by T. Shaw, P. Sinclair, B. Andah, and A. Okpoko, pp. 61–70. Cambridge: Cambridge University Press, 1993.

Clutton-Brock, Juliet. "Origins of the Dog: Domestication and Early History." In *The Domestic Dog*, edited by James Serpell, pp. 8–19. Cambridge: Cambridge University Press, 1995.

Clutton-Brock, Juliet. "The Legacy of Iron Age Dogs and Livestock in Southern Africa." *Azania*, 29–30, 1994–1995 (1996a), pp. 161–167.

Clutton-Brock, Juliet. "Horses in History." In *Horses through Time*, edited by S. Olsen, pp. 83–102. Niwot: Robert Rinehart for Carnegie Museum of Natural History, 1996.

Clutton-Brock, Juliet. *A Natural History of Domesticated Mammals*. 2nd ed. Cambridge: Cambridge University Press/The Natural History Museum, 1999.

Clutton-Brock, Juliet. "Cattle, Sheep, and Goats South of the Sahara: An Archaeozoological Perspective." In *Origins and Development of African Livestock: Archaeology, Genetics, Linguistics, and Ethnography*, edited by R. M. Blench and K. C. MacDonald, pp. 30–37. New York: Routledge, 2000.

Clutton-Brock, J., and N. Hammond. "Hot Dogs: Comestible Canids in Preclassic Maya Culture at Cuello, Belize." *Journal of Archaeological Science* 21 (1994): 819–826.

Coleman, K.M. "Fatal Charades: Roman Executions Staged as Mythological Enactments." *Journal of Roman Studies* 80 (1990): 44–73.

Coleman, K.M. "Ptolemy Philadelphus and the Roman Amphitheater." In *Roman Theater and Society*, edited by W.J. Slater, pp. 49–68. Ann Arbor: University of Michigan Press, 1996.

Collier, M., and B. Manley. *How to Read Egyptian Hieroglyphs*. London: British Museum Press, 1998.

Collins, Paul. "A Goat Fit for a King." *ART News* 102, no. 7 (2003): 106, 108.

Collon, D. "Bull-Leaping in Syria." *Egypt and the Levant: International Journal of Egyptian Archaeology* 40 (1994): 80–88.

Columella, Lucius Junius Moderatus. *On Agriculture, I, Books 1–4*, trans. H. B. Ash. Cambridge: Harvard University Press, Loeb Classical Library, 1941.

Columella, Lucius Junius Moderatus. *On Agriculture, II, Books 5–9*, trans. E. S. Forster and Edward H. Heffner. Cambridge: Harvard University Press, Loeb Classical Library, 1954.

Cranstone, B.A.L. "Animal Husbandry: The Evidence from Ethnography." In *The Domestication and Exploitation of Plants and Animals*, edited by Peter J. Ucko and G. W. Dimbleby. Chicago: Aldine, 1969.

Crosby, Alfred W. *Ecological Imperialism: The Biological Expansion of Europe, 900–1900.* Cambridge: Cambridge University Press, 1986.

Csapo, E. "Deep Ambivalence: Notes on a Greek Cockfight." *Phoenix* 47 (1993): 1–28, 115–124.

D'Ambra, Eve. "The Cult of Virtues and the Funerary Relief of Ulpia Epigone." In *Roman Art in Context: An Anthology,* edited by Eve D'Ambra, pp. 104–114. Englewood Cliffs, NJ: Prentice-Hall, 1993.

David, Ephraim. "Hunting in Spartan Society and Consciousness." *Echos du Monde Classique/Classical Views* 37 (1993): 393–413.

Davis, E. *The Vapheio Cups and Aegean Gold and Silver Ware.* New York: Garland, 1977.

Dawson, Warren. *Magician and Leech: A Study in the Beginnings of Medicine with Special Reference to Ancient Egypt.* London: Methuen & Co., 1929.

Deloria, Vine, Jr., *God Is Red.* New York: Grosset and Dunlap, 1973.

Dembeck, Hermann. *Animals and Men.* Garden City, NY: Natural History Press, 1961.

Dessau, H. *Inscriptiones Latinae Selectae.* 1916. Reprint, Berlin: Weidman, 1954.

Dickerman, Sherwood O. "Some Stock Illustrations of Animal Intelligence in Greek Psychology." *Transactions of the American Philological Association* 42 (1911): 123–130.

Diels, Hermann, and Walther Kranz, eds. *Die Fragmente der Vorsokratiker.* Berlin: Weidmann, 1951.

Dierauer, Urs. "Das Verhältnis von Mensch und Tier im griechisch-römischen Denken." In *Tiere und Menschen: Geschichte und Aktualität eines prekären Verhältnisses,* edited by P. Münch and R. Walz, pp. 37–85. Paderborn: Schöningh, 1988.

Dobney, K., and G. Larson. "Genetics and Animal Domestication: New Windows on an Elusive Process." *Journal of Zoology* 269 (2006): 261–271.

Dombrowski, Daniel A. *The Philosophy of Vegetarianism.* Amherst: University of Massachusetts Press, 1984.

Dombrowski, Daniel A. "Porphyry and Vegetarianism: A Contemporary Philosophical Approach." *Aufstieg und Niedergang der römischen Welt* 2, 36. 1 (1987): 774–791.

Doumas, C. *The Wall-Paintings of Thera.* Athens: The Thera Foundation, 1992.

Dumont, J. "Les combats du coq furent-ils un sport?" *Pallas* 34 (1988): 33–47.

Dunbabin, Katherine M.D. *The Mosaics of Roman North Africa.* Oxford and New York: Clarendon Press, 1978.

Dunbabin, K.M.D. *Mosaics of the Greek and Roman World.* Cambridge: Cambridge University Press, 1999.

Edelstein, Ludwig, and I.G. Kidd, eds. *Posidonius I: The Fragments.* Cambridge: Cambridge University Press, 1972.

Eggebrecht, Arne. *Schlachtungsbräuche im alten Ägypten unf ihre Wiedergabe im Flachbild bis zum Ende des Mittleren Reiches.* München: Ludwig-Maximilians-Universität, 1973.

Epstein, H. *Domestic Animals of China.* Farnham Royal, Bucks: Commonwealth Agricultural Bureaux, 1969.

Evans, A.J. *The Palace of Minos at Knossos.* Vol. 3. London: Macmillan, 1930.

Evans-Pritchard, E.E. *The Nuer: A Description of the Modes of Livelihood and Political Institutions of a Nilotic People.* Oxford: Clarendon Press, 1940.

Faulkner, R.O. *A Concise Dictionary of Middle Egyptian.* Oxford: Griffith Institute, 1962.

Faulkner, R.O. *The Ancient Egyptian Pyramid Texts.* Oxford: Clarendon Press, 1969.

Faulkner, R.O. *The Ancient Egyptian Coffin Texts.* Vols. 1–3. Warminster: Aris & Phillips, 1977–1978.

Foertmeyer, V. "The Dating of the *Pompe* of Ptolemy II Philadelphus." *Historia* 37 (1988): 90–104.

Foley, H. *Ritual Irony.* Ithaca and London: Cornell University Press, 1985.

Foster, Benjamin R. "Animals in Mesopotamian Literature." In *A History of the Animal World in the Ancient Near East,* edited by Billie Jean Collins, pp. 271–288. Leiden: Brill, 2002.

Foucault, Michel. *Discipline and Punish.* New York: Vintage, 1977/1995.

Frankfort, Henri. *Kingship and the Gods.* Chicago: University of Chicago Press, 1948.

Frazer, James George. *The Golden Bough: A Study of Magic and Religion.* New York: Macmillan, 1935.

Freeman, Kathleen. *Ancilla to the Pre-Socratic Philosophers.* Cambridge: Harvard University Press, 1978.

Friedländer, Ludwig. *Roman Life and Manners under the Early Empire.* 4 vols. London: George Routledge and Sons, 1909–1913.

Futrell, Alison. *Blood in the Arena: The Spectacle of Roman Power.* Austin: University of Texas Press, 1997.

Galan, Jose M. "Bullfight Scenes in Ancient Egyptian Tombs." *Journal of Egyptian Archeology* 80 (1994): 81–96.

Gardiner, Alan. *Ancient Egyptian Onomastica.* Vols. 1–3. Oxford: Oxford University Press, 1947.

Geertz, C. "Deep Play: Notes on the Balinese Cockfight." In *Myth, Symbol, and Culture,* edited by C. Geertz, pp. 1–37. New York: W.W. Norton and Company, 1971.

Gentry, A., J. Clutton-Brock, and C.P. Groves. "The Naming of Wild Animal Species and Their Domestic Derivatives." *Journal of Archaeological Science* 31 (2004): 645–651.

Ghalioungui, Paul. *The House of Life: Magic and Medical Science in Ancient Egypt.* Amsterdam: B.M. Israël, 1973.

Gifford-Gonzalez, Diane. "Animal Disease Challenges to the Emergence of Pastoralism in Sub-Saharan Africa." *African Archaeological Review* 17 (2000): 95–139.

Gimbutas, Marija. *Goddesses and Gods of Old Europe, 7000–3500 B.C.* Berkeley: University of California Press, 1982.

Ginzberg, Louis. *The Legends of the Jews.* Vols. 1–7. Philadelphia: Jewish Publication Society of America, 1909–1966.

Gordon, Andrew. "Origins of Ancient Egyptian Medicine. Part 1: Some Egyptological Evidence." *KMT* 1 (1990): 26–29.

Gordon, Andrew. "The *K3* as an Animating Force." *Journal of the American Research Center in Egypt* 33 (1996): 31–35.

Gordon, Andrew, and Calvin Schwabe. " 'Live Flesh' and 'Opening-of-the-Mouth': Biomedical, Ethnological, and Egyptological Aspects." In *Proceedings of the Seventh International Congress of Egyptologists, Cambridge, 3–9 September 1995,* edited by C.J. Eyre. Leuven: Peeters, 1998.

Gordon, Andrew H., and Calvin W. Schwabe. *The Quick and the Dead: Biomedical Theory in Ancient Egypt.* Egyptological memoirs, 4. Leiden: Brill, 2004.

Gordon, R. "The Moment of Death: Art and the Ritual of Greek Sacrifice." In *World Art: Themes of Unity in Diversity*, edited by I. Lavin, pp. 567–573. University Park: Pennsylvania State University Press, 1989.

Gossen, Gary H. "Animal Souls, Co-essences, and Human Destiny in Mesoamerica." In *Monsters, Tricksters, and Sacred Cows: Animal Tales and American Identities*, edited by A. James Arnold, pp. 80–107. Charlottesville: University Press of Virginia, 1996.

Grapow, Hermann. *Grundriss der Medizin der alten Ägypter*. Vols. 1–9. Berlin: Akademie Verlag, 1973–1974.

Griffith, F. Ll. *Hieratic Papyri from Kahun and Gurob (Principally of the Middle Kingdom)*. Vols. 1–2. London: Bernard Quaritch, 1898.

Grivetti, L. "Goat Kraal Gardens and Plant Domestication: Thoughts on Ancient and Modern Food Production." *Ecology of Food and Nutrition* 10 (1980), 5–7.

Groves, C. *Ancestors for the Pigs: Taxonomy and Phylogeny of the Genus* Sus. Department of Prehistory, Research School of Pacific Studies, Australian National University, Technical Bulletin No. 3 (1981).

Halioua, Bruno, and Bernard Ziskind. *Medicine in the Days of the Pharaohs*. Cambridge: Belknap Press, 2005.

Hallager, B., and E. Hallager. "The Knossian Bull—Political Propaganda in Neopalatial Crete." In *Politeia: Society and State in the Aegean Bronze Age*, edited by R. Laffineur and W. D. Niemeier, pp. 547–556. Liege: Université de Liege and UT-PASP, 1995.

Hammond, M., trans. *Homer: The Iliad*. New York: Penguin Books, 1987.

Handford, S. A., trans. *Caesar: The Conquest of Gaul*. New York: Penguin Books, 1951.

Hansen, Donald P. "Art of the Royal Tombs of Ur: A Brief Interpretation." In *Treasures from the Royal Tombs of Ur*, edited by Richard L. Zettler and Lee Horne, pp. 43–59. Philadelphia: University of Pennsylvania Museum, 1998.

Harris, J. R. "Medicine." In *The Legacy of Egypt*, edited by J. R. Harris, pp. 112–137. 2nd ed. Oxford: Clarendon Press, 1971.

Harris, Marvin. *Cannibals and Kings: The Origins of Cultures*. New York: Random House, 1977.

Hart, Donna, and Robert W. Sussman. *Man the Hunted: Primates, Predators, and Human Evolution*. New York: Westview Press, 2005.

Healy, John F. "The Life and Character of Pliny the Elder." In Pliny the Elder, *Natural History: A Selection*, edited by John F. Healy, pp. ix–xxxx. London: Penguin, 2004.

Heath, J. *The Talking Greeks: Speech, Animals, and the Other in Homer, Aeschylus, and Plato*. Cambridge: Cambridge University Press, 2005.

Hoage, R. J., Anne Roskell, and Jane Mansour. "Menageries and Zoos to 1900." In *New Worlds, New Animals: From Menagerie to Zoological Park in the Nineteenth Century*, edited by R. J. Hoage and William A. Deiss, pp. 8–18. Baltimore: Johns Hopkins University Press, 1996.

Hodder, I. "The Lady and the Seed." In *Archaeology beyond Dialogue*, edited by I. Hodder, pp. 155–163. Salt Lake City: University of Utah Press, 2003.

Hoffmann, H. "Hahnenkampf in Athen: Zur Ikonologie einer attischen Bildformel." *Revue Archeologique* (1974): 195–220.

Hood, S. *The Arts in Prehistoric Greece*. Harmondsworth: Penguin, 1978.

Hopkins, Keith. *Death and Renewal: Sociological Studies in Roman History*. New York: Cambridge University Press, 1983.

Houlihan, Patrick F. *The Animal World of the Pharaohs*. London: Thames and Hudson, 1996.

Houlihan, Patrick F. "Animals in Egyptian Art and Hieroglyphs." In *A History of the Animal World in the Ancient Near East,* edited by Billie Jean Collins, pp. 97–144. Leiden: Brill, 2002.

Huffman, R. *Nuer-English Dictionary.* Berlin: Dietrich Reimer, 1929.

Hughes, J. Donald. "Artemis: Goddess of Conservation." *Forest and Conservation History* 34 (1990): 191–197.

Hughes, J. Donald. *Pan's Travail: Environmental Problems of the Ancient Greeks and Romans.* Baltimore: Johns Hopkins University Press, 1994.

Huskinson, J. "Routes to Reception: The Case of Orpheus in Early Christian Art." *The Reception of Classical Texts and Images, Open University Conference January 1996.* http://www2.open.ac.uk/ClassicalStudies/GreekPlays/conf96/huskinson.htm.

Hussey, Edward. *The Presocratics.* New York: Scribners, 1972.

Ingold, T. *Hunters, Pastoralists, and Ranchers.* Cambridge: Cambridge University Press, 1980.

Inwood, Brad. *The Poem of Empedocles: A Text and Translation with Introduction.* Toronto: University of Toronto Press, 1992.

James, T.G.H. *Egyptian Painting and Drawing in the British Museum.* London: British Museum Press, 1985.

Jameson, M.H. "Sacrifice and Animal Husbandry in Classical Greece." In *Pastoral Economies in Classical Antiquity,* edited by C.R. Whitaker, pp. 87–119. Cambridge: Cambridge University Press, 1988.

Jenkins, I. *The Parthenon Frieze.* London: British Museum Press, 1994.

Jennison, George. *Animals for Show and Pleasure in Ancient Rome.* Manchester: University of Manchester Press, 1937. Reprint, Philadelphia: University of Pennsylvania Press, 2005.

Johansen, Donald C., and James Shreeve. *Lucy's Child: The Search for Our Beginnings.* New York: Morrow, 1989.

Johnson, William M. *The Rose-Tinted Menagerie: A History of Animals in Entertainment, from Ancient Rome to the Twentieth Century.* London: Heretic Books, 1990.

Jones, H.L., trans. *The Geography of Strabo.* 8 vols. Cambridge: Harvard University Press, Loeb Classical Library, 1983.

Junker, Hermann. *Giza III: Die mastabas der vorgeschrittenen V. Dynastie auf dem Westfriedhof.* Wien and Leipzig: Hölder, Pichler-Tempsky, 1938.

Kadwell, M., M. Fernandez, H. Stanley, R. Baldi, J. Wheeler, R. Rosadio, and M. Bruford. "Genetic Analysis Reveals the Wild Ancestors of the Llama and the Alpaca." *Proceedings of the Royal Society of London* B 268 (2001): 2575–2584.

Kahil, Lilly. "The Mythological Repertoire of Brauron." In *Ancient Greek Art and Iconography,* edited by Warren G. Moon, pp. 231–244. Madison: University of Wisconsin Press, 1983.

Kalof, Linda. *Looking at Animals in Human History.* London: Reaktion Books, 2007.

Kees, Herrmann. *Ancient Egypt: A Cultural Topography.* Chicago: University of Chicago Press, 1951.

Keswani, N.H. "The Concepts of Generation, Reproduction, Evolution and Human Development As Found in the Writings of Indian (Hindu) Scholars during the Early Period (up to 1299 A.D.) of Indian History." *Bulletin of the National Institute of Science, India* 21 (1963): 206–255.

Khazanov, A.M. *Nomads from the Outside World.* Translated by J. Crookenden. Cambridge: Cambridge University Press, 1984.

Kisling, Vernon N., Jr. "Ancient Collections and Menageries." In *Zoo and Aquarium History: Ancient Animal Collections to Zoological Gardens,* edited by Vernon N. Kisling, Jr., pp. 1–47. Boca Raton: CRC, 2001.

Klingender, Francis. *Animals in Art and Thought to the End of the Middle Ages,* edited by Evelyn Antal and John Harthan. Cambridge: MIT Press, 1971.

Klingender, Francis. *Animals in Art and Thought to the End of the Middle Ages.* Edited by Evelyn Antal and John Harthan. Cambridge: MIT Press, 1971.

Koler-Matznick, J., I. Brisbin, M. Feinstein, and S. Bulmer. "An Updated Description of the New Guinea Singing Dog (*Canis hallstromi* Troughton, 1957)." *Journal of Zoology* 261 (2003): 109–118.

Kyle, Donald G. *Spectacles of Death in Ancient Rome.* New York: Routledge, 1998.

Lahanas, Michael. "Galen." www.mlahanas.de/Greeks/Galen.htm (accessed November 18, 2004).

Leakey, Richard E., and Roger Lewin. *Origins: What New Discoveries Reveal about the Emergence of Our Species and Its Possible Future.* New York: E.P. Dutton, 1977.

Leeds, Anthony, and Andrew P. Vayda, eds. *Man, Culture, and Animals: The Role of Animals in Human Ecological Adjustments.* Washington, DC: American Association for the Advancement of Science, 1965.

Lenski, Gerhard, and Jean Lenski. *Human Societies: An Introduction to Macrosociology.* 4th ed. New York: McGraw-Hill, 1982.

Lenski, Gerhard, Patrick Nolan, and Jean Lenski. *Human Societies: An Introduction to Macrosociology.* 7th ed. New York: McGraw-Hill, 1995.

Lerner, Gerda. *The Creation of Patriarchy.* New York: Oxford University Press, 1986.

Lewinsohn, Richard. *Animals, Men, and Myths.* New York: Harper and Bros., 1954.

Lincoln, B. *Priests, Warriors, and Cattle: A Study in the Ecology of Religions.* Berkeley: University of California Press, 1981.

Linzey, Andrew. *Animal Theology.* Urbana: University of Illinois Press, 1995.

Lloyd-Jones, Hugh. "Artemis and Iphigeneia." *Journal of Hellenic Studies* 103 (1983): 87–102.

Lopez, Barry Holstun. *Of Wolves and Men.* New York: Charles Scribner's Sons, 1978.

Lovejoy, A.O. *The Great Chain of Being.* Cambridge: Harvard University Press, 1948.

Majno, Guido. *The Healing Hand: Man and Wound in the Ancient World.* Cambridge: Harvard University Press, 1975.

Marinatos, N. "The 'Export' Significance of Minoan Bull Hunting and Bull-Leaping Scenes." *Egypt and the Levant: International Journal of Egyptian Archaeology* 40 (1994): 89–93.

Marinatos, S., and M. Hirmer. *Crete and Mycenae.* London: Thames and Hudson, 1960.

Marshall, J., ed. *Mohenjo-Daro and the Indus Civilization.* Vol. 1. London: Arthur Probsthaim, 1931.

Mason, Jim. *An Unnatural Order: The Roots of Our Destruction of Nature.* New York: Lantern Books, 2005.

Matz, David. *Daily Life of the Ancient Romans.* Westport, CT: Greenwood Press, 2002.

Mellaart, James. *Çatal Hüyük: A Neolithic Town in Anatolia.* London: Thames and Hudson, 1967.

Meskell, Lynn M., and Rosemary A. Joyce. *Embodied Lives: Figuring Ancient Maya and Egyptian Experience.* London: Routledge, 2003.

Michaelides, D. *Cypriot Mosaics.* Picture Book 7. Nicosia, Cyprus: Department of Antiquities, 1987; 2nd ed., 1992.

Millet, Kate. *Sexual Politics.* Garden City, NY: Doubleday, 1970.

Mitsis, Phillip. *Epicurus' Ethical Theory: The Pleasures of Invulnerability.* Ithaca: Cornell University Press, 1988.

Morenz, Siegfried. *Egyptian Religion.* Ithaca: Cornell University Press, 1973.

Morgan, L. "Of Animals and Men." In *Klados: Essays in Honour of J. N. Coldstream,* edited by C. Morris. London: Institute of Classical Studies, 1995.

Morgan, M. Gwyn. "Three Non-Roman Blood Sports." *Classical Quarterly* 25 (1975): 117–122.

Morris, Christine E. "In Pursuit of the White Tusked Boar: Aspects of Hunting in Mycenaean Society." In *Celebrations of Death and Divinity in the Bronze Age Argolid,* edited by Robin Hagg and Gullog C. Nordquist, pp. 151–156. Stockholm: Paul Astroms Forlag, 1990.

Newmyer, Stephen T. "Just Beasts? Plutarch and Modern Science on the Sense of Fair Play in Animals." *Classical Outlook* 74, no. 3 (1997): 85–88.

Newmyer, Stephen T. "Speaking of Beasts: The Stoics and Plutarch on Animal Reason and the Modern Case against Animals." *Quaderni Urbinati di Cultura Classica,* n.s., 63, no. 3 (1999): 99–110.

Newmyer, Stephen T. "Philo on Animal Psychology: Sources and Moral Implications." In *From Athens to Jerusalem: Medicine in Hellenized Jewish Lore and in Early Christian Literature,* edited by Samuel Kottek and Manfred Horstmanshoff, pp. 143–155. Rotterdam: Erasmus Publishing, 2000.

Newmyer, Stephen T. "Paws to Reflect: Ancients and Moderns on the Religious Sensibilities of Animals." *Quaderni Urbinati di Cultura Classica,* n.s., 75, no. 3 (2003): 111–129.

Newmyer, Stephen T. *Animals, Rights, and Reason in Plutarch and Modern Ethics.* Oxford: Routledge, 2006.

Nitecki, Matthew H., and D. V. Nitecki, eds. *The Evolution of Human Hunting.* New York: Plenum Press, 1987.

Nunn, John. *Ancient Egyptian Medicine.* Norman: University of Oklahoma Press, 1996.

Obbink, Dirk. "The Origin of Greek Sacrifice: Theophrastus on Religion and Cultural History." In *Theophrastean Studies on Natural Science, Physics and Metaphysics, Ethics, Religion, and Rhetoric,* edited by William W. Fortenbaugh and Robert W. Sharples, pp. 272–295. New Brunswick: Transaction Books, 1988.

Padgett, J. M. *The Centaur's Smile: The Human Animal in Early Greek Art.* New Haven: Princeton University Press, 2003.

Pasquier, A. *The Louvre: Greek, Roman and Etruscan Antiquities.* Paris: Scala, 1991.

Pembroke, S. J. "Oikeiôsis." In *Problems in Stoicism,* edited by A. A. Long, pp. 114–149. London: Athlone, 1971.

Pharr, C., trans. *The Theodosian Code and Novels and the Sirmondian Constitutions.* Princeton: Princeton University Press, 1952.

Phillips, Dorothy. *Ancient Egyptian Animals.* New York: Metropolitan Museum of Art Picture Books, 1948.

Phillipson, D. W. *African Archaeology.* 2nd ed. Cambridge: Cambridge University Press, 1993.

Piggott, S. *The Earliest Wheeled Transport: From the Atlantic Coast to the Caspian Sea.* London: Thames and Hudson, 1983.

Pinsent, J. "Bull-Leaping." In *Minoan Society,* edited by O. Krzyszkowska and L. Nixon, pp. 259–271. Bristol: Bristol Classical Press, 1983.

Plass, Paul. *The Game of Death in Ancient Rome.* Madison: University of Wisconsin Press, 1995.

Pliny the Elder. *Natural History: A Selection*. Translated by John F. Healy. London: Penguin, 2004.

Pliny the Elder. *The Natural History*. Book IX, *The Natural History of Fishes*. Edited by John Bostock and H. T. Riley. http://www.perseus.tufts.edu/cgi-bin/ptext?doc=Perseus%3Atext%3A1999.02.0137&query=toc:head%3D%23418 (accessed November 14, 2005).

Pliny the Elder. *The Natural History*. Book VIII, *The Nature of the Terrestrial Animals*. Edited by John Bostock and H. T. Riley. http://www.perseus.tufts.edu/cgi-bin/ptext?doc=Perseus%3Atext%3A1999.02.0137&query=toc:head%3D%23333 (accessed November 14, 2005).

Plutarch. "Pyrrhus." http://penelope.uchicago.edu/Thayer/E/Roman/Texts/Plutarch/Lives/Pyrrhus*.html (accessed April 22, 2005).

Pollard, John Richard Thornhill. *Birds in Greek Life and Myth*. London: Thames and Hudson, 1977.

Postgate, N. *The First Empires*. Oxford: Elsevier Phaidon, 1977.

Poynting, Jeremy. "From Ancestral to Creole: Humans and Animals in a West Indian Scale of Values." In *Monsters, Tricksters, and Sacred Cows: Animal Tales and American Identities*, edited by A. James Arnold, pp. 204–229. Charlottesville: University of Virginia Press, 1996.

Preece, Rod, and Lorna Chamberlain. *Animal Welfare and Human Values*. Waterloo: Wilfrid Laurier University Press, 1993.

Prioreschi, Plinio. *Roman Medicine*. Omaha, NE: Horatius Press, 2003.

Probert, W., trans. *The Ancient Laws of Cambria*. London: E. Williams, 1823.

Quibell, J. E. *The Ramesseum*. London: Bernard Quaritch (Egyptian Research Account, 1896), 1898.

Radcliffe, William. *Fishing from the Earliest Times*. Chicago: Ares Publishers, 1974.

Radice, B., trans. *Pliny Letters, Books I–VII*. Cambridge: Harvard University Press, Loeb Classical Library, 1969.

Ramsay, K., L. Harris, and A. Kotzé. *Landrace Breeds: South Africa's Indigenous and Locally Developed Farm Animals*. Pretoria: Farm Animal Conservation Trust, Pretoria, 1999.

Rasmussen, Knud. "Intellectual Life of the Iglulik Eskimos." *Report of the Fifth Thule Expedition 1921–24*. The Danish Expedition to Arctic North America. Vol. 7, no. 1. Copenhagen, 1929.

Rawlinson, G., trans. *The Histories of Herodotus*. London: J. M. Dent & Sons, 1970.

Reade, J. *Mesopotamia*. London: British Museum Press, 1991.

Reeder, E. D. *Pandora: Women in Ancient Greece*. New Haven: Princeton University Press, 1995.

Renehan, Robert. "The Greek Anthropocentric View of Man." *Harvard Studies in Classical Philology* 85 (1981): 239–259.

Reydams-Schils, Gretchen. "Human Bonding and *Oikeiōsis* in Roman Stoicism." *Oxford Studies in Ancient Philosophy* 22 (2002): 221–251.

Rice, E. E. *The Grand Procession of Ptolemy Philadelphus*. Oxford: Oxford University Press, 1983.

Rieu, E. V., trans. *Homer: The Odyssey*. Baltimore: Penguin Books, 1946.

Rodman, John. "The Dolphin Papers." *North American Review* 2 (spring 1974): 13–26.

Rogers, Katharine M. *The Cat and the Human Imagination: Feline Images from Bast to Garfield*. Ann Arbor: University of Michigan Press, 1998.

Rosivach, K. J. *The System of Public Sacrifice in Fourth-Century Athens*. Atlanta: Scholars Press, 1994.

Rostovtzeff, Mikhail. *The Social and Economic History of the Roman Empire.* 2nd ed. 2 vols. Oxford: Clarendon Press, 1957.

Ryder, Richard D. *Animal Revolution: Changing Attitudes towards Speciesism.* Oxford: Blackwell, 1989.

Saad, Zaki. *Ceiling Stelae in Second Dynasty Tombs from the Excavations at Helwan.* Le Caire: l'Institut français d'Archéologie orientale, 1957.

Saad, Zaki. *The Excavations at Helwan: Art and Civilization in the First and Second Egyptian Dynasties.* Norman: University of Oklahoma Press, 1969.

Sandars, N.K., trans. *The Epic of Gilgamesh.* Harmondsworth: Penguin Books, 1960.

Sanday, Peggy Reeves. *Female Power and Male Dominance: On the Origins of Sexual Inequality.* Cambridge: Cambridge University Press, 1981.

Sauneron, Serge. "Le germe dans les os." *Bulletin de l'Institut français d'Archéologie orientale* 60 (1960): 19–27.

Schwabe, Calvin W. "Animals in the Ancient World." In *Animals and Human Society: Changing Perspectives,* edited by Aubrey Manning and James Serpell, pp. 36–58. London: Routledge, 1994.

Schwabe, Calvin, Joyce Adams, and Carleton Hodge. "Egyptian Beliefs about the Bull's Spine; An Anatomical Origin for Ankh." *Anthropological Linguistics* 24 (1982): 445–479.

Schwabe, Calvin, and Andrew Gordon. "The Egyptian *w3s*-Scepter: A Possible Biological Origin as a Dried Bull's Penis in Relation to an Ancient Theory on Bones as the Source of Semen." Working Paper Series No. 53. Davis: Agricultural History Center, University of California, 1989.

Schwartz, M. *A History of Dogs in the Early Americas.* New Haven and London: Yale University Press, 1997.

Scullard, Howard Hayes. *The Elephant in the Greek and Roman World.* Ithaca: Cornell University Press, 1974.

Scurlock, JoAnn. "Animals in Ancient Mesopotamian Religion." In *A History of the Animal World in the Ancient Near East,* edited by Billie Jean Collins, pp. 361–387. Leiden: Brill, 2002.

Seligman, C. G. "Egyptian Influence in Negro Africa." In *Studies Presented to F. Ll. Griffith.* London: Egypt Exploration Society, 1932, 457–462.

Semple, Ellen Churchill. *The Geography of the Mediterranean Region: Its Relation to Ancient History.* New York: Henry Holt and Co., 1931.

Serpell, James. *In the Company of Animals: A Study of Human-Animal Relationships.* London: Basil Blackwell, 1986.

Sharp, Henry S. "The Null Case: The Chipewyan." In *Woman the Gatherer,* edited by Frances Dahlberg, pp. 221–244. New Haven: Yale University Press, 1981.

Shelton, Jo-Ann. "Contracts with Animals: Lucretius, *De rerum natura.*" *Between the Species* 11 (1995): 115–121.

Shelton, Jo-Ann. "Dancing and Dying: The Display of Elephants in Ancient Roman Arenas." In *Daimonopylai: Essays in Classics and the Classical Tradition,* edited by Mark Joyal and Rory B. Egan, pp. 363–382. Winnipeg: University of Manitoba, Centre for Hellenic Civilization, 2004.

Shepard, Paul. *Thinking Animals: Animals and the Development of Human Intelligence.* New York: Viking Press, 1978.

Shepard, Paul. *Nature and Madness.* San Francisco: Sierra Club Books, 1982.

Sherratt, A., and G. Clark, eds. *The Cambridge Encyclopedia of Archaeology.* Cambridge: Cambridge University Press, 1980.

Sigerist, H. E. *A History of Medicine*. Vol. 1, *Primitive and Archaic Medicine*. New York: Oxford University Press, 1967.

Singer, Peter. *Animal Liberation: A New Ethics for Our Treatment of Animals*. New York: Avon, 1975.

Smith, A.B. *Pastoralism in Africa: Origins and Development Ecology*. London: Hurst and Co., 1992.

Smith, A.B. "The Origins of the Domesticated Animals of Southern Africa." In *Origins and Development of African Livestock: Archaeology, Genetics, Linguistics, and Ethnography*, edited by R.M. Blench and K.C. MacDonald, pp. 222–238. New York: Routledge, 2000.

Smith, G. Elliot, and Warren Dawson. *Egyptian Mummies*. New York: Dial Press, 1924.

Sorabji, Richard. *Animal Minds and Human Morals: The Origins of the Western Debate*. Ithaca: Cornell University Press, 1993.

Sperber, D. "Why Are Perfect Animals, Hybrids and Monsters Food for Symbolic Thought?" *Method and Theory in the Study of Religion* 8, no. 2 (1996): 143–169.

Spivey, Nigel. *Etruscan Art*. London: Thames and Hudson, 1997.

Steiner, Gary. *Anthropocentrism and Its Discontents: The Moral Status of Animals in the History of Western Philosophy*. Pittsburgh: University of Pittsburgh Press, 2005.

Straten, F. van. "Greek Sacrificial Representations: Livestock Prices and Religious Mentality." In *Gifts to the Gods,* edited by T. Linders and G. Norquist, pp. 159–170. Uppsala: Boreas, 1987.

Straten, F. van. *Hiera Kala: Images of Animal Sacrifice in Archaic and Classical Greece*. Leiden: Brill, 1995.

Striker, Gisela. "The Role of *Oikeiosis* in Stoic Ethics." *Oxford Studies in Ancient Philosophy* 1 (1983): 145–167.

Strutt, Joseph. *The Sports and Pastimes of the People of England*, edited by J.C. Cox. London: Augustus M. Kelley, 1903.

Tambiah, Stanley J. "Animals Are Good to Think and Good to Prohibit." In *Culture, Thought, and Social Action*, pp. 169–211. Cambridge: Harvard University Press, 1985.

Tarn, W.W. "Two Notes on Ptolemaic History." *The Journal of Hellenic Studies* 53 (1933): 57–68.

Tarn, W.W. *Hellenistic Civilization*. London: Arnold, 1952.

Terian, Abraham. *Philonis Alexandrini de Animalibus: The Armenian Text with an Introduction, Translation, and Commentary*. Chico: Scholars Press, 1981.

Thomas, Keith. *Man and the Natural World: A History of the Modern Sensibility*. New York: Pantheon Books, 1983.

Toynbee, J.M.C. *Animals in Roman Life and Art*. 1973. Reprint, Baltimore and London: Johns Hopkins University Press, 1996.

Tsekourakis, Damianos. "Pythagoreanism or Platonism in Ancient Medicine? The Reasons for Vegetarianism in Plutarch's 'Moralia.'" *Aufstieg und Niedergang der römischen Welt* 2, 36. 1 (1987): 366–393.

Tuan, Yi-Fu. *Dominance and Affection: The Making of Pets*. New Haven: Yale University Press, 1984.

Underhill, Ruth. *Red Man's Religion: Beliefs and Practices of the Indians North of Mexico*. Chicago: University of Chicago Press, 1965.

Veltre, Thomas. "Menageries, Metaphors, and Meanings." In *New Worlds, New Animals: From Menagerie to Zoological Park in the Nineteenth Century,* edited by

R.J. Hoage and William A. Deiss, pp. 19–29. Baltimore: Johns Hopkins University Press, 1996.

Veyne, Paul. *Bread and Circuses: Historical Sociology and Political Pluralism.* Translated by Brian Pearce. London: Penguin Press, 1990.

Vigneron, P. *Le cheval dans l'antiquite greco-romaine.* Nancy: Annales de L'est, 1968.

Waddell, W.G., trans. *Manetho.* Cambridge: Harvard University Press, 1940.

Wainwright, G.A. "A Pair of Constellations." In *Studies Presented to F. Ll. Griffith.* London: Egypt Exploration Society, 1932, 373–382.

Walker, R.E. "The Veterinary Papyrus of Kahun." *Veterinary Record* 76 (1964): 198–201.

Ward, A. "The Cretan Bull Sports." *Antiquity* 42 (1968): 117–122.

Watson, J.S., trans. *Xenophon's Minor Works.* London: George Bell and Sons, Bohn's Classical Library, 1884.

White, Lynn, Jr. *Medieval Technology and Social Change.* Oxford: Oxford University Press, 1962.

Wiedemann, Thomas. *Emperors and Gladiators.* London and New York: Routledge, 1992.

Wilkinson, Toby. *Genesis of the Pharaohs: Dramatic New Discoveries Rewrite the Origins of Ancient Egypt.* New York: Thames and Hudson, 2003.

Willetts, R.F. *The Civilizations of Ancient Crete.* Berkeley and Los Angeles: University of California Press, 1977.

Xenophon. "On Hunting." Translated by H.G. Dakyns. http://www.gutenberg.org/dirs/etext98/sport10.txt (accessed April 2005).

Xinran, Xue. *Sky Burial: An Epic Love Story of Tibet.* New York: Random House, 2005.

Yablonsky, L.T. "Burial Place of a Massagetan Warrior." *Antiquity* 64 (1990): 288–296.

Younger, J.G. "Bronze Age Representations of Aegean Bull-Leaping." *American Journal of Archaeology* 80 (1976): 125–137.

Younger, J.G. "Bronze Age Representations of Aegean Bull-Games III." *Aegaeum* 12 (1995): 507–545.

Yoyotte, Jean. "Les os et la semence masculine à propos d'une théorie physiologique égyptienne." *Bulletin de l'Institut français d'Archéologie orientale* 61 (1962), 139–146.

Zeimbeki, M. "Nurturing the Natural: A Cognitive Approach in the Study of the Xeste 3 Aquatic Imagery." In *Authochthon: Papers Presented to O.T.P.K. Dickinson on the Occasion of His Retirement,* edited by A. Dakouri-Hild and S. Sherratt, pp. 242–251. Oxford: British Archaeological Reports, 2005.

Zettler, Richard L., and Lee Horne, eds. *Treasures from the Royal Tombs of Ur.* Philadelphia: University of Pennsylvania Museum of Archaeology and Anthropology, 1998.

Zeunon, F. *A History of Domesticated Animals.* London: Hutchinson & Co., 1963.

Zhang, Z. "Goldfish." In *Evolution of Domesticated Animals,* edited by I.L. Mason, pp. 381–385. London and New York: Longman, 1984.

NOTES ON CONTRIBUTORS

Bill Cambray was born and educated in England where he studied geology at Kings College London. Following his doctoral work he taught at London University, the University of the West Indies, Wayne State University, and Michigan State University. He was chairman of the Geology Department at Michigan State and director of the Center for Integrative Studies in General Science. His lifelong interest in photography was stimulated by the need to capture the subtleties of rock formations for teaching and research. He is now retired and resides in Okemos, Michigan.

Juliet Clutton-Brock, B.Sc., Ph.D., D.Sc, FZS, FSA, is retired after 25 years in a research post as archaeozoologist at the Natural History Museum in London. In that position, she published more than 90 scientific papers and several books on archaeozoology and the history of domesticated mammals, notably *The Natural History of Domesticated Mammals* (Cambridge University Press, 1999), *The Walking Larder* (Unwin Hyman, 1989), and *Horse Power* (Harvard University Press, 1992). For the past 13 years she has been an editor of the *Journal of Zoology* and is presently an associate editor of the *Archives of Natural History*.

Andrew H. Gordon has an M.S. in paleontology from the University of Rochester and a Ph.D. in Egyptology from the University of California, Berkeley. He specializes in ancient Egyptian history, archaeology, and lexicography, as well as the origin of ancient Egyptian medicine. He has published in a number of journals, including the *Journal of the American Research Center in Egypt*, *Journal of Near Eastern Studies*, *Mitteilungen des Deutchen Archäologischen Instituts Abteilung Kairo*, *Göttinger Miszellen*, and others. For more than 20 years he has also written articles and authored a book, *The Quick and the Dead: Biomedical Theory in Ancient Egypt* (Brill, 2004), with the late Calvin W. Schwabe, a veterinary medicine and epidemiology specialist. He co-owns Archaeologia Books in Oakland, California, and lives with his wife, Nancy, on a lake in northern New Jersey.

J. Donald Hughes is John Evans Distinguished Professor of History at the University of Denver, Colorado. Author of several books including *An Environmental History of the World: Humankind's Changing Role in the Community of Life* (Routledge, 2001), *The Mediterranean: An Environmental History* (ABC-CLIO, 2005), and *Pan's Travail: Environmental Problems of the Ancient Greeks and Romans* (Johns Hopkins University Press, 1994), and articles including "Europe as Consumer of Exotic Biodiversity: Greek and Roman Times," (*Landscape Research* 28, no. 1 [theme issue, "The Native, Naturalized and Exotic—Plants and Animals in Human History"] January 2003: 21–31). He is a founding member of the American Society for Environmental History (ASEH) and the European Society for Environmental History (ESEH), and past editor of *Environmental Review*, a predecessor of *Environmental History*, the quarterly journal of ASEH.

Linda Kalof is professor of sociology at Michigan State University. She studies the cultural representations of humans and other animals and the links between culture and nature. Her recent books include *Looking at Animals in Human History* (Reaktion, 2007), *The Animals Reader: The Essential Classic and Contemporary Writings* (Berg, 2007), and *Environmental Values* (Earthscan Reader/James and James, 2005). In addition to serving as a general editor for the multivolume *A Cultural History of Animals,* she also edits *A Cultural History of the Human Body* (forthcoming in 2008 from Berg) and *Human Ecology Review*, a peer-reviewed academic journal on the interaction between humans and the natural world. Her published articles on animal studies include animals in art; the display of dead animals in trophy photography; and the connection among animals, women, and sexuality in the discourse of blood sports.

Jim Mason is an author and attorney who focuses on human and animal concerns. His latest book, coauthored with Princeton professor and ethicist Peter Singer, is *The Way We Eat: Why Our Food Choices Matter* (Rodale Press, 2006). The authors trace the foods eaten by three American families back to their sources and explore the ethical questions that arise along the way. The book discusses factory farming and alternatives, fair trade, buying local, organic farming, commercial fishing, and other food matters of concern to consumers today. Mason is also the author of *An Unnatural Order: The Roots of Our Destruction of Nature* (Lantern Books, 2005) and coauthor with Peter Singer of *Animal Factories* (Harmony Books, 1990). He is a contributor to *In Defence of Animals* (Blackwell, 2005), edited by Peter Singer. His writings have appeared in *Audubon, The New York Times, New Scientist, Newsday, Country Journal, Orion Nature Quarterly*, and other publications.

Christine Morris is Leventis Senior Lecturer in Greek Archaeology and History, and head of the Department of Classics, at Trinity College Dublin. Her main area of research is the Aegean Bronze Age. She has published extensively on pottery, figurines, and iconography, and is working on the primary publication of material from Ayia Irini on Kea in the Cyclades, and from the Minoan peak sanctuary of Atsipadhes in western Crete. With Lucy Goodison she has edited *Ancient Goddesses* (University of Wisconsin Press, 1998), and she is currently working on the nineteenth- and early twentieth-century historiography of goddesses as well as a project on the ritual life of animals in the Mediterranean.

Stephen T. Newmyer is professor of Classics at Duquesne University, Pittsburgh. He has published a monograph on the *Statius Silvae* (Bryn Mawr Commentaries, 1987), textbooks on Statius and Herodotus, and a study of Plutarch's animal-related treatises titled *Animals, Rights and Reason in Plutarch and Modern Ethics* (Routledge, 2006), as well as numerous articles on post-Augutan Roman literature, ancient medical science, and the classical tradition in Western music. He is currently at work on an anthology of translations from Greek and Roman philosophical literature that relates to animal issues, with commentary and bibliography, scheduled for publication by Routledge.

Jo-Ann Shelton is a professor of Classics at the University of California, Santa Barbara. Her research focuses on the cultural and social history of the ancient Roman world, with particular attention to human attitudes toward animals. Her publications include *As the Romans Did* (Oxford University Press, 1998) and articles on the moral status of animals in both the ancient and the modern world. In addition to courses in the Classics Department, she teaches a class on ethical issues of animal use in the Environmental Studies Department at the University of California, Santa Barbara.

INDEX